"Anyone contemplating buying a second, or even third, home owes it to himself or herself to read and benefit from this comprehensive book."

Christopher A. Brown
Co-president, Prudential New Jersey Properties

"This book is an essential guide for anyone who's thinking about buying a second home. The advantages, challenges and pitfalls of second-home ownership are clearly explained and the book details purchase strategies that every potential buyer should consider."

Liz Pulliam Weston
MSN Money columnist and author of *Your Credit Score*

"This book is a helpful tool for those looking to understand the process of purchasing a second home. It's a must read for anyone looking to buy for investment, vacation or future retirement."

Lori Collins
Senior vice president and general manager, LendingTree

"Buying a Second Home *visually guides you through the process of finding and purchasing a second home while providing great examples and real-life situations. I will definitely add a copy of this well-written book to my reference library!"*

Mallory Anderson
Executive director, National Association of Home Inspectors

"For anyone thinking of owning a second home... Buying a Second Home *offers practical and comprehensible information that will help you think through the process of becoming a successful second home owner."*

Francis Carlet
Publisher, *2nd Home Journal*

Casey McNamara

About the Author

Craig Venezia has worked as an executive for several Fortune 500 companies, focusing on financial services. A leading expert on private mortgages, Craig is a contributing editor to the *San Francisco Chronicle*, has appeared on CNN and NPR, and been quoted by the *Los Angeles Times*, *Chicago Tribune*, and more. He makes his home near Boston. To see Craig's latest articles and more, visit www.craigvenezia.com.

always up to date

The law changes, but Nolo is on top of it! We offer several
ways to make sure you and your Nolo products are up to date:

1 **Nolo's Legal Updater**
We'll send you an email whenever a new edition of this book is
published! Sign up at **www.nolo.com/legalupdater**.

2 **Updates @ Nolo.com**
Check **www.nolo.com/update** to find recent changes
in the law that affect the current edition of your book.

3 **Nolo Customer Service**
To make sure that this edition of the book is the most
recent one, call us at **800-728-3555** and ask one of
our friendly customer service representatives.
Or find out at **www.nolo.com**.

please note

We believe accurate, plain-English legal information should help you solve many of your own legal problems. But this text is not a substitute for personalized advice from a knowledgeable lawyer. If you want the help of a trained professional—and we'll always point out situations in which we think that's a good idea—consult an attorney licensed to practice in your state.

Buying a Second Home

Income, Getaway, or Retirement

by Craig Venezia

FIRST EDITION	JANUARY 2007
Editor	ILONA BRAY
Book Design	SUSAN PUTNEY
Cover Design	SUSAN PUTNEY
Production	MARGARET LIVINGSTON
Proofreading	SUSAN CARLSON GREENE
Index	MEDEA MINNICH
Printing	DELTA PRINTING SOLUTIONS

Venezia, Craig, 1966-
    Buying a second home : income, getaway, or retirement / by Craig Venezia. -- 1st ed.
        p. cm.
    ISBN-13: 978-1-4133-0556-2 (alk. paper)
    ISBN-10: 1-4133-0556-3 (alk. paper)
    1. Second homes. 2. Real estate investment. I. Title.

    HD7289.2.V46 2007
    643'.12--dc22

                                                    2006046792

Quantity sales: For information on bulk purchases or corporate premium sales, please contact the Special
Sales department. For academic sales or textbook adoptions, ask for Academic Sales. Call 800-955-4775,
or write to Nolo at 950 Parker St., Berkeley, CA 94710.

Acknowledgments

Writing a book of this nature is by no means a solitary venture. While the concept may have originated with me, it took the involvement, expertise, and belief of many to bring it to life. First off, this book would never have seen the light of day if not for Sigrid Metson and Kelly Perri, my dear friends in Nolo's Business Division, who brought my idea to the attention of Nolo's editors. You guys are the best.

Special thanks also goes to Nolo Acquisitions Editor Marcia Stewart, who saw the potential in this book from the start and, more importantly, took a chance on a first-time author. I thank you for opening that door for me.

I owe a debt of gratitude to my incredible editor, Ilona Bray. You made my words dance without losing meaning or impact. You continually challenged the content to make sure that we left no stone unturned and that the reader always came first. I couldn't have asked for a better partner to introduce me to the world of publishing.

Special thanks goes to Nolo Managing Editor Janet Portman who, along with Marcia Stewart, lent their expertise to the landlord chapter. I tip my hat to Nolo Senior Vice President of Editorial Mary Randolph for adding flair to the chapter titles.

I am indebted to everyone in Nolo's Sales and Marketing and Business Divisions for their amazing work in bringing this book to market. Thank you to Group Marketing Director Pat Jenkins, who involved me every step of the way, from soliciting my feedback on the book's cover design to involving me in brainstorming meetings. I'm in awe of Publicist Clark Miller who started publicizing this book long before it hit the shelves. And a warm thank you to Vice President of Sales and Marketing Tom Cosgrove, who had enthusiasm for this book from day one. Also thanks to Nolo's Production Department, for handling the cover and final product, including Susan Putney and Margaret Livingston, and to Ellen Bitter and Andre Zivkovich for work on the forms and CD-ROM.

My gratitude extends beyond those at Nolo. In particular, to Karen Toms-Brown, mortgage broker with Adamarc Financial Company, Inc. (www.adamarc.com) in Menlo Park, California. Your keen eye, professionalism, and integrity kept the mortgage chapter focused. Thank you to accountants Janet Downey of Butte, Montana, and Joe Serrecchia of Liberty Tax Service in Salem, Massachusetts. Both of you gave the tax chapter the perspective it needed from experts in the field. I applaud former *San Francisco Chronicle* reporter Ulysses Torassa, who pitched in to help research and draft some selected chapters, and opened the door to writing feature articles for the *Chronicle.* And finally, to Paul Genovese, a residential individual producer with Walter A. Wilkins Insurance Agency in Gloucester, Massachusetts, who gave me a crash course in insuring a second home.

Writing this book required burning the midnight oil many a night. I would be remiss if I didn't say "mahalo" to folks at Hawaii Coffee Company (www.lioncoffee.com) who made sure my coffee shipments arrived promptly each month. Also, thank you to San Francisco's KKSF 103.7, smooth jazz which I still tune in through streaming on the Internet. You set the right mood each night when I sat down at the computer to write.

Saving the best for last, I owe a big hug to my wife, Claire, for her unconditional love and support over the last year, which commanded so much of my time. Not only did you keep me going personally, but you also helped me professionally by exhaustively researching and drafting key sections for this book. No matter what happens in life, you've always been there for me. Finally, my heart goes out to my four wonderful children, three of whom are still with us. Luke, you may only be three and a half, but I still appreciate all those times you offered to help me write, even if it was just an excuse not to go to bed. And, to my wonderful babies Jack and Grace, who weren't even born yet when I started this book. Somewhere along the way, I think during the writing of Chapter 7, the two of you came into our lives. And to Sean, who left this world much too early. It's been several years now, but you're still in our hearts and you'll always live on through The Sean W. Venezia Foundation (www.smafund.org).

—Craig Venezia

Preface

first had the idea for this book several years ago. At the time, I was working for a small financial services company that set up private loans between families and friends. As I spoke with clients, I noticed that many of these loans were being used to help buy second homes. Intrigued, I began to look into just how many people owned a second home. To my surprise, I discovered the number to be quite high. Some time later, the National Association of Realtors came out with a research study that quantified the number. The study stated that 40% of all homes sold in the U.S. were bought as second homes.

Even more surprising, I found that it wasn't the wealthy who were buying—it was everyday people from all walks of life. They were buying for a multitude of reasons: some solely to earn money from rental income and home value appreciation, others to escape the daily grind, and still others to establish a place where they'd eventually retire.

Armed with these findings, I spent months researching existing books on the topic to learn more. To my dismay, many of those books were dated or limited in scope. None contained in-depth information on innovative financing strategies, such as buying jointly with others or arranging private family loans. Thus, the concept for a comprehensive, yet easily read, up-to-date book on how to buy a second home was born.

Now, as the housing market shifts in favor of buyers, there are even more reasons and available opportunities to buy a second home for income, getaway, or future retirement. This book will arm you with the knowledge needed to do it right.

—Craig Venezia

Table of Contents

14   Tax-Saving Strategies

APPENDIX A – How to Use the CD-ROM

APPENDIX B – Forms and Checklists

Forms for Calculating Costs and Affordability
HUD-1 Settlement Statement

Affordable Monthly Expenditures Worksheet

Estimated Maximum Loan Amount Worksheet

Maximum Purchase Price Worksheet

Forms for Evaluating Individual Houses
Initial Walk-Through Checklist

Rental Property Annual Pretax Cash Flow Worksheet

Return on Investment (ROI) Worksheet

Forms for Interviewing Professionals
Real Estate Agent Interview Questionnaire

Mortgage Broker Interview Questionnaire

Attorney Interview Questionnaire

Home Inspector Interview Questionnaire

Forms for Evaluating Fixer-Uppers
Fixer-Upper State-of-Mind Quiz

Fixer-Upper Walk-Through Checklist

Fixer-Upper Cost-Tracking Form

Forms to Facilitate Down Payment and Other Informal Loans
Annual Nonessential Expenditures Adjustment Worksheet

Borrowing Against Home Equity: Comparison Worksheet

Promissory Note

Form for Choosing Management Company
Property Management Company Interview Questionnaire

INDEX

The Seven Rules of Buying a Second Home

One out of every three homes in the United States today was bought as a second home. We're in the midst of a second-home ownership boom, fueled by such factors as the shrinking American family, older and wealthier households, and new technologies for working from home.

And now you're thinking about taking the plunge. Maybe you're looking for an alternative to other investments and will rent or resell the house. Or maybe a cabin by your favorite lake or ski area is calling to you. And if you're thinking ahead toward retirement, you may want to find a manageable, well-located home now.

Whether you plan to buy a second home for investment, vacation, or future retirement, this book is for you. It covers everything you need to know, from how to locate a house that meet your needs, to ways to stay within your budget, to a crash course in being a landlord. We cover topics you may be curious about but won't find in other home-buying books, such as how to buy jointly with friends, how to arrange loans from family members, and how to choose the best place to retire. And we help you understand some complex legal and financial matters, to make sure your home is a good investment no matter your reason for buying it.

What's Your Main Reason for Buying a Second Home?

Before you so much as open the real estate section of your newspaper, decide what you really want out of your second home. And, of course, discuss your goals with anyone who'll be buying, or moving, along with you.

Most people looking for a second home are doing so for either:

- investment, or to earn money from rental income or home-value appreciation
- vacation, or to find a destination to escape the daily grind, or
- future retirement, or to establish a place to enjoy the post-workforce years.

Choosing and staying focused on your main goal will help you make later decisions, for example regarding the type of home you choose, where it will be located, and whether or not you will rent it out.

You may already know which goal is uppermost in your mind. But take a moment to review the characteristics of each type of second-home buyer, below. This is your chance to feel certain about your choice and learn what's unique about your home-buying needs.

Curious About Your Fellow Second-Home Buyers?

The following fun facts were revealed in a 2006 survey by the National Association of Realtors®:

- The typical vacation-home owner is 59 years old and earns $120,600 per year.
- 18% of vacation-home owners plan to retire there eventually.
- The typical investment-home owner is 55 years old, and earns $98,600 per year.
- Most second-home owners are married couples—83% of vacation-home owners, and 75% of investment-home owners.
- Minorities are playing an increasing role in the second-home market, accounting for 11% of vacation-home purchases and 17% of investment-home purchases between the years 2003 and 2005.
- Buyers must be enjoying the second-home experience—21% of vacation-home owners go on to buy one or more additional vacation homes, and 34% of investment-home owners go on to buy additional investment properties.

Buying a Second Home for Investment

If you see a home with deeded beach rights and the first thought that pops into your head is, "Wow! Imagine how much I could sell that for after a few years and a paint job," then you're probably motivated by investment goals.

Investors heed one thing above all others—getting a healthy return on their second home, be it through rental income or, more likely, appreciation. Everything else takes a back seat. Investors view buying a second home as simply an alternative to putting money into stocks, bonds, or other investment vehicles, and their decisions about purchasing a second home are methodical and financially based. Instead of scouting for a home in their favorite vacation destination, investors might buy one in a town where they'd never go, but which has had a track record of steady appreciation in home values.

Are You a Tortoise or a Hare Investor?

In the childhood story, "The Tortoise and the Hare," slow and steady always wins out over fast and furious. In real estate investing, both approaches can win—but you'll probably want to stick to one or the other, depending on your level of patience and willingness to take risks.

- **A tortoise** will purchase a second home with the idea of holding onto it over a long period of time: ten, 20, even 30 years. Tortoises aren't looking to make a quick buck. Their strategy is to weather the ups and downs of the real estate market and profit through long-term rises in home values. Tortoises often also rent out their property, ideally to achieve monthly profits, but at a minimum to offset expenses.

- **A hare** will purchase a second home with the idea of reselling it as soon as a reasonable profit can be gained. This is commonly referred to as "flipping" a property. Hare investors often try to add value to the property by fixing it up, preferably with low-cost cosmetic changes. Hares want to see house values increase sharply over a short period of time. While some hares may rent out their properties, most don't, because that would get in the way of a quick sale.

It doesn't matter whether you're a tortoise or a hare, so long as you recognize your tendencies and make well-researched decisions around them. You can also change in midrace. For example, during the housing boom that started in the mid- to late 1990s, many tortoises sold their properties after holding onto them for only a few years, because house values had increased so fast and furiously. Conversely, when house values flattened, and even dipped, in the mid 2000s, many hares decided to hold onto their properties longer than anticipated, because they weren't achieving the desired profits.

INVESTOR

If you're an investor, pay special attention to this symbol. It will alert you to advice and tips tailored to people with your home-buying goals.

Buying a Second Home for Vacation

If you see a home with deeded beach rights and the first thought that pops into your head is, "Wow, a private beach where I could relax and leave the craziness of life behind," then you're thinking like a vacationer. You're probably already fantasizing about using your second home during your free time, holidays, or peak sport seasons. While almost every vacationer wants a second home to be a good financial investment, turning a profit is not the main motivation.

WARNING

Don't confuse a vacationer with an investor who buys a vacation home. A true vacationer buys a second home for personal enjoyment above all else. If the property is rented out, it's usually only as a means to offset expenses. When an investor buys a vacation home, the purpose is to profit from rental income, appreciation, or a combination of the two. In many cases, an investor won't even use the home personally.

For vacationers, decisions about purchasing a second home are driven by emotion more than by logic. For example, a vacationer who has always dreamed of owning a condo on Poipu Beach in Kauai isn't going to buy one on the other side of the island in Hanalei Bay just because it promises to appreciate at a faster rate or would command a higher rental price. That's not to say a vacationer doesn't ever rent out a second home to offset expenses, or even look for the home to appreciate in value. Rental or other profits are not, however, the driving factor behind a vacationer's buying decisions.

VACATIONER

If you're a vacationer, pay special attention to this symbol. It will alert you to advice and tips tailored to people with your home-buying goals.

Buying a Second Home as a Future Retiree

If you see a home with deeded beach rights and instantly think, "What a great place to live after I've stopped working," you're thinking like a future retiree. It doesn't matter whether your retirement date is just around the corner or decades away.

With people living longer (current life expectancies are around 75 years for men and 80 years for women), retirement has the potential to be the start of life, not the end. Buying a second home now for future retirement could give you a jump start on the good life.

Like vacationers, future retirees often rent out their second homes to offset expenses, and even look for the home to appreciate in value. However, rental or other profits are not the driving factor behind future retirees' buying decisions. Rather, their goal is to have a second home they can ultimately call "home."

FUTURE RETIREE

If you're a future retiree, pay special attention to this symbol. It will alert you to advice and tips tailored to people with your home-buying goals.

Buying a Second Home for Mixed Reasons

Of course, you may have a mix of motivations. Perhaps you want the home primarily for vacation purposes, but will also treat it as an investment property by renting it out for parts of the year, and will maybe even retire in it afterwards. That's fine—but decide which of your goals (investment, vacation, or future retirement) is number one, so that you'll stay focused as you enter the homebuying fray.

Your secondary motivations for buying can, however, be important in helping you develop a backup plan for your property. You know what they say about the best-laid plans: An investor who planned on flipping the property may watch house values plunge 10%; a vacationer may receive an unexpected job transfer to the other side of the country, meaning significantly less time spent at the weekend getaway; a future retiree whose second home sits at 3,500 feet above sea level may discover that high altitudes aggravate asthma.

As you look at potential houses, it's worth thinking, "If I can't use it for this, maybe I can use it for that." Here are some likely backup plans:

- The investor who planned on flipping the property could plan to rent it out and use the income to offset expenses until house values rise again.

- The vacationer facing an unexpected job transfer could plan to rent out the property for most of the year, using it for vacations only a few times a year.

- The future retiree with asthma could either sell the property at a profit or rent it out year-round and wait for house values to climb.

Seven Steps Toward a Successful Second-Home Purchase

If you're ready to embark on your home search, let's not waste a minute. Your seven most important steps toward finding and buying your dream second home are right here. Once you've got these down, we'll fill you in on the details in later chapters.

One: Decide Whether a Second Home Makes Financial Sense

Whether or not you consider yourself an investor, you no doubt want your second-house purchase to be a sound financial move. Yet many second-home owners complain that the house cost more than they'd ever imagined. You'll want to tally up your likely expenses, work on building up your cash reserve, and determine how much you can expect from rental income. This book will give you worksheets and detailed information to do all these things.

Two: Decide Where, and What Type of Home, You'll Buy

A home in a badly chosen location won't serve anyone's goals—the investor can't sell or rent it, the vacationer won't enjoy it, and the future retiree may have to pick up and move again. You'll need to rely on both market research and your own personal preferences. The type of home you buy is similarly important. The demands of owning a single-family home are different from those of owning a condominium, townhouse, or co-op. Which type of home serves you best will depend on factors such as cost, location, and upkeep. Finally, you'll want to look into unique possibilities such as a fixer-upper or a for-sale-by-owner (FSBO) property, all described further in this book.

Three: Understand the Tax Implications Before You Take the Plunge

Taxes on your second home come in all shapes and sizes, yet have one thing in common—they can be a burden. However, you can, with some advance planning, save thousands of dollars a year in taxes. For example, sometimes buying a home just over a town's border can significantly trim your annual property tax bill. If you plan to both vacation in and rent your home, understanding how the IRS treats combined uses of the home, and what deductions you can claim, may also save you a bundle. And, if you sell your second home at a profit down the road, a like-kind exchange can, in certain situations, help you defer paying capital gains tax.

Four: Come Up With Short-Term Cash and Long-Term Financing

Most people pay for their home with a combination of a down payment and a loan for the remaining amount. The higher your down payment, the lower the loan amount, and the more house you can therefore afford. In order to come up with down payment cash (ideally, 20% of the purchase price) you may need to get creative. Using equity in your primary home, borrowing against a life insurance policy, and reducing your spending are among the possibilities explored in this book.

Most buyers will also need to get a home loan to help with the rest of the financing. The number of mortgage options available today could make anyone's head spin. And some of them may tempt you into highly risky behavior, such as paying only the interest you owe for several months or years, only to be walloped with a large, lump sum payment at the end of the loan period. However, by reviewing various mortgage options and sample payment schedules, and factoring in your own short- and long-term goals, you'll be able to choose a mortgage type that suits you.

Five: Consider Nontraditional Financing Methods

With real estate prices at record highs, you may have a harder time affording a second home than your parents or grandparents did. One unique way to help finance your second home is to tap the "Bank of Family and Friends." That lets you keep the tens of thousands of dollars in interest you'll pay over the life of your mortgage loan within your circle of friends or family, rather than handing it over to an institutional lender. We'll explain how to approach prospective friend-and-family lenders with a written proposal, and create the appropriate legal documentation when the loan is made.

Another money-saving approach is to partner with another purchaser, for example sharing a vacation home in the sun. A growing number of people have already discovered that partnering with a family member, a friend, or even a stranger who's looking to invest can make second-home ownership a reality. You'll want to start by determining whether co-ownership with a particular person is likely to work, and draft a written agreement to deal with likely sources of contention in advance.

Six: Be Prepared If You'll Be a Landlord

Some second-home owners plan to rent out their properties long-term with the intention of eventually turning a profit, while others just want to rent out their property periodically as a means to offset expenses. Either way, you're taking on the role of a landlord, which means more than just following your instincts. Finding good tenants or trustworthy vacation renters, understanding and preparing leases or short-term agreements, and dealing with ongoing management and repairs are just a few of the issues involved with being a landlord. Also, the obligations of managing a long-term rental are quite different from those of a periodic or vacation rental. This book will delve into these differences and provide advice on how to be an effective landlord in both situations.

Seven: Take Steps to Protect Your Second-Home Investment

Whether you're buying a second home as a pure investment, for a weekend getaway, or as a place to enjoy your retirement, it's an investment all the same. And a large one, at that. Protecting your investment starts before you buy and continues long afterwards. For example, you'll want to get a proper home inspection prior to purchasing the property, so as to deal with some repair issues up front and get a sense of what repairs may be looming. You may want to purchase title insurance in case past claims on the property surface after the purchase. And, your lender will require that you carry homeowners' insurance, to protect your property against damage from such causes as theft, fire, flooding, or windstorms. Taking these protective steps will guard not only your home, but your peace of mind.

Icons Used in This Book

 This icon asks you to slow down and consider potential problems.

 This icon alerts you to a practical tip or good idea.

 This icon tells you when you can skip certain material that may not be relevant to your situation.

 This icon alerts you to information of special interest to people buying second homes for investment.

 This icon alerts you to information of special interest to people buying second homes for their own vacations and enjoyment.

 This icon alerts you to information of special interest to people buying second homes for future retirement.

 This refers you to organizations, books, websites, and other resources for more information.

 This icon lets you know when to seek the advice of a lawyer, accountant, or other expert.

 This icon highlights a summary of the most important points in every chapter.

What a Second Home Really Costs

f you haven't bought a house in a while, you may be in for some sticker shock. House prices have gone up nationwide, dramatically in some areas. And although the median home price is currently $230,000, the median in certain popular areas is double that or more. Then again, if you live in a high-cost housing area, buying a second house elsewhere may feel like discount shopping on a grand scale.

But the sale price is just the baseline—it never tells the whole story. On the day the sale closes, every homebuyer inevitably gets zonked with costs above and beyond those expected. And later down the road, your second house will cost money to repair and maintain, even when you're not living there.

This chapter will help you systematically plan and prepare for the various incidental costs that come with buying and keeping a second home. The point is not to scare you out of buying (you knew this wasn't going to be small change, right?), but to help you start budgeting appropriately.

Initial Costs to Buy the House

Your second home's sale price will certainly constitute the lion's share of your costs. However, at the settlement or closing on your second home (when the formalities of the sale are finalized and the property legally changes hands), you'll also feel the sting of numerous incidental costs. Some of these will be dependent on the sale price, others on local custom. By planning ahead, you can avoid last-minute panics or raids on other sources of funds.

A great way to plan ahead is to review a blank HUD-1 Settlement Statement. You may or may not remember this from your first home sale. The HUD-1 is a standard, federally mandated form that your lender or mortgage broker (if you use one) will give you a few days before the sale closing. (In fact, you might want to come back to this chapter at that time, for help in reviewing the real thing.)

Remember Those Unexpected Costs for Your Current Home?

Reminding yourself how much you've spent on your current home can be a helpful reality check. Try taking out a piece of paper and writing down the amount you think you paid for it, including the purchase price and other expenses such as closing costs, property taxes, and hazard insurance.

Then run to your filing cabinet, safe, junk drawer, or wherever you keep your important home documents and pull out a copy of your settlement statement (the document that itemizes all charges associated with the sale of a house). Look at all the incidental costs you had to pick up—loan fees, title charges, government and transfer fees, escrow for property taxes and hazard insurance, and more.

Odds are, the number on your settlement statement is higher—by a good several thousand dollars—than the number you just wrote down. For the select few of you who correctly remembered your total purchase cost, kudos to you. But the point remains—houses cost more than their base purchase price would suggest.

Now jog your memory again, and think about any unforeseen expenses that you've encountered since moving into your current home. For example, maybe your old, clunky furnace decided to call it quits, the interest rate went up on your adjustable rate mortgage, or your property taxes increased because your town needed a new high school. Your second home won't be immune to such twists of fate, either.

The form itemizes all the purchase costs and who pays them, as between the buyer and the seller. It won't be your earliest warning of these costs—another form, called a Good Faith Estimate or GFE, does that—but it will one day be the final word on exactly how much you'll be asked to pay.

Refer to the blank version of the HUD-1 that appears below (and in the Appendix and on the CD-ROM in the back of the book). We'll walk you through line by line, explaining what each cost entails and how much you might expect to pay—or how much is too much. If you know approximately what priced home you expect to buy, you can write down your estimates now, either on a HUD-1 form or on the Anticipated Closing Costs worksheet provided below.

The total purchase cost of your home will be summarized on page one. For the breakdown, look at Section L, page two of the document.

> **WARNING**
>
> **Some line items can be used to disguise junk fees.** The form is blank and innocent now, but later, as you review a filled-in HUD-1 statement, be on the lookout for "junk fees" (also referred to as "garbage fees"). These are invented fees tacked onto your loan by unscrupulous mortgage lenders, in order to up their profits but continue to advertise low rates. They may call them underwriting fees, loan review fees, processing fees, documentation fees, or administration fees—all services that should have been part of the deal in the first place. For example, you may be charged $75 for an administration fee that includes nothing more than having an assistant spend a whopping two minutes putting all the pages in your file right-side up. We'll let you know which lines below make the best junk fee hiding places.

Sales/Broker's Commission (HUD-1 Line 700)

Most home sales are conducted with the help of a real estate agent, and often separate agents representing both buyer and seller. Line 700 displays the amount of commission they'll be paid (usually a percentage of the selling price). These days, a 5% commission is standard, with half going to the seller's agent and half to the buyer's. While in most cases the seller covers this cost, in certain situations, such as a "for sale by owner," the buyer may cover all or some of it.

Items Payable in Connection With Loan (HUD-1 Line 800)

Your mortgage lender will no doubt charge you fees in order to process and approve your loan. Among the legitimate fees you may see listed on the HUD-1 are:

- *Loan origination fee (Line 801):* Also referred to as "points," this is the amount your mortgage lender charges you to process the loan. The fee is usually calculated as a percentage of your loan. For example, two points on a $200,000 loan would be 2%, or $2,000. The IRS ordinarily considers points to be prepaid interest, making this cost tax deductible. It's not uncommon for a buyer to negotiate down the loan origination fee.

- *Loan discount (Line 802):* This is a fee charged by your mortgage lender in return for lowering your interest rate. Similar to the loan origination fee, it's measured in points or "discount points," and calculated as a percentage of your loan, with one point equaling 1% of the loan. The more points, the lower the interest rate. You'll sometimes see this fee lumped in with the loan origination fee, and it's also tax deductible.

- *Appraisal fee (Line 803):* This is the fee charged by a licensed appraiser to examine the property and provide a written report of its current market value. It usually runs between $200 and $1,000.

- *Credit report (Line 804):* This fee covers the detailed report of your credit, employment, and residence history that your mortgage lender will order from a credit reporting agency to help determine your likelihood of repaying the loan. The credit report will also mention any judgments, tax liens, bankruptcies, or similar matters on your financial record. The credit report fee can run between $15 and $100.

- *Lender's inspection fee (Line 805):* If your home is being newly built, you'll probably have to pay for a final inspection or "442 inspection." Such an inspection verifies, even after other, more preliminary inspections have been done, that all of the work, such as installing new carpets and flooring, adding countertops, and more, has finally been completed. This fee runs in the neighborhood of $100. Be sure not to confuse this fee with that for the home inspection for an existing home, covered under the section of the HUD-1 entitled "Additional Settlement Charges" (see below).

- *Mortgage insurance application fee (Line 806):* If you'll be borrowing more than 80% of the value of your second home, most mortgage lenders will require you to carry private mortgage insurance (PMI), to protect it in the event that you default on the loan. This line item covers the application and processing costs for PMI. (The monthly premium costs are a separate issue.) Expect to pay around $50.

- *Assumption fee (Line 807):* In certain situations, a buyer can take over or assume the seller's mortgage with no change in such terms as the interest rate and remaining loan period. To assume a mortgage can be particularly beneficial to the buyer during periods of rising interest rates. If you go this route, you'll probably be charged an assumption fee by the seller's lender. The cost can vary greatly, from a few hundred dollars to 1% of the outstanding balance of the loan.

- *Mortgage broker fee (Usually handwritten into Line 808):* If you use a mortgage broker (a person or company that helps you select and obtain a mortgage), this is the fee that you'll pay for the broker's services. It's usually a percentage of the amount you borrow—1% is considered standard. In most situations, this line will be left blank, because the mortgage broker's fee will be included in the loan origination fee (Line 801, above).

- *Underwriting fee (Usually handwritten into Line 809):* A fee charged by some mortgage lenders to cover the cost of an analysis of the risk associated with the loan. This fee can range from $300 to $600. It's a big-time junk fee, so don't plan it into your budget—instead, plan to negotiate with your mortgage broker or lender to have it removed.

- *Tax service fee (Usually handwritten into Line 810):* Sometimes a lender will set up a service in which a third party monitors the borrower's property tax payments to ensure that payments are made on time and to help prevent tax liens. The cost, which is passed on to the borrower, can range from $25 to $75.

- *Flood certification (Usually handwritten into Line 811):* Federal law requires that homeowners obtain flood hazard insurance if their property resides in a designated flood zone. To find out whether you need insurance, your lender will obtain a report from the Federal Emergency Management Agency (FEMA) indicating whether your property is, in fact, in a flood zone. Expect to pay from $15 to $50.

Items Required by Lender To Be Paid in Advance (HUD-1 Line 900)

This section of the HUD-1 focuses on any recurring costs that your mortgage lender will collect from you in advance. Prime examples include initial interest on your loan and your hazard insurance premiums. Here's the line-by-line breakdown:

- *Interest (Line 901):* Your lender will usually require you to pay enough interest on your loan to cover the period between your closing date and your first monthly payment due date. That amount will depend on your interest rate and the length of that time gap.

- *Mortgage insurance premium (Line 902):* If you're required to carry PMI (see Line 806, above), your lender may also require you to pay the first year's PMI premium or even a lump sum for the life of the loan. The total amount will depend on your loan-to-value ratio, your type of loan, and the amount of your PMI coverage. Plan on paying anywhere from 1/2% to 1% of your loan amount.

- *Hazard insurance premium (Line 903):* Your lender will normally insist that you pay your first year's premium for hazard insurance. Similar to the homeowners' policy on your primary home, second homes (both rentals and nonrentals) usually have what is called a "dwelling policy," which covers the house against exterior or interior damage. A dwelling policy is geared towards nonowner-occupied homes, which tend to be more at risk for damage due to vacancies and, where applicable, having renters. Covered damage may be caused by fire, theft, vandalism, or certain natural hazards such as tornadoes or a windstorm. Depending on where your property is located, you may be required to get additional insurance coverage, for example, if the property is located in a flood zone. See Line 904, below. The cost of your premium will depend primarily on the type of property and how high your coverage is. Also note that you yourself should buy additional insurance, particularly to cover your personal possessions and your liability to other people injured on your property.

- *Flood insurance (Usually handwritten into Line 904):* Depending on where the property is located, federal law may require that you carry insurance against floods, which are not covered under standard hazard insurance policies. Refer to Line 903, above. The additional cost varies based on the type and location of the property.

Reserves Deposited With Lender (HUD-1 Line 1000)

Mortgage lenders in some states will require you pay into a separate account, known as an escrow or impound account, to cover certain future payments. The lender usually asks for funding of approximately three months' worth of hazard insurance, PMI (if applicable), and property taxes.

- *Hazard insurance (Line 1001):* We've already discussed hazard insurance in connection with Line 903, which covers prepaying the first year's premium. However, your lender may also require you to fund a reserve of three or more months to cover future payments.

- *Mortgage insurance (Line 1002):* We've already discussed private mortgage insurance (PMI) in connection with Line 902, which covers the first year's premium. However, your lender may also require you to fund a reserve of three or more months to cover future payments.

- *City and county property taxes (Lines 1003 and 1004):* Whether you'll pay city property taxes, county taxes, or both, and how high the taxes will be, depends on where your property is located as well as its assessed value. A good way to guesstimate the monthly cost is to take $12 per $1,000 in assessed value and divide by 12. For example, a house valued at $300,000 might have an annual property tax bill of $3,600 per year or $300 per month. Therefore, you could estimate that you'd need $900 at the closing to cover the first three months of property taxes.

- *Annual assessments (Line 1005):* Your lender may require you to set aside funds for use in periodically assessing your property to make certain that its current market value remains at a level appropriate for the loan. This way, if your lender ever had to foreclose, it would be assured that the market value of the property would cover the outstanding balance of your loan.

Title Charges (HUD-1 Line 1100)

This section of the HUD-1 covers all of the fees typically charged to you, the buyer, by the attorneys or title companies who help transfer the property title from the seller. (Whether it's an attorney or a title company that plays this role depends on the state where the property is located.)

- *Settlement or closing fee (Line 1101):* This line usually applies only in states that use title companies for the closing. It's the fee paid to the title company. Who pays it is usually a matter for negotiation between seller and buyer. The fee can run between $500 and $1,000. If a charge appears on this line, you will not usually have a charge on Line 1107, Attorney's fees (see below).

- *Abstract or title search (Line 1102):* This is the fee to prepare a written history of the property based on the results of the title search (see Line 1103, below). The result is reviewed and used to prepare the Title insurance binder (see Line 1104, below). This cost varies, but averages around $150.

- *Title examination (Line 1103):* This is the fee for performing the actual title search. A title search involves reviewing all the public records affecting ownership or allowed use of your property. Title searches typically cover documents filed during the previous 30 years, but can go back much further. This fee can run between $150 and $300, depending on where the property is located and how detailed an examination is performed. Sometimes this fee will be added to the cost of Line 1102, above.

- *Title insurance binder (Line 1104):* Also known as a "commitment to insure," this is the fee charged by the title insurer to produce a preliminary report stating the condition of the title, plus make a commitment to issue you a title insurance policy when certain conditions are met and you've paid the premium (which is listed on Line 1108).

- *Document preparation (Line 1105):* Here's another fee that you should plan not to pay. This is a charge to cover your mortgage lender's work in physically preparing the mortgage, deed of trust, note, or deed. Typically around $200, this is a classic junk fee. If it later comes up, try to remove it or, at least negotiate it down considerably.

- *Notary fees (Line 1106):* This is the fee to pay a licensed notary public who authenticates that the people named on the mortgage and loan documents are the same ones who actually sign the papers. Expect to pay between $15 and $50.

- *Attorney's fees (Line 1107):* This is the cost for legal services, if you use an attorney. (You'll have to, in certain states that require an attorney to handle the closing.) The fee is likely to range from $500 to as much as $1,500. If a charge appears on this line, you will usually not have a charge on Line 1101, Settlement or closing fee (see above).
- *Title insurance (Line 1108):* This is your actual cost for title insurance, which protects the lender and you against loss resulting from any defects in the title or claims against the property that were not uncovered in the title search. This line reflects the sum of the subsequent two lines, Line 1109 (Lender's coverage) and Line 1110 (Owner's coverage).

Government Recording and Transfer Charges (Line 1200)

This section of the HUD-1 covers the state and local government fees that you can expect to pay in conjunction with buying a home.

- *Recording fees (Line 1201):* This is the cost to record the mortgage with the county where the property is located. Depending on the state, this will be done at either the registry of deeds or the county clerk's office. Recording the mortgage makes it a public record, thus advising the rest of the world that your lender holds a lien on your property. These fees normally run from $50 to $250.
- *City/county and state taxes/stamps (Lines 1202 - 1203):* These are taxes charged by state and local governments whenever property changes hands. For some localities, the amount can be rather large. As of 2006, the states that charge some type of tax, usually a stamp or intangible tax (refer to Chapter 14 for more on tax implications) on the purchase of property are: Alabama, Florida, Georgia, Hawaii, Kansas, Maryland, New York, Oklahoma, Tennessee, and Virginia.

Additional Settlement Charges (HUD-1 Line 1300)

This section covers miscellaneous costs that you may be charged, or choose to pay, when buying a second home. For example, although your mortgage lender probably won't require a full home inspection (though it will, especially in certain geographic areas, probably require a pest inspection), you're likely to want one in order to feel comfortable about the condition of the home.

- *Survey (Line 1301):* Your lender may require a survey of the property in order to determine or confirm its boundaries. Expect to pay between $200 and $2,000, depending on the size of the property and its location.

- *Pest inspection (Line 1302):* This is the cost, usually between $75 and $175, to hire someone to inspect for dry rot and other fungus, as well as termites, carpenter ants, and other pests that can cause major damage to the property.

- *Inspections (Lines 1303 - 1305):* This includes the costs for various inspections, some of which may be required by your lender or by state or federal law, such as for lead-based paint ($500), radon ($50 to $100), or the condition of your septic system ($200 to $400). These lines are also where you'll see the cost for a standard home inspection (examining electrical, plumbing, heating, and the like) on an already built home. The average cost is $350.

Use the worksheet below to keep a running tally of your anticipated closing costs. If you've already applied for a loan, you should have received a Good Faith Estimate. (Your lender or mortgage broker is required to give you a GFE within three days of receiving your loan application.) A close estimate of many of these costs can be pulled from that GFE. Work with your real estate agent to estimate the remainder of the costs.

Ongoing Ownership Costs

Given that you may spend several hundred thousand dollars to buy a second home, you probably don't want to contemplate the tens of thousands of dollars you can easily spend each year to maintain it. With a little knowledge and proper budgeting, however, you'll be able to stay on top of these ongoing financial demands. They are likely to include:

- repairs and maintenance
- property taxes, and
- rising mortgage interest rates (if you have an adjustable rate mortgage).

HUD-1 Settlement Statement

A. **Settlement Statement**	U.S. Department of Housing and Urban Development	OMB Approval No. 2502-0265 (expires 11/30/2009)

B. Type of Loan

1. ☐ FHA 2. ☐ FmHA 3. ☐ Conv. Unins.	6. File Number:	7. Loan Number:	8. Mortgage Insurance Case Number:
4. ☐ VA 5. ☐ Conv. Ins.			

C. Note: This form is furnished to give you a statement of actual settlement costs. Amounts paid to and by the settlement agent are shown. Items marked "(p.o.c.)" were paid outside the closing; they are shown here for informational purposes and are not included in the totals.

D. Name & Address of Borrower:	E. Name & Address of Seller:	F. Name & Address of Lender:

G. Property Location:	H. Settlement Agent:	
	Place of Settlement:	I. Settlement Date:

J. Summary of Borrower's Transaction		K. Summary of Seller's Transaction	
100. Gross Amount Due From Borrower		**400. Gross Amount Due To Seller**	
101. Contract sales price		401. Contract sales price	
102. Personal property		402. Personal property	
103. Settlement charges to borrower (line 1400)		403.	
104.		404.	
105.		405.	
Adjustments for items paid by seller in advance		Adjustments for items paid by seller in advance	
106. City/town taxes to		406. City/town taxes to	
107. County taxes to		407. County taxes to	
108. Assessments to		408. Assessments to	
109.		409.	
110.		410.	
111.		411.	
112.		412.	
120. Gross Amount Due From Borrower		**420. Gross Amount Due To Seller**	
200. Amounts Paid By Or In Behalf Of Borrower		**500. Reductions In Amount Due To Seller**	
201. Deposit or earnest money		501. Excess deposit (see instructions)	
202. Principal amount of new loan(s)		502. Settlement charges to seller (line 1400)	
203. Existing loan(s) taken subject to		503. Existing loan(s) taken subject to	
204.		504. Payoff of first mortgage loan	
205.		505. Payoff of second mortgage loan	
206.		506.	
207.		507.	
208.		508.	
209.		509.	
Adjustments for items unpaid by seller		Adjustments for items unpaid by seller	
210. City/town taxes to		510. City/town taxes to	
211. County taxes to		511. County taxes to	
212. Assessments to		512. Assessments to	
213.		513.	
214.		514.	
215.		515.	
216.		516.	
217.		517.	
218.		518.	
219.		519.	
220. Total Paid By/For Borrower		**520. Total Reduction Amount Due Seller**	
300. Cash At Settlement From/To Borrower		**600. Cash At Settlement To/From Seller**	
301. Gross Amount due from borrower (line 120)		601. Gross amount due to seller (line 420)	
302. Less amounts paid by/for borrower (line 220)	( )	602. Less reductions in amt. due seller (line 520)	( )
303. Cash ☐ From ☐ To Borrower		**603. Cash** ☐ To ☐ From Seller	

Section 5 of the Real Estate Settlement Procedures Act (RESPA) requires the following: • HUD must develop a Special Information Booklet to help persons borrowing money to finance the purchase of residential real estate to better understand the nature and costs of real estate settlement services; • Each lender must provide the booklet to all applicants from whom it receives or for whom it prepares a written application to borrow money to finance the purchase of residential real estate; • Lenders must prepare and distribute with the Booklet a Good Faith Estimate of the settlement costs that the borrower is likely to incur in connection with the settlement. These disclosures are manadatory.

Section 4(a) of RESPA mandates that HUD develop and prescribe this standard form to be used at the time of loan settlement to provide full disclosure of all charges imposed upon the borrower and seller. These are third party disclosures that are designed to provide the borrower with pertinent information during the settlement process in order to be a better shopper.

The Public Reporting Burden for this collection of information is estimated to average one hour per response, including the time for reviewing instructions, searching existing data sources, gathering and maintaining the data needed, and completing and reviewing the collection of information.

This agency may not collect this information, and you are not required to complete this form, unless it displays a currently valid OMB control number.

The information requested does not lend itself to confidentiality.

HUD-1 Settlement Statement (cont'd.)

L. Settlement Charges

		Paid From Borrowers Funds at Settlement	Paid From Seller's Funds at Settlement
700. Total Sales/Broker's Commission based on price $ @ % =			
Division of Commission (line 700) as follows:			
701. $	to		
702. $	to		
703. Commission paid at Settlement			
704.			
800. Items Payable In Connection With Loan			
801. Loan Origination Fee	%		
802. Loan Discount	%		
803. Appraisal Fee	to		
804. Credit Report	to		
805. Lender's Inspection Fee			
806. Mortgage Insurance Application Fee to			
807. Assumption Fee			
808.			
809.			
810.			
811.			
900. Items Required By Lender To Be Paid In Advance			
901. Interest from to @ $ /day			
902. Mortgage Insurance Premium for months to			
903. Hazard Insurance Premium for years to			
904. years to			
905.			
1000. Reserves Deposited With Lender			
1001. Hazard insurance	months @ $	per month	
1002. Mortgage insurance	months @ $	per month	
1003. City property taxes	months @ $	per month	
1004. County property taxes	months @ $	per month	
1005. Annual assessments	months @ $	per month	
1006.	months @ $	per month	
1007.	months @ $	per month	
1008.	months @ $	per month	
1100. Title Charges			
1101. Settlement or closing fee	to		
1102. Abstract or title search	to		
1103. Title examination	to		
1104. Title insurance binder	to		
1105. Document preparation	to		
1106. Notary fees	to		
1107. Attorney's fees	to		
(includes above items numbers:)			
1108. Title insurance	to		
(includes above items numbers:)			
1109. Lender's coverage	$		
1110. Owner's coverage	$		
1111.			
1112.			
1113.			
1200. Government Recording and Transfer Charges			
1201. Recording fees: Deed $; Mortgage $; Releases $			
1202. City/county tax/stamps: Deed $; Mortgage $			
1203. State tax/stamps: Deed $; Mortgage $			
1204.			
1205.			
1300. Additional Settlement Charges			
1301. Survey to			
1302. Pest inspection to			
1303.			
1304.			
1305.			
1400. Total Settlement Charges (enter on lines 103, Section J and 502, Section K)			

Source: U.S. Department of Housing and Urban Development

Anticipated Closing Costs

HUD-1 Line #	Cost Description	Estimated Cost
700	Sales/broker's commission	$
801	Loan origination fee	$
802	Loan discount fee	$
803	Appraisal fee	$
804	Credit report	$
805	Lender's inspection fee	$
806	Mortgage insurance application fee	$
807	Assumption fee	$
808	Mortgage broker fee	$
809	Underwriting fee	$
810	Tax service fee	$
811	Flood certification fee	$
901	Initial interest payment on loan	$
902	Mortgage insurance (PMI) premium	$
903	Hazard insurance premium	$
904	Flood insurance premium	$
1001	Hazard insurance reserve	$
1002	Mortgage insurance (PMI) reserve	$
1003	City property taxes	$
1004	County property taxes	$
1005	Annual assessments	$
1101	Settlement or closing fee	$
1102	Abstract or title search charge	$
1103	Title examination charge	$
1104 ·	Title insurance binder charge	$
1105	Document preparation charge	$
1106	Notary fees	$
1107	Attorney's fees	$
1108	Title insurance premium	$
1201	Recording fees	$
1202	City/county tax/stamps	$
1203	State tax/stamps	$
1301	Survey charge	$
1302	Pest inspection charge	$
1303	Other inspection fees	$
	Radon	$
	Septic tank	$
	Lead paint	$
	General home inspection	$
	Total	$

Home Repair and Maintenance

All houses are subject to wear and tear. How fast a house goes downhill depends on how well it was built, where it's located (for example, houses by the ocean usually get beat up more than inland houses), and how diligent the previous owners were about basic maintenance. Don't assume that your current house's repair costs are a good indicator of the next one's.

INVESTOR

Planning to rent the property out? Budget for the fact that careless tenants may bang up walls, stain carpets, crack windows, or otherwise accelerate your house's need for repair.

Repairs can range from minor (fixing leaky gutters, recaulking windows, replacing old faucets) to complex (installing a new furnace, repairing a leaky roof, installing new carpets). But they have one thing in common—they all cost money. Below is a list of common home repairs and approximately how much you can expect to pay for them if a professional does the work. Of course, the materials you choose to use, the experience and honesty of the contractor, and the size, existing features, and location of your property will affect the accuracy of these estimates. Before having any work done, request a written estimate from the contractor—and sign a written contract for services before the work begins.

To avoid being surprised or overwhelmed by these costs, you'll want to:

• budget in advance for home maintenance, and

• consider buying a home warranty.

Budgeting for Home Maintenance

It's worth starting a home maintenance fund now, so that you'll have money available for ongoing maintenance as well as unexpected repairs. Of course, larger-scale repairs such as replacing a furnace may drain your fund for a time, but at least the fund will help offset some of the expense.

The generally accepted rule of thumb is to set aside 1% of the purchase price of your home each year. That means, for example, that if you paid

Home Repair Cost List	
Electrical	
Replace light switches or outlets	$25 each
Replace ceiling fan	$250 plus cost of fan
Replace light fixtures	$25 per fixture
Exterior	
Resurface asphalt driveway	$3 to $5 per square foot
Replace windows	$400 to $600 each
Paint exterior	$3,500 to $10,000
Heating and air conditioning	
Replace furnace	$3,500 to $7,000
Replace hot water heater	$400 to $600, depending on cost of water heater unit
Interior	
Paint room	$400 to $800 per room
Install new carpeting	$10 to $30+ per square yard (installed)
Refinish wood floors	$3 per square foot
Plumbing	
Replace faucets	$200 to $300, depending on cost of faucet
Install new toilet	$300 to $400, depending on cost of toilet
Roofing	
Install new rain gutters	$6 to $10 per foot
Install new roof	$5,000 to $11,000

$300,000 for your second home, your annual contribution should be $3,000 a year. To make your saving plan more manageable, divide the annual amount by 12 and focus on saving that amount each month (around $250 in the above example).

If you have a more expensive home, say, over $500,000, you can place a cap on your annual contribution. There's a limit to how many repairs you can do on a home, even an expensive one. A cap of $5,000 works for most single-family houses, whether the house cost $500,000, $750,000, or $1 million. (If you'll be buying a $12 million estate, the analysis might be different, but in that case you're probably not worried about a set-aside fund.)

Also, if you have an older home (more than ten years old) or you're a landlord, you'll probably need to tinker with the accepted rule of thumb a bit. A 50-year old house is, for example, likely to demand more maintenance and repairs than a five-year old house. And, landlords tend to experience higher maintenance costs than nonlandlords, since tenants seem to accelerate wear and tear on houses. To account for these situations, adjust the accepted rule of thumb as follows:

- *If your home is more than ten years old,* take 10% of your annual contribution to your maintenance fund, multiply that amount by the number of ten-year increments that add up to the age of your home, and add the total to your annual repair fund. Let's do those calculations for the $300,000 home described above, assuming also that the home is 50 years old. First, 10% of the recommended $3,000 annual repair fund contribution comes out to $300. At 50 years old, it's got five ten-year increments. (If the age of your home doesn't divide evenly by ten, round up to the nearest ten-year increment.) Multiplying $300 by five, we come up with $1,500. Adding this number to the initial repair fund of $3,000 brings you to a more realistic repair fund of $4,500 a year.

- *If you're a landlord,* add a 25% premium to your annual contribution from the start. Therefore, rather than setting aside 1% of the cost of your home, up it to 1.25%. Continuing with the $300,000 example, you would need to put aside $3,750 (as opposed to $3,000) each year for home maintenance.

In the end, budgeting for a home maintenance fund is more art than science. While you should use the rules of thumb as a starting point, be sure to adjust your annual contribution up or down depending on the outcome from previous years.

Buying a Home Warranty

Unlike hazard insurance, which you'll buy in order to cover damage to your home in the event of a natural catastrophe, a home warranty policy covers the various mechanical problems that may crop up in a house. (Existing houses only: Newly built ones usually receive a warranty straight from the builder.) These mechanical problems might include a furnace breaking down, water pipes springing leaks, or appliances going haywire. It's optional coverage—many people go without it.

A basic home warranty policy can, however, be particularly useful for older homes. The coverage usually costs between $250 and $600 a year (coverage on multifamily homes will be higher since several units are involved). The home warranty company ordinarily partners with a local repair company that will fix or replace the damaged item or part. After you file a claim, you will pay a set service fee, ranging from approximately $25 to $75 per visit. These fees tend to be much lower than the bill for an entire repair would be.

INVESTOR

Landlords of older homes, in particular, out-of-state ones, may find home warranties useful. It's like having a repairperson on call. Of course, the landlord or property management company (if you chose to use one) will still need to coordinate the home visit and ensure that the repairperson can gain access to the house.

Like any insurance, home warranty policies have their limitations—not everything is covered. Preexisting conditions are often excluded, as are problems that can be attributed to your own (or your tenants', if you're a landlord) negligence. Buyers have been heard to complain that the part that breaks on an appliance is inevitably the part that's not covered. Before committing to a home warranty policy, make sure you understand which items are covered and which ones can be added for an additional cost or are excluded altogether.

TIP

Consider asking the seller to cover the first year's cost of a home warranty. Some sellers will offer to do this on their own, as a way of making the house more attractive and reducing nervousness and disputes during the closing and soon after the sale. If the house you're looking at has older appliances or heating and plumbing systems, you're in a particularly good position to ask the seller for coverage.

At the very least, it's worth contacting one or more home warranty companies to discuss your coverage options and receive a quote, especially since the only cost involved at this point is your time. Some of the more established home warranty companies include:

• American Home Shield (www.ahswarranty.com)

• Home Warranty of America (www.hwahomewarranty.com), and

• Mutual Warranty (www.mutualwarranty.com).

Property Taxes

Just like your primary residence, property taxes are probably the most expensive recurring cost that you will have to deal with in your second home—and when they go up, it can be in the thousands of dollars. Property tax rates, assessments, and collections occur at the local government level (your city or township). The purpose of these taxes is usually to fund schools and other public services, such as fire and police departments and libraries. Property taxes are most often due on a quarterly or biannual basis.

Depending upon the state in which your second home is located, as well as your lender's standard practices, you'll need to pay property taxes in one of two ways: either to the town directly, or via your lender, who collects the money from you (in conjunction with your loan payment) and pays on your behalf.

The amount you pay in property taxes is usually based on a percentage of your home's assessed value at the time of purchase. From that point forward, the degree to and pace at which your taxes increase will depend on where your property is located—that is, in which U.S. state, and within which local jurisdiction. For example, in California, property taxes increase at a snail's pace, while in Massachusetts, the sky seems to be the limit.

 FUTURE RETIREE

High property taxes can take a big bite out of a retiree's income. Since most retirees are on a fixed income, many look to retire in states and towns that offer lower property taxes. Refer to Chapter 4 to learn more about how property taxes and overall cost of living can impact where you choose to retire.

TIP

Before you buy a property, pay a visit to the town hall. Since property tax information is a matter of public record, you can ask to pull a tax history on the home you're thinking about buying. Look at how much the property taxes went up for the current owners over the course of their ownership. While you're there, ask whether are any pending town issues, such as tax overrides, might foreseeably raise your property taxes.

Rises in Mortgage Interest Rates

When you choose a mortgage for your home—discussed fully in Chapter 11—you'll need to consider how your loan choice will affect the predictability of your future home costs. A fixed-rate mortgage is obviously the most predictable, because your interest rate remains the same over the life of the loan. By contrast, the interest rate on an adjustable rate mortgage (ARM) adjusts up or down based on a specific index (a published number). The acronym ARM is eerily appropriate, because sometimes these mortgages can cost you just that—and a leg as well.

Rises in Planned Mortgage Payments

The payment structure on your home loan, whether it's a fixed-rate mortgage or an ARM, can also impact your monthly costs. Many borrowers now choose loans where the payments aren't preset at the same amount each month. In some cases, such as with an interest-only loan, your payments start out low, but are raised for the later and greater part of the loan period. (The reason is that each initial payment consists of only the interest due on the loan, but this ends after a specified period of time, such as five or ten years. After that, the principal is amortized over the remaining loan term.) These changes are mostly predictable (although you can have an ARM with a variable payment amount), but they manage to catch some buyers off guard anyway.

For example, suppose you take out a $250,000, 30-year, fixed-rate loan at 6% interest. At the start of this loan, your monthly payments on the interest-only payment structure will be $1,250. However, when you hit year six, your monthly payments will jump to $1,611 per month and stay there for the remaining 25 years of the loan. That year-six switch may feel like a shock, despite your having known it was coming.

INVESTOR

Many "flippers" (investors who buy and sell homes to turn a quick profit) use interest-only loans. Flippers usually hold onto homes for a year or two, at most—just enough time to either fix up the home and sell it or, in a strong real estate market, allow for rapid appreciation in house values to occur. Either way, flippers want to keep their monthly payments as low as possible in order to minimize expenses.

POINTS TO REMEMBER

Purchase price isn't the only thing to consider when budgeting to buy your second home. You'll also need to consider costs associated with the sale itself, as well as ongoing repair and maintenance costs. The secret is to understand these costs before you buy, so that you purchase a house you can afford to maintain.

Crunching the Numbers: How Much Second Home Can You Afford?

nless you're King Midas or Rumpelstiltskin, you probably don't have an endless supply of cash. Like most of us, you probably bring home a fixed amount of money each month, from which you pay a slew of bills for your existing home and other living expenses. Hopefully, you even tuck away a little extra for retirement, your kids' college tuition, or some other major event down the road.

The upshot is that you probably haven't saved up enough to pay for your second home outright. You may be planning to get a loan—or even loans—to help with financing. That's fine, but don't forget to figure out how much this will add to your monthly outflow of cash. The amount is likely to be significant.

To avoid having to sell your second home before the ink has dried on your loan papers, you may want to make some revisions (possibly major ones) to your budget right now. This will require assessing where your money currently goes and how much of it can realistically be redirected toward a second home.

To help you, we've created some handy budget worksheets, below (also found in the Appendix and on the CD-ROM at the back of this book). We'll walk you through each worksheet, explaining what you need to consider along the way toward creating your own second-home budget.

You'll find that our approach to budgeting hinges on how much you can afford to pay on a monthly basis—taking into account not only the obvious cost of your mortgage payment, but also your property taxes, insurance, utilities, and other second-home expenses. This allows you to determine exactly:

- how large a loan you can comfortably take on (as opposed to how much the bank says you qualify for)
- how much you can ultimately spend on a house (both to buy it and maintain it afterwards), and
- how large a down payment you'll need (given the purchase price of your home).

In the end, you'll have a budget that allows you to buy and maintain a second home with a minimum of financial stress.

Don't Let Your Down Payment Dictate Your Budget

"How much cash do I have that I can put down?" is often the first question someone asks when thinking about buying a second home. Based on the answer, the next question is often, "How much of a loan can I qualify for?" And that's where some people's financial problems begin. The fact is that most of us will qualify for a loan for more money than we can actually afford to pay back. That's because, regardless of our income, we're already stretched thin with other debts and savings obligations, such as our current home maintenance or building a nest egg for retirement.

"But why would the bank let me overextend myself?" you might be wondering. "Don't they want their money back?" The truth is that mortgage lenders qualify you for a loan based on how you rate on a risk assessment rather than on how much you can afford. And in the past few years, lenders have been much more lenient about how they assess borrower risk—sometimes to their own detriment, as shown by the rising numbers of foreclosures.

A smarter approach is to build your budget based on what you can comfortably afford to pay back each month, and let that dictate your maximum purchase price (including closing costs, which were covered in Chapter 2). Think of it this way: If you already know you can afford to pay $1,500 a month on a second home, then whether you're able to put down 5% or 50%, the maximum amount you can afford to pay each month is still $1,500. (This assumes you don't supplement your monthly payment with any savings you had tucked away.)

Where the size of your down payment comes into play is in providing a final financial boost. The higher your down payment, the higher-priced house you can buy without exceeding your affordable monthly payment.

By way of example, let's assume that, of your $1,500 available monthly cash, you can safely allocate $1,050 (about 70%) towards your home loan, and will need to set aside the balance to pay taxes, insurance, and other home-related expenses. That means you can handle a $175,000 loan (assuming 6% interest over 30 years).

Now let's bring the down payment into the picture. If you have $30,000 stashed away for a down payment, that's great, but it shouldn't change the amount of loan you take on. It will, however, provide the last puzzle piece for determining the maximum purchase price you should pay on a house, in this case $205,000 (your $175,000 maximum loan amount plus the $30,000 down payment). Knowing this, you would now have the following three options when looking at potential houses:

- Find a house that's less than $205,000, put the full $30,000 down, and pay less than $1,500 each month (leaving yourself a little extra money for other purposes).
- Find a house at $205,000, put $30,000 down, and pay $1,500 each month, which is the most you can afford to pay.
- Find a house that's more than $205,000, but know that if you really want that house, you'll need to up the size of your down payment in order to keep your monthly payments at $1,500.

In a world prone to stretching the financial limits, the concept of spending only within your means may seem like a radical way of thinking. However, it's the only realistic way to buy a second home that will be a source of joy, not panic, in the coming months and years.

How Much Money Comes in Each Month

Since your current monthly income will be carrying the burden of your second home debt, adding up that income is the best starting point in developing your budget.

Monthly income can come from a variety of sources, some of which may be steady (like a salary), while others are sporadic (like profits on investments). While the former is easier to budget around, the latter shouldn't be ignored, especially if they add significantly to your income.

To add up your monthly income, take out the Affordable Monthly Expenditures worksheet (available in the Appendix and on the CD-ROM at the back of this book) and fill out Section A (reproduced below).

Section A - Monthly income:

Net salary/wages (after taxes and other deductions)

Interest income/dividends   + $ _____

Other income:

Profits on investments	$ _____	
Part-time work or home-based business	$ _____	
Other	$ _____	
Total	$ _____	

(Insert total other income)   + $ _____

Rental income (if you plan on renting out your second home)   + $ _____

Line 1: Total monthly income $ = _____

Here's some explanation of the types of monthly income that the worksheet asks you for.

- *Net wages/salary.* This probably accounts for the bulk of your income, whether you receive a paycheck from an employer or you're self-employed. A common mistake in budgeting for a second home (or any home, for that matter) is to base decisions on your gross (before taxes and other deductions) salary. In fact, you'll see this used in many of the worksheets available online. But net salary gives a far more realistic picture—it is, on average, about two-thirds of your gross salary (depending on your monthly deductions).

  EXAMPLE: Morton has a job as a marketing manager for a local restaurant chain, which pays him a gross salary of $72,000 per year or $6,000 a month. He figures he's doing pretty well, and hopes to buy a vacation home in the near future, which he and his family will use exclusively. But if you look at Morton's net (take home) salary, it's down to $3,960 a month after taxes, insurance deductions, 401(k) contributions, and other deductions. That's a $2,040 difference—and one that should make a big difference in Morton's budget.

- *Interest income/dividends.* This is any income you receive (usually on a monthly or quarterly basis) that comes from checking or savings accounts, money market accounts, stock dividends (those that are paid out as opposed to being reinvested), and similar investment vehicles.

- *Other income (the total from the next three lines).* This is incoming cash (steady or sporadic) that comes from such sources as capital gains on investments, a part-time business, alimony payments, or any other form of income beyond your wages/salary and interest income/dividends.

- *Rental income.* If you plan on renting out your second home, you can and should factor into your budget your estimated rental income. Just make sure you're realistic about how much it will amount to each month. You can start by combing through the local newspaper to gauge the "going rates" for comparable rentals. Also recognize that there will be periods of time when your property isn't rented out (maybe because you're using it personally, you're between tenants, or you're only planning to rent out the property seasonally). Either way, assume a vacancy period of around 25% on a year-round or seasonal rental. (This is more or less the percentage a mortgage lender will assume when reviewing your loan application—but don't panic, the U.S. Census Bureau puts the actual nationwide vacancy rate at more like 10%—see www.census.gov.)

Where Your Money Currently Goes Each Month

Unless you're stranded on a desert island, it costs money to live (and even then, your cable bills would probably keep on coming). Even the most determined saver in the world has to spend each month just to survive.

By understanding where you spend your money, you can figure out how much second home you can afford—or whether you can afford one at all. Broadly speaking, there are three areas of spending to look at:

- payments for your current home
- payments for other debts, and
- any regular savings you've imposed upon yourself.

Paying for Your Current Home

If you're thinking about buying a second home, you obviously own a first home, the expenses from which probably make up the bulk of your current spending. To add these expenses up, fill out Section B of the Affordable Monthly Expenditures Worksheet (reproduced below).

Section B - Monthly expenses for your existing home:

Mortgage/loan payment	$_____
Property taxes (annual cost/12)	+ $_____
Property insurance (annual cost/12)	+ $_____
Household bills:	

Electric	$_____	
Heating	$_____	
Water and sewer	$_____	
Internet	$_____	
Phone (landline and cell)	$_____	
Cable	$_____	
Other	$_____	
Total	$_____	

(Insert total household bills)	+ $_____
Maintenance and repairs (average annual cost/12)	+ $_____
Line 2: Total monthly expenses for your existing home	= $_____

As you'll see from the worksheet, it's important to include all of your expenses, not just your mortgage payment. You're probably spending thousands of dollars per year on property taxes and homeowners' insurance (if these aren't already included in your monthly mortgage payment), not to mention household bills for utilities, repairs, and more.

Paying for Other Debt

Debt for items other than your first home can be also be a major factor in your budget. Add it up on Section C of the Affordable Monthly Expenditures Worksheet (reproduced below).

Section C - Other monthly expenses:	
Auto loans	$_____
Credit card payment (bank cards and store cards)	+ $_____
Other loans or debt (student loan, consumer loan, child support, etc.)	+ $_____
Line 3: Total other monthly expenses	= $_____

The two most common and largest areas of "other debt" are usually credit cards (including store cards as well as bank cards) and automobile loans. But don't forget any other lingering debts or obligations, such as student loans, consumer loans (perhaps for a computer, big-screen TV, or other electronic merchandise), or alimony or child support payments.

Self-Imposed Savings

If you're regularly saving money for some future purpose, such as retirement, tuition, a vacation, or a wedding, great. Some people even set up a special savings account that automatically deducts from their checking account. Just don't forget your regular savings plan when budgeting for your second home. If you plan to continue with it, it needs to be viewed as a cost like any other. Account for your savings on Section D of the Affordable Monthly Expenditures Worksheet (reproduced below).

Section D - Monthly savings not related to second home:	
IRA contributions (Note: 401(k) contributions are already factored into the "Net salary/wages" line under "Monthly income.")	$_____
Self-imposed savings, such as for school tuition or wedding	+ $_____
Line 4: Total monthly savings not related to second home	= $_____

The good news is that your self-imposed savings are completely within your control. That means if you come up a bit short in your second-home budget, one possibility is to reduce these savings to make up the difference. Just be realistic about what you're giving up. For example, recommending to your daughter that she transfer from Harvard to a community college so you can pay for your second home probably won't go over very well.

How Much Is Left for Your Second Home Each Month

After filling out Sections A through D of the worksheet, the rest is a cinch. In Section E, simply subtract Lines 2, 3, and 4 (your expenses) from Line 1, your current income. The resulting number will tell you how much you can realistically dedicate toward your second-home loan and other expenses.

Section E - What's left? Calculate what you can spend each month for a second home	
Line 1: Total monthly income	$_____
Line 2: Total monthly expenses for existing home	– $_____
Line 3: Total other monthly expenses	– $_____
Line 4: Total monthly savings not related to second home	– $_____
Amount left for your second home each month	= $_____

That brings you to the end of the first and biggest worksheet in this chapter. A complete version of this worksheet is shown below (and remember, it's available in the Appendix and on the CD-ROM at the back of the book).

Affordable Monthly Expenditures Worksheet

Section A - Monthly income:

Net salary/wages (after taxes and other deductions) $_____

Interest income/dividends   + $_____

Other income:

Profits on investments	$_____
Part-time work or home-based business	$_____
Other	$_____
Total	$_____

                (Insert total other income)   + $_____

Rental income (if you plan on renting out your second home)   + $_____

Line 1: Total monthly income   = $_____

Section B - Monthly expenses for your existing home:

Mortgage/loan payment $_____

Property taxes (annual cost/12)   + $_____

Property insurance (annual cost/12)   + $_____

Household bills:

Electric	$_____
Heating	$_____
Water and sewer	$_____
Internet	$_____
Phone (landline and cell)	$_____
Cable	$_____
Other	$_____
Total	$_____

                (Insert total household bills)   + $_____

Maintenance and repairs (average annual cost/12)   + $_____

Line 2: Total monthly expenses for your existing home   = $_____

Affordable Monthly Expenditures Worksheet (cont'd.)

Section C - Other monthly expenses:

Auto loans	$_____
Credit card payment (bank cards and store cards)	+ $_____
Other loans or debt (student loan, consumer loan, child support, etc.)	+ $_____
Line 3: Total other monthly expenses	= $_____

Section D - Monthly savings not related to second home:

IRA contributions (Note: 401(k) contributions are alreadyfactored into the "Net salary/wages" line under "Monthly income.")	$_____
Self-imposed savings, such as for school tuition or wedding	+ $_____
Line 4: Total monthly savings not related to second home	= $_____

Section E - What's left? Calculate what you can spend each month for a second home

Line 1: Total monthly income	$_____
Line 2: Total monthly expenses for existing home	– $_____
Line 3: Total other monthly expenses	– $_____
Line 4: Total monthly savings not related to second home	– $_____
Amount left for your second home each month	= $_____

How Much to Set Aside for Nonmortgage Second-Home Expenses

The next step in creating your budget is to understand how much your second home will demand of you financially each month. When most people think about the monthly cost of a home, they think about their mortgage payment. But don't forget that you'll also need to cover such expenses as your property taxes and homeowners' insurance (in some cases these costs may be included in your mortgage loan payment), as well as other monthly expenses such as repairs, property management fees, utilities, and possibly a security system.

Since you haven't even shopped for the house yet, there's no perfect way to estimate these expenses. At this point, your best bet is to use a general percentage allocation based on your maximum monthly payment. Of course, this allocation can vary considerably depending on how much you end up putting down on your house, its condition, where it's located, your personal needs, and more.

For now, we're assuming a down payment of about 20% (the current median down payment on second homes is actually 22%) on a house that's in good condition and located in an average-priced market. With this in mind, consider allocating 70% of your maximum affordable payment towards paying off your home loan, with the balance going towards other second-home expenses. If, for example, you can afford to pay a total of $1,500 per month, it's a reasonable bet that about $500 will be needed for expenses other than the loan. This 70% is an average derived from a random comparison of various monthly home expenses (see table below).

If you're planning to rent out your property, the "General maintenance and repairs" could easily be double or triple the percentage listed in the chart. That's because tenants tend to beat up places more than owners do. Plus, if you plan on using a property management company, that's another expense to be added. On the positive side, you'll be able to take advantage of business-expense-related tax deductions, which will help offset the additional expenses. (To learn more about the impact of renting on your second-home budget, see Chapters 5 and 13.) For now, stick with the budget allocations listed below. You can always adjust your budget accordingly once you begin to look at properties and get a more accurate view of the expenses involved.

Typical Home Expense Breakdown	
Description of Monthly Expense	% Allocation of Total Monthly Payment*
Mortgage/loan	70%
Property taxes	15%
Homeowners' insurance	5%
General maintenance and repairs	5%
Household bills (utilities, phone, cable, etc.)	5%

*Based on a random comparison of monthly home expenses, assuming a down payment of 20% on a house in good condition located in an average-priced market.

How Much You Can Spend on Your Second-Home Mortgage

At last, having mentally whittled away your income by calculating and predicting your current and future expenses, you can arrive at a key figure: what size second-home mortgage you can comfortably take on, taking into account the interest you'll be charged on that loan. The worksheet below will walk you through the math, covering both how much you can pay each month and in total. (It's also in the Appendix and on the CD-ROM.)

Estimated Maximum Loan Amount Worksheet

Amount left for your second home each month $_____
(from final line of the Affordable Monthly Expenditures Worksheet)

Percent allocation towards your loan payments (see table above)   x _____ %

Affordable monthly loan payment   = $_____

Number of months for loan term (most likely 360 months)   x _____

Total payback amount (loan principal plus interest)   = $_____

Percentage of payback amount allocated towards loan principal only*   x $_____ %

Estimated maximum loan amount   = $_____

* The easiest way to figure out this loan principal allocation is to use an online mortgage calculator. Simply plug in your anticipated loan terms (such as loan amount, interest rate, and number of years) to determine the total amount paid (principal and interest) at the end of your loan period. To calculate the percentage of principal only, divide the total principal paid by the total amount paid on your loan. For example, a $200,000 loan at 6% interest over 30 years means you'll pay back a total of $431,677 ($200,000 in principal plus $231,677 in total interest). That means your principal-only percentage is 46% ($200,000 divided by $431,677).

How Much You Can Pay for Your Second Home Overall

Having hypothetically allocated your cash in various directions, you can now figure out what price you can pay for your second home. To do this, you'll need to answer the following:

- *How much do you currently have saved up for a down payment?* For second homes, most lenders require a down payment of at least 5% (10% if it's an investment property). But at this point, those percentages are useless, because we haven't yet determined how much you can spend on a home. Rather than think about your down payment as a percentage of the sale price, think of it in terms of raw dollars. Specifically, how much do you have (or will you have) saved up to put towards a down payment? Talk to your financial advisor if you're uncertain about how much of your savings you can safely deplete. Plug that dollar amount into the worksheet below.

- *How much do you estimate your closing costs will be?* As discussed in Chapter 2, on the day your house becomes yours, you'll have to pay several costs and fees above and beyond the sale price. These may include, for example, processing, title, and home inspection fees, as well as prepayments of property taxes and home insurance. While it's difficult to determine the exact dollar amount of closing fees so early in the process, at least plug in an estimate for now. You can always adjust this estimate later when you have a better idea as to your actual closing costs. Bankrate.com has a section on its website that provides average closing costs by state, at www.bankrate.com/brm/news/mortgages/ccmap.asp.

Now you're ready to use the simple worksheet below to determine your maximum purchase price. (It's also in the Appendix and on the CD-ROM.)

Maximum Purchase Price Worksheet

Your estimated maximum loan amount (from Estimated Maximum Loan Amount Worksheet, above)	$_____
Down payment amount (how much you have currently saved)	+ $_____
Estimated closing costs	− $_____
Total amount you can pay for a second home	= $_____

Remember, the down payment amount listed above is strictly for budgeting purposes. Your lender may require you to put down a higher amount based on the sale price of the home and your personal financial situation.

How to Adjust Your Budget Around a More Expensive House

If you find a house you love, but it costs more money than your budget can handle, there are a few ways to adjust while staying within your affordability limits. Subsequent chapters will cover each in depth, but in brief, these methods include:

- *Bolstering the size of your down payment.* A higher down payment gets you one of two things: either lowered monthly payments or the ability to spend more on a house overall. Possible ways of increasing your down payment include modifying your daily spending habits or increasing your savings (see Chapter 9), or getting money from a family member in the form of a gift or a deferred loan (see Chapter 10).

- *Reducing your current monthly expenses.* You can comfortably afford to spend more on a second home without adding a penny to your existing down payment. All you need to do is reduce your current monthly outflow of cash. This can be achieved by lowering or eliminating your current credit card debt, paying down any existing auto or personal loans, or even refinancing the mortgage on your current home if interest rates have fallen.

- *Buying a home with another person.* A surefire way to increase your house-buying capacity is to split the cost of a second home with a relative, friend, or colleague. This works especially well for homes that are bought for pure investment or as a getaway destination. A joint purchase could easily get you twice as much house or more (depending on the split) than if you bought on your own (see Chapter 12).

POINTS TO REMEMBER

It took some work and a bunch of calculations, but now you know exactly how much you can afford to spend on a second home. You've also discovered that it's best to let your affordable monthly payment drive your budget rather than the size of your down payment. The maximum amount you can spend is the uppermost end of your budget. If you find your "perfect" second home for a lower amount, terrific—your monthly second-home payments will be even more manageable. If you find one at a higher amount, it means that you'll probably need to increase the amount of your down payment.

Narrowing Your Search: What and Where to Buy

D amn the torpedoes, full speed ahead" may have worked fine for Admiral David Glasgow Farragut in the Battle of Mobile Bay. You, however, might want to do a tad more research on what's ahead before launching yourself toward a second home. Give some serious thought to:

- what type of home you want to buy (single or multifamily? condominium or co-op? existing home or new build?), and
- where you'll buy it (urban or suburban area? coast or inland? an area with good rental or resale potential?).

This chapter helps you choose a house and a location that's right for you and is also a good investment—which is important even if investing isn't first on your priority list.

Which Comes First? House Type or House Location?

Think about your ideal second home. What immediately comes to mind? Did a specific type of home (two-story Victorian or condominium with pool and golf course access) pop into your head, or did you instead picture a particular location, such as a beach or the mountains? If you plan on buying a second home with someone else (such as a spouse, significant other, or friend), ask that person the same question. There's no wrong answer: It's a matter of personal choice and your home-buying goals.

Knowing whether home type or home location is driving your decision will help you create a balance between the two, especially if and when you have to make tradeoffs. For example, you might decide to buy a condominium instead of a single-family home in order to buy in a more desirable area. Or, you might decide to shift your location if your heart is set on owning a single-family home.

Reviewing Your House-Type Options

Houses vary not just in shape, size, and décor, but also when it comes to how their ownership is legally structured. Here's an overview of the various types of houses:

Single-family home. A dwelling meant for one family or household that is not attached to other homes. Ownership includes both the house (structure) and the land it sits on.

Multifamily home. A dwelling meant for two or more families or households that is not attached to other homes. You've probably heard of them as duplexes (two families), triplexes (three families), or quadruplexes (four families). Ownership includes both the house (structure) and the land it sits on. Homes with five or more units are not addressed in this book, because they're considered commercial properties and are a different ballgame (for one thing, they require a commercial as opposed to a residential mortgage).

Townhouse. The term "townhouse" was originally coined to describe units within row housing tracts, usually in urban areas. Now it refers to a dwelling, usually with two or more floors, that shares one or more common walls with similar, attached structures to the left and right and has its own entrance. That means you can have neighbors on either side of you, but not above or below. Ownership includes both the unit (interior and exterior, meaning walls and roof), and the land it sits on, plus a proportionate interest in the common areas. These common areas are maintained and managed by a homeowners' association, to which you normally pay a monthly fee. Owners abide by a set of covenants, conditions, and restrictions (CC&Rs) governing use of their property and other community matters.

Condominium (condo). A dwelling (usually on one floor) surrounded by similar units within a larger building. The units often share a main entrance. Units are owned individually, while the land and any common areas are owned jointly. The exterior parts of the buildings and the common areas are maintained and managed by a homeowners' association, to which you normally pay a monthly fee. Owners abide by a set of CC&Rs governing use of their property and other community matters.

Cooperative (co-op). A dwelling similar to a condominium, except that the residents are shareholders of a corporation that, in turn, owns the individual units as well as the land. The corporation holds the deed on the property, while you're issued a stock certificate specifying how many shares of the corporation you own. The larger, more desirable units generally require owning a high percentage of shares. You also receive a lease allowing you to occupy your individual unit, much like a tenant would. Shareholders or owners elect a board of directors, which functions like a homeowners' association, setting and collecting monthly dues for maintaining the land and common areas, and upholding the community's rules and regulations.

Distinguishing Between Townhouses, Condos, and Co-Ops

Confusion reigns when it comes to differentiating between these three house types—partly because sellers sometimes use the wrong names themselves. Many people mistakenly believe that the differences are physical, as between a brick row house and an urban loft. In reality, however, the main differences depend on how your property ownership is legally structured.

Let's start with the central commonalities and differences between a townhouse and a condominium, which have to do with how much you own beyond the interior of your own unit, and in what form you own it.

For starters, in both townhouses and condos, any common areas—parking, planted areas, pool areas, and walkways—are partly yours, as you own them jointly with all your fellow owners.

But in a townhouse, you own all of your own unit—both the inside and the outside—plus you own the land upon which it sits. In a condominium development, by contrast, you own the inside of the unit, but not the exterior, and not the land upon which it sits.

As for co-ops, your ownership is defined not by physical portions of the property, but by the number of shares you own in the corporation that owns the property. You have usage rights to an individual unit and to common areas.

> ! **WARNING**
> **You can't tell by looking.** Many condominium developments are built to look like townhouses, some co-ops are built to look like apartments—it's easy to be totally misled. Remember, legal ownership structure is the main determinant of whether a property is a condominium, townhouse, or co-op. That's why it's important to examine the rules of ownership provided by the governing body or association (usually called "covenants, conditions, and restrictions," or CC&Rs).

Choosing a House Type: Price, Privacy, and Property Maintenance Needs

When it comes to choosing between a single-family home, multifamily home, townhouse, condominium, or co-op, the top three factors to think about are price, privacy, and property maintenance. We'll call this combo the "P Factor."

Price: How Much Can You Comfortably Afford?

For most people, cost is the single most important factor in choosing a home type—you can't buy what you can't comfortably afford. (If you're not sure how much you can put towards your second home, refer back to Chapter 3, which helps you create a second-home budget.) For now, understand that your costs will include not only the purchase price of the property, but also your monthly mortgage payments, home-related insurance, property taxes, repairs and ongoing maintenance, and more.

INVESTOR

Planning on renting out your property? Your rental income may help offset your monthly expenses, thus allowing you to buy a more expensive type of home. But be conservative with your rental income projections. Make sure you understand the rental market in the area before adding up your hypothetical earnings. An expensive and desirable area in which to live isn't necessarily a hot rental market. And even in solid markets, it's often unrealistic to expect rental income to cover 100% or more of your second-home expenses.

Privacy: How Much Are You Willing to Give Up?

Privacy is an individual consideration. Some vacationers, for example, may fantasize about a rural getaway, enclosed in greenery, where they won't see another soul for miles. Others may be looking forward to all-night parties on the boardwalk.

Investors aren't ordinarily too concerned with privacy, since they won't be using the property themselves. They require that the property have only as much privacy as is necessary to satisfy their renters or buyers, and thereby increase their own profit margins.

Future retirees may need to think about two sets of privacy needs: their or their renter's current wishes, and the level of privacy that they want—or that will be healthy for them—post-retirement. Let's face it, privacy can turn into loneliness after you stop going to an office every day.

Privacy normally requires added space, and that's almost guaranteed to come with a higher price tag. In urban or developed areas, putting privacy at the top of your P Factor priority list may mean compromising in other ways, for example looking in less-developed locations.

Property Maintenance: Who Will Keep the Place Up?

You probably won't be at your second home as often as your first. Weeks or months might pass between visits to your property. But that doesn't mean the grass will stop growing, the dust will take a break from collecting, or the furnace will refrain from breaking down.

How to handle property maintenance is a huge consideration for anyone buying a second home, especially if you won't live within a comfortable driving distance. Of course, you can hire a property management company to maintain the property and handle repairs. If you plan on being a landlord, the management company can also screen and find tenants, and collect rent on your behalf. But these companies aren't charities. Their services come at a cost, so you'll have to balance the hit to your budget against the potential headaches and travel time involved in doing it yourself.

Comparing House Types Using the P Factor

Let's take a look at how each type of home stacks up using the P Factor described above.

Single-Family Homes and the P Factor

Single-family homes are the clear winner in the high-cost department. But their other charms may make them worth it. Here's a look at the P Factor for single-family homes:

- *Price.* Single-family homes tend to cost more per square foot than most other home types (with the possible exception of some larger, multifamily units). In the mid-2000s, it was big news when median condo prices surpassed single-family homes for the first time ever, due in large part to a higher concentration of condos in more expensive housing markets. In spite of this, single-family homes tend to hold their value better than townhouses and condos over the long haul, and are usually easier to sell.

- *Privacy.* Single-family homes usually offer more privacy than other home types, mainly because of the land surrounding the house. Single-family homes are usually found in less dense urban areas, the suburbs, or the exurbs. (Wondering about "exurbs?" It's short for "extra-urban", a term derived in the 1950s by August Comet Spectorsky in his book *The Exurbanite*, which discussed the formation of housing developments in rural communities.) The more land, the more privacy. But watch out for so-called "zero-lot-line homes," which maximize living space by building right up near the property boundary. Developers squeeze these homes within ten feet of each other in order to increase profits. While these homes still have front and back yards, their postage stamp size can't help but reduce your privacy.

- *Property maintenance.* Single-family homes require more upkeep than other home types. The owner is responsible for maintaining the land as well as the house. And the larger the lot size, the more upkeep is required. Dreaming of a second home on a half-acre lot in the country? Now picture yourself mowing all that grass and trimming the hedges—or writing the check for someone else to do so. The same goes for painting, cleaning gutters, and a slew of other maintenance demands. Don't forget to pack your work clothes (or checkbook).

Multifamily Homes and the P Factor

If you plan on renting out your property, a multifamily home could be a great way to maximize rental income. The tradeoff is that these homes tend to be harder to sell, especially in a soft real estate market. Here's the P Factor analysis for a multifamily home:

- *Price.* Although a multifamily property will usually be more expensive than a single-family in terms of absolute dollars, that should be offset somewhat by your rental income. (Most multifamily homeowners rent out the units even if they use one of them exclusively for themselves.) For investors, multifamily properties are appealing because they tend to generate higher cash flow than single-family dwellings, while diversifying the rental income stream among several tenants.

- *Privacy.* If you're sharing a wall or have people above or below you, you've got to expect less privacy. And the more units on a property, the less privacy for each occupant. Of course, if you don't plan on personally using the property, this is less of a concern. For some, less privacy can be a plus—having neighbors adds to a feeling of community and security. Better yet, if you've got a large family or group of friends and want to spend your time near them, a multifamily property can serve as a family compound.

- *Property maintenance.* It's simple math: The more units on the property, the more chances there are for things to go wrong. However, taking care of a four-unit property is not as burdensome as managing four separate single-family homes. In fact, most property management companies will charge less per unit the more units you have. Multi-unit properties also tend to have easy-to-maintain landscaping and other money- and time-saving features.

Townhouses, Condominiums, and Co-Ops and the P Factor

Part of the attraction of townhouses, condos, and co-ops is that your responsibility often stops at or near your own walls. Still, if you're looking for a home that's maintenance free, you'll soon learn that there's no such thing. A townhouse, condo, or co-op, however, is about as close as you can get. Here's how their P Factor looks:

- *Price.* Townhouses, condos and co-ops are supposed to be relatively low cost. Townhouses and condos came into being in the 1970s as a means of offering homeownership to people who couldn't raise enough cash for a single-family home. Co-ops have been around much longer, having begun in New York City in the late 1800s. Still, the rationale was the same—to provide more affordable housing. However, over the past five or so years, the real estate boom has pushed townhouse, condo, and co-op prices higher and higher. They now tend to be priced just a tad lower than single-family homes of the same square footage in the same area. But purchase price isn't your only financial concern. Your monthly fees (covering such costs as maintenance and repair of the common areas) can really add up: Anywhere from $200 to $1,000 a month is common. And depending on the community's operating rules, you may be assessed special fees to cover things like a major emergency repair or a lawsuit against the association. Find out how much it'll cost you before you buy, by asking for a written copy of any fee statements, the bylaws, and the CC&Rs.

- *Privacy.* Townhouses, condos, and co-ops tend to offer less privacy than single-family homes by virtue of sharing one or more common walls, or in the case of a condo or co-op, having someone above or below you. Also, you may feel like Big Brother is watching you as you're forced to abide by the community's rules. Such rules could restrict you from having pets; limit your exterior paint colors, types of curtains, or what you can keep on your deck or patio; forbid a home business; and much more. If you plan on renting out the property, the bylaws could even limit or eliminate your renters' use of common amenities such as a pool. The upside of giving up some privacy is your greater sense of security knowing that your neighbors are just on the other side of the wall. You might also appreciate rules that prevent your neighbors from doing anything drastic, such as painting the exterior of their unit Pepto Bismol pink.

- *Property maintenance.* Townhouses, condos, and co-ops require far less maintenance than single-family homes. While the inside of the unit (and the small front and back yards commonly found in townhouses) are the responsibility of the owner, exterior maintenance (such as painting, roofing, and landscaping) is usually handled by a homeowners' association or the board of directors. Of course, that comes at a price, which you'll pay monthly. And you may have to shell out more money on your own, in order to comply with design and landscaping standards set forth in the community's rules.

INVESTOR

Hoping to rent out your condo or townhouse? Some developments place limits on how many units can be owned and rented out by non-resident investors. Make sure you know the rules before you buy.

WARNING

Co-ops can be difficult to get into. Getting into a co-op is not guaranteed. Usually, you'll need to be approved by the board of directors and a majority of the owners. Some co-ops can be snooty, or even downright snotty, about who they accept. Also, if and when you try to sell a co-op, those same rules apply. So, while you may have found someone you think is the perfect buyer, the board and owners can deem that person inappropriate to join their select group.

New Build or Existing Home?

The differences between buying an existing home and buying one that will be newly built for you go far beyond their age. For instance, new builds typically require less upkeep and can be built to suit your needs. On the other hand, existing homes are usually found in more developed communities and offer more character and old-world charm. In some ways, choosing between the two is like deciding whether you want soup or salad with your meal.

New Builds: Advantages and Disadvantages

If you have very specific wants and needs for your home, you don't want to deal with an aging structure, or you just love the idea of starting from scratch, a new build may be the way to go. You can either buy into a new development or hire an architect and general contractor to build a custom home. Either way, a newly built home has advantages and disadvantages.

Advantages of newly built homes:

- They tend to be more efficient to maintain and to operate, since everything is new and in compliance with current building codes.
- They offer modern conveniences such as central air conditioning, cable and Internet hookups, a sufficient number of electrical outlets, better insulation, energy-efficient windows, and more.
- They offer more choice in terms of the materials used (particularly with a custom-built home, but also true of homes in developments).
- Builders of developments are nationally known, so you can research their reputation for honesty and quality work.

Disadvantages of newly built homes:

- They tend to cost more than existing homes on a square-foot basis.
- They offer less flexibility on pricing compared to an existing home.
- They are usually built in less-established communities where land is more plentiful. That could mean being further away from cities or towns.

- Some builders try to make sure you don't bring in any independent professionals—they'd prefer you go without your own realtor, inspector, and sometimes even mortgage lender.

- Quality depends on the builder. Particularly in large developments, some contractors cut corners and use lower quality materials to increase their profit margins. Also, since the homes are being built quickly, the developers may run out of skilled labor, or fail to let materials dry or settle the proper amount of time. Don't just take our word for it: *Consumer Reports*, *SmartMoney*, and other publications have recently reported on a so-called epidemic of bad new-home workmanship.

RESOURCES

Want more information about building a new home? The National Association of Home Builders (www.nahb.org) has lots of free information on its website—everything from how to find a builder to resolving problems to accommodating disabilities. Also see the article "Heartbreak Houses," in the *SmartMoney* September 2006 issue.

Existing Homes: Advantages and Disadvantages

If you love charm and character, want to buy into an established area, or appreciate knowing that a particular house has aged to reveal any flaws, then an existing home can be the way to go. Below are the main advantages and disadvantages.

Advantages of an existing home:

- Usually lower priced per square foot than a new build

- More room to negotiate on pricing, especially during a soft housing market

- Usually found in more developed, established communities, with identifiable personalities and such features as cultural amenities, tree-lined streets, and unique local restaurants, and

- May have been built during a time when beams were thicker and construction more solid—and its construction has stood the test of time.

Disadvantages of an existing home:

- Typically less efficient to maintain, unless the house has been completely renovated or is still relatively new
- May lack modern conveniences such as central air conditioning and cable and Internet hookups
- Usually costly to maintain, because aging structural and mechanical systems require more repairs, and
- What you see is what you get. If you want to change something, such as replacing bathroom tile or upgrading kitchen appliances, it usually means doing so after you buy the home.

Starting Your Search for a House Location

Most people have at least a vague idea of where they want to look for a house (such as in the country, the city, the desert, or along the coast). Some even have specific towns or neighborhoods in mind. Your ideas for potential locations may grow out of personal familiarity with certain areas or word of mouth. The media can play a role as well. You pick up a magazine or newspaper or read an online article or book about hot spots for travel, retirement areas, and home appreciation, and your imagination goes to work.

RESOURCES

No idea where to begin your search for a location? Visit:

- www.neighborhoodscout.com/neighborhoods, where you can search for retirement areas, vacation destinations, family-oriented communities, and more. While the site prompts you at times to subscribe, there's a lot of information you can access for free, without providing contact information. Click on "Build a Neighborhood" to select from over 60 characteristics and find neighborhoods that may work for you.
- www.homepages.com, which shows you aerial neighborhood maps. You can zoom in and out and select various "neighborhood filters" that will show you locations of schools, parks, restaurants, and more.

For each location you're considering, ask yourself the questions below (in order of priority).

- *How far will your second home be from your primary home?* You don't want to spend all your free time traveling, especially if you plan on frequent visits to your second home. If you're a prospective landlord, you may have to stop by on short notice, particularly if you won't be hiring a property management company. The more time it takes to get to your second home, the less time you have to enjoy the place or deal with on-site tenant and home maintenance issues. While mileage is one way to measure distance, time is actually a better indicator. How many hours will it take door to door, in your car, on a plane, or in a shuttle? Try it at least once, if possible—you may be surprised how traffic patterns or other issues add hours to your travel time.

RESOURCES

Driving? Check out the distance between the two locations. Go to www.mapquest.com, click on the "Directions" icon at the top of the page, and then plug in the addresses of both locations. You'll get driving directions as well as mileage and an estimated drive time.

- *Do you like your neighbors and the other people who live there?* People make up communities. They define the personality of an area and even influence its surrounding amenities and activities. If you're going to be spending personal time at your second home, you'll want to be able to relate to the people around you. And if you plan on renting out your property (either full-time or for only part of the year), the people in the area will define the types of renters you'll most likely attract. You can easily research such factors such as gender, age, ethnicity, and family size (known as demographics), using the resources listed below. Use this information to create a mental picture of the typical person who lives in the area. Then visit in person and really get to know what the people are like.

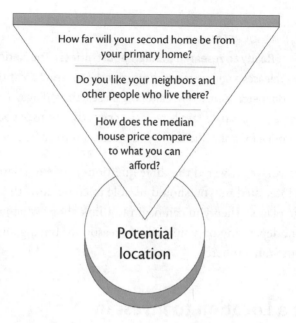

How far will your second home be from your primary home?

Do you like your neighbors and other people who live there?

How does the median house price compare to what you can afford?

Potential location

RESOURCES

Interested in finding out what type of people live or rent somewhere? The U.S. Census offers demographic data on individual towns. Visit www.fact finder.census.gov/home/saff/main.html and input the name of a town. For populations under 65,000 residents, the data is over five years old. Still, you'll get a general sense of gender, age, ethnicity, and other demographics of the people in the area. Another helpful website is www.bestplaces.net, providing general information on age, education, average income, crime rate, and more, plus other handy tools. You can also flip through the local newspaper to get a sense of the people and overall character of a town.

- *How does the median house price compare to what you can afford?* After determining how much money you can put toward a house (covered in Chapter 3), your best bet is to look in areas where that amount is as close to the median selling price as possible. That's not to say that you can't look in areas where the median is higher than what you can afford, but as a practical matter, you'll find fewer houses there that fit your budget.

RESOURCES

Ready to research median house prices? The National Association of Realtors releases a survey every three months covering areas that are roughly 50 miles in diameter. Visit www.realtor.org/Research.nsf/Pages/MetroPrice and select between existing single-family homes or condos/co-ops. If you want to find the median price for a specific town, your best bet is to contact a local realtor.

Once you've answered the three questions above in relation to the locations you're interested in, you should be able to come up with a list of a few specific places. Then you can begin to think about which of them works best for you, depending on your primary reason for buying and whether you'll rent out your property.

Choosing a Location to Invest In

If your primary second-home goal is to buy for investment, decide first whether you're a tortoise or a hare. As a reminder, tortoises buy, hold, and rent out their properties to generate ongoing rental income and long-term appreciation, while hares buy, fix up (if necessary), and sell properties to make quick money on appreciation.

We'll discuss the different types of research that tortoises and hares will need to do below. However they do share one thing: When it comes to choosing the ideal location, both are looking for a healthy market with signs of growth. And both should avoid areas described by Bruce Springsteen's lyrics, "Now Main Street's whitewashed windows and vacant stores, seems like there ain't nobody wants to come down here no more."

RESOURCES

For quick and easy access to local market data: Go to www.city-data .com, where you can plug in a location name and get a wealth of information: the population, weather, median income, and more. Be sure to click on the "[*Location name*] residents, houses, and apartments details" link. You'll see housing data such as rental rates and sale prices. (Some of the information on this site is dated, and you'll have to deal with some Google ads, but it's still an excellent starting point.) Your real estate agent or town clerk can confirm or update the data.

Planning to Rent? Know the Local Market

As a tortoise, driven by rental income, you need to select a location with a good pool of potential renters. First, decide which of the following you'll be offering.

• *A short-term rental,* in which you rent out your property for periods of a few days, a week, a month or even several months. We'll discuss these under "Choosing a Location to Vacation In," further on in this chapter.

• *A long-term rental,* in which you rent out your place to someone who may stay in it year after year. Your rental property probably serves as their primary home.

If you're interested in a long-term rental, you'll want to balance all the considerations described below before settling on a location.

• *How much people pay in rents.* Get a snapshot of what other landlords are charging by picking up a copy of the local newspaper and looking at the available rentals comparable to the size and type of house that you're interested in. Keep in mind that these are asking rents and don't reflect how much people are actually paying. However, they should be close enough to provide a general sense of whether rents are high enough to cover your likely mortgage payments in that area. Also realize that if you're in an area with rent control laws, you'll only be able to raise their rent by a certain amount. If you're looking to buy in California, District of Columbia, Maryland, New Jersey, or New York, you may, in certain areas, be subject to rent control laws.

• *Which way rental rates are headed.* Your snapshot view won't tell you whether you can raise the rent next year—or might have to lower it. Find out the average amount by which local rents have increased or decreased over the last five or so years. (You'll need to know this when you calculate your cash flow, in Chapter 5). Your best bet is to contact a local property management company or ask a real estate agent who also handles property management in the area. You can also call the local newspaper and request back issues from previous years so you can search through the classifieds. And keep your eye on the local news, too. If, for example, a major local employer or industry is experiencing a boom or a bust, you can expect rents to follow suit.

- *Vacancy rates.* Usually expressed as a percent, this tells you how many months out of the year you can expect to have your place sit empty. The best way to find vacancy rates on a local level is to contact local property management companies or real estate agents who also function as property managers. A strong rental market has a vacancy rate of 15% or lower. Try to stay away from areas with vacancy rates greater than 25%.

- *Crime rate.* Everyone's worried about crime these days—and crime at your investment property can make a hash of your budget. You'll usually see the crime rate measured as an index that uses 100 as the average. The lower the index, the lower the crime rate. For example, an index of 50 means that the city has half the crime rate of the average city, where an index of 200 means that the city has double the crime rate of the average city. Areas with lower crime rates tend to attract good tenants—families and professionals. In addition, a lower crime rate means less chance of vandalism, break-ins, or other problems at your property. Such events are double trouble if your tenants can trace some fault back to you—for example, if you didn't fix a broken lock on the front door and an intruder assaults your tenants and steals their TV and computer. You might end up having to pay for the loss (though your insurance might cover portions of it). Visit www.homefair.com/homefair/calc/crime.html to research crime rates at various locations. Of course, a citywide average may not reflect the level of crime in a particular neighborhood, so talk to the neighbors for a more local perspective.

- *School quality.* Better schools attract families who can't afford to buy a home in the area but want to provide their children with a good education. These are usually stable renters who will remain in your place at least until their children graduate. Visit www.greatschools.net to compare ratings of schools (K-12) in the area where you're looking to buy.

- *Unemployment rate.* You'll find this measured as a percentage of the number of people out of work in a given area. The average unemployment rate in a so-called "healthy" economy is about 5%. The fewer people who are unemployed, the more who can afford to pay rent. You can find unemployment rates down to the county level at the Bureau of Labor Statistics website at data.bls.gov/map/servlet/map.servlet.MapToolServle t?survey=la&map=county&seasonal=u. (Note: Don't put "www" in front of this Web address.) Select a state, click on "Draw Map," and then place your cursor over the appropriate county.

Gather these various figures for each location in which you're potentially interested, then compare them to see which is most favorable to your investment goals.

> **TIP**
> **Curious where other second-home investors are buying?** Six out of ten buy properties in metropolitan areas, according to the National Association of Realtors®' 2006 survey. Half of these properties were single-family homes, 21% were duplexes or apartments in two-to-four unit buildings, 13% were condominiums, and 8% were townhouses. Two-thirds of investors bought with the goal of earning rental income, though eight out of ten ended up renting out anyway (probably while they wait for their properties to appreciate).

Planning to Flip? Gauge Where the Housing Market Is Headed

If you're a hare, also known as a flipper, you're searching for markets that promise strong appreciation, ideally over a short period of time, so you can sell your house quickly and pocket the profit.

Cracking open the real estate section of a local newspaper will give you a general idea of the market there. However, it takes more than that to gain an acute sense of what's happening. Specifically, you should:

• *Review key housing indicators.* Start by identifying such so-called housing indicators as the median house price and existing home sales. (See "Key Housing and Market Indicators," below.) These paint a historical picture of the market and establish a trend (ideally, going back at least five years). Then you can begin to draw conclusions about whether the market is headed upwards at a promising rate. The quickest way to find local housing indicators is to ask your real estate agent (if you're already working with one). Another option is to visit your town clerk and ask, as this is all publicly available information. Unfortunately, we've found no centralized website where you can plug in a specific location and pull up all this information, but you may be able to devise a search focusing on your own location of interest.

> **WARNING**
> **History is no guarantee of future performance.** As the name implies, a market indicator is, at best, an indication or suggestion as to where the market is going. Unless you're able to hitch a ride with H.G. Wells back to the start of a housing trend, don't rely on market indicators as a predictor of what the future holds.

- *Overlay local market data.* While housing market indicators establish a trend, the state of the local market will help you determine whether that trend may continue. For example, if crime rates are starting to increase in one town, but just a few miles away in a comparable town the crime rate has remained low, you may want to consider buying in the latter town.

After analyzing these various figures for each location in which you're potentially interested, compare them to see which is most favorable to your goal of reselling at a profit.

Choosing a Location for Your Vacation House

Buying a vacation home is about finding a place where you can relax and be yourself, so choosing the right location is critical. As you continue your search, think about the nuances that exist between the communities and neighborhoods in which you're interested. Two towns may share a border, but the activities each offers and the people who live or rent there can differ greatly. That's why you need to assess the features of each potential town based on your personal preferences.

Key Housing and Market Indicators

Here are your main clues as to whether you're looking at a profitable market for investor hares:

- **Median home price.** This tells you the dollar amount of the midpoint in home prices, with half the homes being above and half below. It's a key measure of how the housing market is performing. If median prices are going up month by month, then home prices are appreciating and the housing market is potentially good for hares. But you can't stop with this measurement—the other ones described below could foretell a change.

- **Existing home sales.** This number tells you how many existing single-family homes or condos, townhouses, and co-ops have changed hands month by month. It indicates the level of demand for housing. As more and more houses sell, the market tends to rise. When fewer houses sell, it typically starts to fall.

- **New home sales.** This measures the number of new single-family homes that have been sold each month. Like existing home sales, it helps you track the demand for housing.

- **Housing starts.** This figure estimates the number of housing units (both single-family and multifamily) on which ground has been broken for new construction. Housing starts add to the existing supply of houses available for sale. If more houses are being built, it's a good indication that the housing market is growing. However, if too many new houses end up being built, the supply of homes may exceed demand, which can, in turn, cause the housing market to level off or even drop.

- **Crime rate.** This is typically measured as an index that uses 100 as the average. The lower the index, the lower the crime rate. For example, an index of 50 means that the city has half the crime rate of the average city, while an index of 200 means that the city has double the crime rate of the average city. Houses in areas with lower crime rates tend to appreciate faster than those in areas with problems, for reasons of personal security and resale value.

- **School quality.** Good schools attract stable renters and keep property values high over the long term. Visit www.greatschools.net to compare ratings of schools (K-12) in the area where you're looking to buy.

Key Housing and Market Indicators (cont'd.)

- **Unemployment rate.** This is measured as a percentage of the number of people out of work in a given area. The average unemployment rate for what is considered a healthy economy is about 5%. The fewer people who are unemployed, the more who can afford to pay rent. You can find unemployment rates down to the county level by visiting the Bureau of Labor Statistics website at data.bls.gov/map/servlet/map.servlet.MapToolServlet?survey=la& map=county&seasonal=u. (Note: Don't put "www" in front of this Web address.) Select a state, click on "Draw Map," and then place your cursor over the appropriate county.

TIP

Curious what other vacationers look for when buying a second home? Oceans, rivers, and lakes top the list of desired locations—around 66% of people surveyed by the National Association of Realtors® in 2006 said they chose a property because it was near water. Around 39% made their choice based on recreational or sporting activities (boating, hunting or fishing, golf, biking, hiking or horseback riding, ski or winter sports, or tennis, in that order). And 31% went for a place close to mountains or other natural attractions.

What's Important to You Personally

Finding that perfect location isn't just a matter of intuition and impulse. It helps to establish some personal criteria, such as those suggested below. Then systematically evaluate how each prospective location matches up to your criteria. We're talking here only about criteria that meet your personal needs—also see "Planning to Rent? Make Sure You'll Find Vacation Renters," below, if that fits your plans.

- *Recreational activities.* Your location should, of course, support the activities that you—and any family who will be vacationing with you— are most interested in. Ask other locals why they enjoy vacationing there and what the drawbacks are. You wouldn't, for example, want to discover that the ski area charges more than you can afford for lift tickets, that mosquitoes make the area unlivable in summer, or that local childcare is nowhere to be found.

- *Cultural and commercial offerings.* After many vacation days of doing the same old thing, you may find you need a cultural fix—say a jaunt to the symphony, a visit to the theatre, or a stroll in a museum. And some people don't consider their vacation complete without a visit to a nice restaurant or some charming shops. Check the map to be sure you won't spend half your weekend driving to these places.

- *What's the area like during the off season?* In areas with a high percentage of second homes, such as the Jersey shore or Cape Cod, Massachusetts, your neighborhood will become a virtual ghost town for a good seven to eight months out of the year. That means that you yourself probably won't want to spend much time there, and neither will would-be renters. You'll also need to consider whether this will make your home a target for burglars or vandals during the off season. Find out by checking out the local crime rate, as discussed below. But to make doubly sure, talk to other second-home owners in the area, especially those who've owned for many years.

- *Crime rate.* We're guessing you want to avoid crime on your vacations— as will your vacation renters, if you're planning on having any. You'll usually see crime rate measured as an index that uses 100 as the average. The lower the index, the lower the crime rate. For example, an index of 50 means that the city has half the crime rate of the average city, while an index of 200 means that the city has double the crime rate of the average city. Visit www.homefair.com/homefair/calc/crime.html to compare the crime rates of various locations. Of course, a citywide average may not reflect the level of crime in a particular neighborhood, so talk to the neighbors for a more local perspective.

Planning to Rent? Make Sure You'll Find Vacation Renters

A good vacation location for you isn't necessarily the best location in which to find short-term renters. For example, if it's well off the beaten track, no one may have even heard of the place, much less think to search for a vacation rental there. Here's what to consider in choosing your likely location:

- *Local vacation rental rates.* Get a copy of the local newspaper and look at the available vacation rentals comparable to the size and type of house that you're interested in. This will help you gauge what your competitors are charging and whether you'll likely be able to charge enough to cover your costs. (We'll show you how to analyze this for an individual house in Chapter 5.) Keep in mind that many vacation rentals have varying rates depending on the time of year. It's best to look at rental rates during the high and low season and create an average. The quickest way is to ask your real estate agent to do some legwork. Have your agent find out when the rental rates change and what these rates are. You can also ask other landlords in the area. Also, realize that all houses in a given area aren't created equal: For example, a house that's walkable to the beach will rent for more than an equivalent one that's a two-minute drive away. Of course, that house will also cost you more to buy.

- *Which way rental rates are headed.* Your snapshot view won't tell you whether you can raise your asking rent next year—or might have to lower it. Find out the average amount by which local vacation rents have increased or decreased over the last five or so years. (You'll need to know this when you calculate your cash flow, in Chapter 5). Your best bet is to contact a local property management company or ask a real estate agent who also handles property management in the area. You can also call the local newspaper and request back issues from previous years so you can search through the classifieds. And keep your eye on the local and national news, too. Rents on vacation properties can shift up or down considerably based on the state of the national and local economy. When the economy is down, vacations are among the first nonnecessities that people cut.

- *Vacancy rates.* Usually expressed as a percent, this tells you how many months out of the season you can expect to have your place sit empty. A strong vacation rental market would have a vacancy rate of 10% or lower during the peak season. Ask your real estate agent for the median vacancy rates during the peak and off-peak seasons.

- *Surrounding activities.* Aside from the main attraction drawing prospective renters—a lake, mountain, golf course, or whatever—it helps if your location supports auxiliary activities such as dining out, renting

DVDs, shopping for food, forgotten toothbrushes, and souvenirs, and more. Make sure these are within a reasonable driving distance (usually 20 minutes or less).

- *Crime rate.* As discussed above, high crime will deter vacation renters. Criminal activity also adds to your headaches as a landlord, since you'll have to think about security measures, what to warn your tenants about, and the like.

Choosing a Location for Your Retirement

Retirement is supposed to be when we harvest the fruits of our lifetime of labor. It contains the promise of finally being able to live for yourself and not for others—no more job commitments, childrearing, or similar demands. Just remember to evaluate your potential locations based on your needs down the road as opposed to what they are today. There may be vast differences between the two.

RESOURCES

Want to learn more about finding a retirement location? Consider subscribing to *Where to Retire* magazine, available at www.wheretoretiremagazine .com. Each issue (five per year) contains informative, well-researched articles, quizzes, charts, and photographs of retirement areas. You can request a free trial issue.

What's Important to You Personally

To make sure you're choosing a location you won't outgrow, consider your current and eventual needs, such as:

- *Agreeable climate.* Many future retirees want to be able to don a T-shirt and shorts instead of a survival suit in the dead of winter. If so, you can choose among the 14 or so states with cooperative weather patterns. But if you live in a colder weather state and staying close to family is important to you, then you may have to forgo a move that puts you closer to the equator.

- *Surrounding activities.* On average, about 40% of our preretirement waking hours are spent on the job. When some or all of those hours become yours again, you'll be looking for interesting ways to fill them: perhaps attending classes, playing golf or tennis, swimming, fishing, and more. Make certain the community in which you buy your second home can support your interests.

- *Cultural offerings.* If you need a regular cultural fix, say a jaunt to the symphony, a visit to the theatre, or stroll in a museum, you'll want to be within a reasonable drive of a major, or at least a minor, city.

- *Proximity to family:* If you want to see your children, grandchildren, other family members, and friends on a regular basis, don't buy a second home that's more than a few hours' drive or short plane ride away. Distance may make the heart grow fonder, but it also makes visits an ordeal—and therefore less likely to happen as often as you'd like.

- *Accessibility to medical care:* To best enjoy your retirement, you'll need to take good care of your health. If you already know you're prone to certain conditions, make sure the specialists you require are not far away. In any case, since health problems are not always predictable, make sure that medical care is within easy driving distance.

- *Available public transportation.* Studies have shown that retirees in remote locations get depressed if and when they become unable to drive. Look for areas with mixed residential and commercial uses, or with good public transport options.

- *Reasonable cost of living.* This is probably on everyone's wish list, so we've addressed it separately, below.

It's worth systematically researching these considerations for each location you're considering. Compare your results to see which place will best meet your expected retirement needs.

How Much It Will Cost to Live There

It costs money to live—and in some areas of the country it costs a lot more than in others. Since retirement usually means a fixed income, gauging cost of living is especially important. Your choice of state or even town could make a difference of thousands of dollars every year. Here are some cost of living indicators to look into:

- *Food and groceries.* Your basic living needs can cost you a pretty penny, particularly if you retire to Hawaii, Alaska, or any other area that has to ship in the majority of its food. Even in some less remote areas, food prices run on the high side. A quick, nonscientific way to compare food prices between various areas is to call a major grocery store in each location. Ask for the prices of a handful of basic items such as one gallon of whole milk, one dozen large brown eggs, and a pound of 85% lean ground beef. Then consider how those price differences will add up and affect your monthly budget.

- *Utilities.* Electricity, water, natural gas, and oil are vital to keep your house operating. Other utilities, such as telephone and cable, are a staple in most people's lives. Utility rates are usually, though not always, regulated by individual states. Either way, you'll find dramatic price differences across the states. To see electric rates by state, visit: www.eia .doe.gov and type in "residential electricity prices: a consumer's guide" in the search box. Click on the link for this guide and scroll down to the U.S. map. For water rates, you're better off contacting the town in which you might buy. For natural gas or oil rates, contact the local provider.

- *Transportation.* Whether it's the cost of a bus ticket, a taxi fare, or the gas you pour into your car, this will be another important part of your living costs. Gas tends to account for the lion's share of most people's transport costs. A 50 cent per gallon price difference between the highest and lowest regions of the United States is not uncommon. If you drive 10,000 miles a year and your car gets 20 miles to the gallon, that difference can mean an extra $250 a year in gas alone. To compare average gas prices by state, visit www.fueleconomy.gov and click on "state prices."

RESOURCES
For general information about the cost of living in different areas: See Sperling's "Best Places" (www.bestplaces.net), which offers a cost of living index calculator. The site also contains a host of other information, ranging from crime rates to climate profiles, for towns and cities throughout the United States.

- *State income tax.* Seven U.S. states (Alaska, Florida, Nevada, South Dakota, Texas, Washington, and Wyoming) don't tax your income at all. The income tax rates vary in all other states. See www.bankrate.com to check on state-by-state income tax rates.

TIP
Many retirees are lured to states with no income tax in hopes of protecting income from their investments. But before you follow their lead, realize that states need money to run on. Check into the host of other taxes (such as property and sales taxes) that such states often charge, which might have an even greater impact on your finances.

- *Property tax.* Imposed by local governments and used to fund schools, libraries, police and fire departments, and other community services, property taxes can vary dramatically by locale, especially as cash-strapped towns look for ways to generate more revenue. Buying a property just over the border from a high-tax town may save you thousands of dollars a year. Call or pay a visit to the town hall and ask how much the taxes have increased over the past five to ten years. (This is usually tracked as a percentage increase based on the median home price). Also make sure you understand the town's policy about raising property taxes (for example, is there an annual cap?) and whether any changes are pending, such as overrides (allowing the town to increase property taxes beyond the annual cap, usually after approval by voters).

- *Sales tax.* Also called a purchase tax, sales tax is collected by state and local governments. It's usually calculated as a percentage of the selling price of goods or services. Sales tax too can vary significantly based on location. A high local sales tax can take a significant bite out of your wallet.

RESOURCES

Need more information on state taxes? Bankrate.com provides a state-by-state summary of income, personal, and state sales taxes. Visit www.bankrate.com/brm/itax/state/state_tax_home_text.asp and click on the state that interests you.

POINTS TO REMEMBER

What type of house you want to buy, and where you hope to buy it, are among the biggest decisions you'll make. Apply the P Factor (price, privacy, and property management) to help you choose between a single-family or multifamily home, condo, townhouse, or co-op. Evaluate locations in terms of accessibility, type of community and activities, and affordability. In the end, you'll have narrowed your search down to a type of house and a location that will truly deliver what you're looking for.

Picking the Right House

A t last, having chosen a type of home and zeroed in on your location, you can start engaging in the great American Sunday pastime: going to open houses! (Individual appointments work, too.)

Whole books have been written on the process of house hunting, and you yourself have done it at least once before. So, we'll stick to some of the most important points here, including how to:

- evaluate the house's physical condition

- protect yourself in your purchase agreement

- identify special considerations depending on whether you're an investor, vacationer, or future retiree, and

- determine whether your investment will pay off.

Whether or not you think of yourself as primarily an investor, it's worth reading the last section of this chapter, called "Choosing a House That's a Good Investment." Your second home will probably be one of the largest investments you make in your lifetime. It can be a source of retirement income for you or an asset that will benefit your heirs or remain in your family for generations. We'd like to help you evaluate your house's potential to rise in value, and show you how to calculate whether renting out the house can offset your expenses.

CONSULT AN EXPERT

Finding a house will be much easier if you've enlisted the help of a quality real estate agent. (Finding a good agent is covered in Chapter 6.) Your agent will research houses in the area, arrange for you to view the ones in which you're interested, accompany you on the walk-through, and help you make an appropriate offer based on an analysis of comparable houses.

House-Hunting Resources

You may decide to get a jump start on the process before you have an agent on board, for example by combing through the classifieds in the local paper and visiting houses before you're ready to make an offer. These are great ways to get a feel for the local market. In addition, check out the following websites to find house-hunting tips and actual homes for sale:

- www.realtor.com, the official site of the National Association of Realtors®. Though parts of the site are for members only, home buyers can access national listings of homes for sale, plus current real estate news items and articles on home buying.

- www.homebuilder.com, by the National Association of Home Builders. This site will help you find a newly built home in your chosen location.

- www.nolo.com, by Nolo, the publisher of this book. Covers both the legal and other aspects of house hunting in free articles under the "Property & Money" tab. For example, check out "Beginning Your Home Search," and "Making an Offer on a House."

- www.inman.com or Inman News, an independent real estate website and media news service. The site features a variety of syndicated columns (some for free, some for an annual subscription) and fun features such as the "See Cool Neighborhoods" link, which leads you to videos of places to live.

Evaluating the House's Physical Condition

FAST TRACK

Buying a newly built home? You don't need to read this section, which explains how to evaluate an existing home. You do, however, still need to insist on having professional home inspections done, both during the building and before the closing, to protect yourself against construction defects. Your lender will also probably require what's called a "final inspection" or "442 inspection," which verifies that all of the work, such as installing new carpets and flooring, adding countertops, and more, has finally been completed.

The first time you visit a house can be overwhelming—you're trying to be open to falling in love with the place while keeping a sharp eye out for any of its flaws. And if it's worth avoiding buying a first home with hidden physical problems, it's doubly so with a second home, since you don't want to be coping with surprise maintenance issues long distance.

Your agent can play an important role here. During your visits, the agent acts as another set of eyes, hopefully spotting such things as a water stain on the ceiling indicating a possible leaky roof or a lack of closet space. While these visits are by no means a substitute for a thorough inspection by a licensed home inspector, your and the agent's observations may help you realize that the house isn't worth an offer at all, or that you should adjust your price or terms based on your findings.

After your first visit, you'll walk away with a property information sheet, and, in most states, a disclosure form revealing some or all of what the seller knows about the house's physical problems (the level of detail varies from state to state). In many states, however, you won't be given the seller's disclosures until you make an offer—and in a few states, either the seller has no obligation to make disclosures or the required disclosures are quite minimal, so investigating the property falls largely to you.

Initial Walk-Through Checklist

Use this list (also included in the Appendix and on the CD-ROM to remind you what to look for during your initial visit or "walk-through." It's also good to bring a camera or video recorder along for future reference.

❏ **General appearance.** How the house rates, on a scale from shabby to spiffy, can tell you a lot about how it's been maintained over the years. On the outside, look to see whether it needs new paint and whether the shingles on the roof or siding are buckled or broken. Also make sure there are no broken or cracked windows. Inside, observe whether the home is dirty and cluttered. Are the walls chipped and crying for a fresh coat of paint? If the owner hasn't bothered to keep the house looking clean and attractive, other, possibly worse problems may be lurking.

❏ **Water leaks.** Water can rot wood, cause foundations to fail, and breed unhealthy mold and mildew. While not always easy to spot, telltale signs of leaks include yellowish-brown stains, bulges, or soft spots on ceilings and walls.

❏ **Appliances and fixtures.** Test all light switches, faucets, toilets, thermostats, and major appliances to make sure that they're working.

❏ **Floors.** All floors should be smooth, even, and solid. If you feel soft, springy sections or hear squeaking, repairs may be needed.

❏ **Doors and windows.** Check that doors and windows fit snugly and operate smoothly. Look for flaked paint and loose caulking. Check for gaps that can create drafts.

❏ **Grout and caulking.** If the grout and caulking around bathroom and kitchen tiles are loose and crumbling, there's a chance water is finding its way behind the wall or under the floor.

❏ **Furnishings.** Think about the furniture (either yours or a potential renter's) that will need to fit into the rooms. Be sure to bring a measuring tape. Rooms can be deceptive, particularly after savvy sellers remove most of their own possessions and artfully decorate the rooms to look spacious.

❏ **Storage space.** Make sure the house has enough storage space for your belongings or those of potential renters. Check the size of the closets, the attic, the basement, and the garage.

Even after you do your own walk-through and read the disclosures, you'll want to make your purchase offer contingent on your satisfaction with the results of one or more professional inspections.

RESOURCES
Looking for more tips on home inspections and seller disclosures?
See the free articles on Nolo's website, www.nolo.com, including " Get a House Inspection Before Buying," and "Required Disclosures When Selling Real Estate."

Adding Contingencies to Your Purchase Offer

If you're lucky, your first home sale went through without a hitch—the bank made you the loan, the seller wasn't hiding any major repair needs, and the closing went according to schedule. But don't let that make you lackadaisical about protecting your interests this time around. By simply including some critical clauses called "contingencies" in your purchase offer, you can make sure you're covered against nasty surprises.

Below are the most useful contingencies for both existing and newly built homes. If any of them can't be accomplished after good faith efforts by you or the seller in the days leading up to the closing, you can call off the sale, with no repercussions. Of course, matters don't usually come to such a drastic end. With some back-and-forth negotiation with the seller, you should be able to deal with problems, such as getting the seller to cover the cost of eliminating termites discovered during the pest inspection.

- *Financing contingency.* Allows you to make sure you can obtain a suitable home loan by a certain date with which to buy the house.
- *Appraisal contingency.* Allows for the property to be appraised by a licensed home appraiser and the value of the property to be a least what you've agreed to pay for it.
- *Home inspection contingency.* Allows for an inspection to be completed by a licensed home inspector who evaluates the structural and mechanical condition of a property—and for you to be satisfied with the results.

On new builds, your lender will require a "final inspection" or "442 inspection," as described earlier in this chapter.

- *Pest inspection contingency.* Allows for the house to be inspected for termites, ants, and other pests, as well as wood rot. Again, you must be satisfied with the results before the sale will go through. And by the way, your lender probably won't approve your loan unless you've included this contingency.

- *Building code compliance contingency (for homes that have had recent renovations).* Requires that you be given proof that the proper building permits were pulled and that the local building inspector has approved the completed work.

Fortunately, most of these contingencies will be found in the standard-form contracts used by qualified real estate agents in almost every state. Nevertheless, you should read your contract to be sure they're all there, and that you're comfortable with any time limits filled in by your agent.

You might also want to add contingencies that aren't in the standard form contract, depending on your particular concerns, or on local conditions. In areas with natural hazards that make homes difficult to insure, for example, some buyers add a contingency allowing them time to find adequate homeowners' insurance.

House-Hunting Considerations for Investors

Earlier in the book, we talked about investors being either tortoises (planning to rent and waiting for long-term appreciation) or hares (planning to flip). Regardless of which you'll be, when looking at houses, the questions to ask include:

- **Does the house have high appreciation potential?** A house that will rise in value is critical for any investor, whether planning to hold onto the house for a long time or to sell quickly, hopefully after a sharp spike in appreciation. This is covered in depth in "Appreciation: Will Your House Rise in Value?" below.

- **Does the house have good resale potential?** The resale value of a house is impacted by several factors. The one most within your control is its physical condition, particularly if you're buying a fixer-upper (described in Chapter 7). After you make the necessary repairs, the house usually increases in value immediately. Other factors that can drive up a house's resale value include future local development, such as a new school, shopping center, or movie theater. Neighborhoods that were undesirable—but appear to be in transition with new businesses coming in, other houses in the area being renovated, or an increase in new home construction, may also be good for your house's resale potential.

- **Will the house be attractive to renters?** While this is a key question for tortoises, hares should consider rentability as well, just in case their resale plans don't work out as expected. Factors to look at include the home's proximity to public transportation (especially important if you're buying in a lower-income area), neighborhood noise level (houses on quieter streets are more appealing and safer than those on busy streets), and the availability of other amenities within close proximity (public parks, food stores, and other shopping). Also look at the size and other features of the house to make sure they suit the demographic profile of your likely renters. For example, if you think your most likely renters will be families with children, avoid a house in a bad school district, or a one-bedroom condominium. Even a single-family home with only one full bath could be a problem. Finally, watch out for luxury houses in general—anyone who can afford the high rent you'll need to charge will more likely be looking to buy his or her own house.

- **Will the house command a high enough rent to significantly offset your expenses?** No matter how long you plan to hold onto the home, look for one that will rent for enough to cover its costs—or at least come close enough to tide you over until you sell at a profit. We've already discussed how to research likely rents in the area. Also see "Cash Flow: Will the House Earn a Regular Income?", below, to learn about how to do a cash flow analysis on a particular house.

- **Will the house be a pain to maintain and keep habitable?** If you're going to be a landlord, you'll have certain obligations to provide a livable house. For starters, make sure it doesn't present physical hazards or issues like cracking stairs on the front walk, creaky old windows, and inadequate water flow or old pipes. Unless you're hiring a property management company, picture yourself making regular visits to this house in order to show it to potential renters, deal with late-night plumbing emergencies, prune bushes, and more. If it's in the same city as you live, a neighborhood that's not too far for you to drive to is ideal. And a neighborhood where you feel safe hanging around is an outright necessity.

House-Hunting Considerations for Vacationers

As a vacationer, you don't need us to tell you to look for a house that's a pleasant escape or provides a portal to recreational activities. In addition, when looking at individual houses, consider the following:

- **How close is the house to recreational activities?** The more convenient a home is to recreational activities, the more fun you'll have—and, perhaps more importantly, the higher the rates you can command from renters (if you'll have them). Of course, this truth isn't lost on sellers: They'll set a higher price on houses close to the region's main attraction. You'll need to look for a house that strikes a comfortable balance between proximity and price.

- **Is the house in an area with high insurance premiums?** Houses in areas where Mother Nature is at her most dramatic may be beautiful one day, but dangerous the next—and the insurance industry knows it. If, for example, you're buying a house steps away from pounding ocean waves or an avalanche-prone slope, check with some insurers to see what you'll pay for coverage.

- **Does the house present seasonal access or maintenance issues?** For example, many Northern lake retreats become snowbound in winter. You'll need to find out who's going to deal with shoveling snow from the road leading to your prospective house in winter. If it's not publicly maintained, you could, at a minimum, need to foot the bill for snowplowing. Even if you don't plan to spend time there during the off season, you or your property manager may need to reach your home to check on it or make repairs.

- **Does the house have areas for private storage and laundry?** If you'll be renting out your property as well as using it personally, make sure there's an area you can keep locked to hold your personal belongings. Otherwise, you'll be burdened with schlepping your stuff back and forth in between renters. Something as simple as an oversized closet in a bedroom or closed storage in the garage may do the trick. Just make sure you're not reducing the value of your rental by making an area—say, the second bedroom—off limits. In many vacation rentals, guests are asked to do their own laundry (sheets and the like), so also make sure there's convenient space for machines.

- **Is the house resistant to renter wear and tear?** Vacation rentals are like a revolving door for people staying relatively short periods of time. Unlike long-term renters who have to live with whatever messes they make, vacation renters may be less concerned with property upkeep. Look for a house that can withstand some careless use. For example, a marble floor in the entryway will scratch much more easily than ceramic tiles, and a granite kitchen counter will chip much more easily than Formica.

House-Hunting Considerations for Future Retirees

Future retirees have the double task of figuring out what to look for in a home both preretirement and postretirement. If you'll be renting out the place before you retire, apply the house-hunting considerations covered in the investor (for long-term rentals) or vacationer (for short-term rentals) sections above. If you'll be using the place as a personal getaway before you retire, also review the vacationer house-hunting tips.

But keep in mind that someday this property will become your primary home—the place you spend each day, invite old and newfound friends, and lay your head down at night. As you transition from active adult to aging senior, you'll want to make sure that you don't outgrow your house. The questions to ask about a particular house include:

- **Will it challenge someone with limited mobility?** At some point, you or your significant other may develop limitations on walking or climbing stairs, or need to use a wheelchair or walker. Avoid homes with lots of hilly landscaping or staircases. Look instead for single-level homes, or condo complexes with elevators. You may also want to measure each house's doorways, and give preference to those that can accommodate a wheelchair. A standard wheelchair is 24"to 27" wide, so doorways should be a minimum of 32" wide. If the doorway leads to an average-sized hallway where you must make an immediate turn, you'll need a 36" door. Also check out the bathrooms. A standard tub is difficult for someone in a wheelchair or even with restricted mobility. Look for a house where at least one bathroom has a wide, walk-in shower with a low threshold.

- **Was it designed for looks rather than safety?** For example, many luxury homes have floor surfaces that become slippery when wet. Marble may look great in the entry way, but you may come in from the rain one day and find yourself sliding all the way to the hospital with a broken hip.

- **Are there hand-friendly grips and handles or can they easily be added later?** Serious falls are one of the major issues seniors face. Most can be avoided with properly installed railings and grips, especially important in bathrooms. Unless you're buying a house from a senior, these probably won't be there. That's okay, just make sure there's enough wall space to add them around showers and toilets later. Also make sure that any stairs around the house—even one- or two-step rises—have adequate handrails. And give points to any house that has lever handles instead of traditional doorknobs, the latter being difficult for stiff or arthritic hands to turn.

- **What other safety features does the house have?** You'll be lucky to find a house with many of the conveniences or safety features already mentioned. But as long as you're creating a wish list, you might add faucets with a built-in scald prevention mechanism, an intercom for communicating with others within the house when it's difficult to get around, and an alarm system (since seniors are common targets for burglars and other undesirables).

The more senior-friendly your house is when you buy, the less time and money you'll need to put into it prior to making it your permanent residence.

Choosing a House That's a Good Investment

No one likes to see the house they've invested in drop in value, let alone cost significantly more to keep up each month than is covered by any rental income. So before you make a final decision on a house, see how it's likely to fare according to the three key measures of profitability, which include:

- cash flow, or the amount of cash your property generates minus any debt or expenses
- appreciation, or the increase in value of your property over time, and
- return on investment (ROI), or the actual or perceived value of your investment in your property.

If investment is your main reason for buying, whether for resale or rental, you've got every reason to learn about these various profitability measurements. If you're a noninvestor, but will be dependent on rental income to help deal with your expenses, you, too, will need to learn to run the numbers. But even if you're buying for your own use and enjoyment, you may want to keep reading, to help assess whether and how your house is quietly adding to your investment portfolio.

Cash Flow: Will the House Earn a Regular Income?

If you're planning on renting out your property, either seasonally or year-round, the obvious critical question is: In the race between house-related income and expenses, which will win? Sure, you'll have rent coming in—your tenants may even pay beyond their rent, such as for parking and coin-operated laundry. But will it be anywhere near enough to cover the mortgage, tax, and insurance payments you need to pay each month, not to mention the less predictable expenses such as maintenance?

You can measure all of these using an analysis called "cash flow." The result will tell you how much money you're likely to make or lose over a given period of time, whether monthly, annually, or longer—we prefer to track it annually and then break it down monthly. A profitable situation is called "positive cash flow." You can guess what "negative cash flow" refers to. By the way, learning to do a cash flow analysis now will serve you well in the future. After you've bought the house, you'll want to get into the habit of running the exact same analysis using real, rather than projected numbers.

> ⚠ **WARNING**
>
> **The only taxes we factored into this cash flow analysis are property taxes.** In a perfect world, you would also factor in income tax you paid on rental income and tax savings you realized through deductions such as depreciation. However, this requires a more complex analysis than is possible before you've bought the house. Plus, not factoring in tax implications makes our approach to cash flow more conservative than others', which is probably safest for a first-time investor. So, we'll look at cash flow on what we're calling a "pretax basis."

Use the worksheet below (also found in the Appendix and on the CD-ROM at the back of the book) to estimate your likely pretax cash flow on an annual basis. Here's how to deal with the line items.

- *Annual rental income.* This is the total amount of rent that you expect to receive during the year. Base your estimate on current rental prices, by asking your real estate agent or checking comparable rental listings in the local newspaper or online. For longer term rentals, go to www.craigslist.org and click on the city nearest your property. For vacation rentals, try www.vacationrentals.com, www.vrbo.com (vacation rentals by owner), www.cyberrentals.com, and www.vacationhomerentals.com. If you're considering a corporate rental, go to www.corporatehousingbyowner.com. If the property is currently rented out, ask the seller what the current monthly rent is. Once you've determined your rental rate, calculate your likely actual income by assuming a vacancy rate of at least 25% during the rental period within a given year. For long-term rentals, that usually means a full 12-month period. Therefore, you'd plan on having the place rented for nine months out of the year (12 x .25 = 9). For short-term rentals, the rental period is typically less than 12 months due to peak vacation times. For example, if the vacation season for your property were six months long, you'd plan on having the place rented out for a total of 4½ months (6 x .25 = 4.5). (Over the years you'll most likely increase your rent to keep pace with the market, but this won't impact your first-year cash flow analysis.)

Rental Property Annual Pretax Cash Flow Worksheet

Annual rental income	$_____
Annual mortgage payments (include principal and interest plus property taxes and insurance)	− $_____
Annual operating expenses	

Liability insurance	$_____
Utilities (if not covered by tenant)	$_____
Upkeep and maintenance fees (if not covered by property management fees if you're using an outside company)	$_____
Advertising and tenant screening costs (if not covered by property management fees if you're using an outside company)	$_____
Property management fees (if you're using a management company)	$_____
Professional services fees (legal, accounting, etc.)	$_____
Prorated repair and improvement costs	$_____
Total	$_____

(Insert total annual operating expenses)	− $_____
Cash flow (+ or −)	= $_____

- *Annual mortgage payments.* This is the amount you'll pay on your mortgage for the year. It will probably be your single largest expense, reflecting the amount of your principal plus interest (unless your loan charges you only interest at the beginning). Some states and lenders require that you pay your property taxes and homeowners' insurance premiums along with your mortgage payment. If this isn't true in your case, be sure to separately calculate these costs and add them to the worksheet. If you have an adjustable rate mortgage, try to allow for the fact that your payments will move up or down based on the index to which the loan is tied. (In later years, any increases in property taxes or insurance premiums years will impact your cash flow as well.)

- *Annual operating expenses.* These are the yearly expenses incurred to keep your property running.

- *Liability coverage.* This is coverage against injuries or losses suffered by others as a result of defects with your property or even caused by you or members of your family. For example, if you're fixing something on the property and accidentally drop a hammer on your tenant's head, this should be covered. (See Chapter 13 to learn more about the importance of such insurance, and how to tailor your coverage to a rental property.)

- *Utilities.* Electricity and natural gas or oil are vital to keep your house operating. Usually, it's the long-term tenant's responsibility to cover these costs—but in a vacation rental, you will most likely be responsible. Also, you, as opposed to your tenant, will probably cover services such as water and garbage, particularly with a vacation rental.

- *Upkeep and maintenance.* Plan on doing basic maintenance such as painting and minor repairs. The results of your Walk-Through Checklist, above, will help you estimate your first year's repair needs. Chapter 7 will help you estimate the likely cost of these repairs. If you're looking at a townhouse, condo, or co-op, find out how much your homeowner's dues will be, and add them here. Also, if you'll be using a property management company, you may be able to subtract out certain repair costs that will be included in its fee, but you'll need to check to make sure.

- *Advertising and tenant-screening costs.* You'll probably advertise your property on rental websites and in local newspapers—check local rates, or ask local landlords for a cost estimate. As people respond to your ads, you'll need to check their credit, at least for a long-term rental. Credit checks cost approximately $20 per person. If you'll be using a property management company, its package of services may cover some of these costs, but you'd need to check with individual companies to make sure.

- *Property management fees.* A property management company can handle some or all of the following: advertising your rental, finding and screening tenants, preparing leases or rental agreements and other paperwork, keeping files on applicants as well as tenants, and managing security deposits, monthly payments, and late fees. The company can also take care of general upkeep of the property and managing repairs and improvements in a timely manner and in accordance with local housing codes, as well as addressing ongoing tenant issues or complaints. A typical property management company will charge 6% to 10% of the monthly rent for a long-term rental, and upwards of 30% or more for a short-term rental.

- *Professional service fees.* If you expect to use any professional services, such as a lawyer to draw up contracts or provide advice or an accountant to do your books, add their fees into your costs. Also, if you're using a financial or estate planner to advise you on your second-home investment, that person's fees should be added here as well.

- *Prorated repair and improvement costs.* Decide what major repairs the house might need during the first year—such as a new furnace, roof, or fence— and add their cost here. See Chapter 7, which discusses fixer-uppers, for some cost estimates. Try to get a list of work that's been done on the house over the past several years. Expect older houses to have higher prorated costs than newer houses, unless the latter was poorly constructed.

EXAMPLE: Ralph is contemplating buying a two-bedroom house as an investment property. He expects to pay $200,000, using a 20% down payment ($40,000) and a mortgage of $160,000 at a fixed rate of 6% over 30 years. His plans are to rent the house out full-time for the next ten years, at which point he'll either sell the place and pocket the profit or move into it permanently, when he retires. To decide whether this house is worth buying, Ralph calculates its potential cash flow.

Ralph knows that comparable places in the area are renting for $1,000 a month ($12,000 annually). He discounts that by 25% to allow for vacancy periods, and calculates that he'll take in $9,000 in rent during the first year (more if the place is vacant less than 25% of the time). Ralph then calculates his first year's projected expenses to be $16,500 ($11,500 for mortgage payments, $2,400 for taxes, $600 for insurance, $500 for other home-related expenses, and $1,500 for closing costs). Putting it all together, Ralph sees that this property would have a negative cash flow of $7,500 or $625 per month its first year ($9,000 rental income minus $16,500 in expenses). He'd have to pull that money from his own pocket—the rent would cover 55% of Ralph's annual expenses.

After you've added up the projected cash flow on a property, you might be shocked, like Ralph in the example above, to see a negative number. Welcome to the realities of your first years in an investment property. While the ideal—and the advice given by many authors promising you can make a million in real estate—is to generate break-even or even positive cash flow on a property, the reality is that the debt on the house is usually much higher than the income it can generate. A more realistic goal would be to use rental income to reduce the expenses on a house you'll enjoy for vacations or retirement, and that may eventually be resold for a profit.

> **TIP**
> **Year two will almost always look better than year one.** That's because your closing costs are a heavy-hit expense in year one, but they won't be repeated. For example, Ralph, from above, paid $1,500 in closing costs. Assuming his rent and expenses remain the same, his second-year cash flow (still negative), would be ($6,000) or ($500) per month. But at least now the rent would cover 60% of Ralph's annual expenses.

Fortunately, you haven't bought the property yet. There are several ways to reduce a negative cash flow, as described below. Let's start with the ones you can do before buying the property (short of simply looking at different houses—if that turns out to be your best option, see Chapter 4, concerning different types of houses, and Chapter 7, concerning fixer-uppers).

- *Reduce your offer to below the asking price.* While bidding low on a house may not have been practical during the housing craze of the late 1990s and early 2000s, it's a viable and realistic option in a correcting market that shifts in favor of buyers. If the home you're looking at is overpriced, you're in the driver's seat. Look for houses that have been on the market for more than 90 days in an area where there are lots of other, comparable homes for sale (your real estate agent can check this out for you). Taking Ralph's example from above, if he or his agent negotiates a price that is just 10% lower, and Ralph still puts down $40,000, he'll see his total expenses drop from $16,500 to $15,800 in the first year. That means his negative cash flow will be $6,800 annually ($566 a month) instead of $7,500 annually ($625 per month).

- *Make a larger down payment.* The less you borrow, the lower your expenses will be. Put another way, the more money you put down on a property, the lower your mortgage payment. You can increase the size of your down payment by borrowing against the equity in your current home, tapping a life insurance policy, or increasing your savings (see Chapter 9). Another option is to borrow from family, in the form of a gift or a private loan (see Chapter 10).

- *Shop carefully for a mortgage.* Your mortgage is usually the largest expense you'll have to contend with. It could easily account for 70% or more of your total expenses. One way to reduce your potential mortgage payment is to get the lowest possible interest rate. That could mean going with an adjustable rate instead of fixed-rate mortgage, which could easily shave a point or two off your initial interest rate. The downside is that if overall interest rates rise, you might quickly end up paying a higher rate than if you'd gone with a fixed-rate mortgage from the start. Another way to get a lower interest rate is to make sure that you qualify for a conforming loan (described in Chapter 11, along with other details on how to get a low interest rate).

After you've bought the property, some additional possibilities may open up to you.

- *Raise the rent.* You can increase your income by raising the rent each year after the first. Just remember that the amount by which you're able to raise it will depend on what the market will bear and whether you're in a rent-controlled area. You may even decide to keep the rent the same, in order not to lose a good tenant. A few percentage points each year is usually the most you can raise rent. And realize that some, if not most of the increase may be wiped out by rises in your expenses, such as property taxes.

- *Charge tenants for items other than rent.* You may be able to charge extra for optional items such as parking (a common charge associated with homes in a city or other congested area, such as a hot vacation spot). You can also add features such as a coin-operated laundry, which could make sense if you're buying a multifamily unit. If there's no laundry equipment in place, however, you'll need to weigh the added cost of purchasing it against the income it will generate.

- *Reduce other expenses.* The majority of expenses outside your mortgage, such as property taxes, insurance, maintenance, and repairs, are fixed or beyond your control—but look for ways to reduce them if you can. For example, new and higher property tax assessments can be appealed—and the nation-wide success rate is 75% for such appeals, because over-assessments are all too common. Another way to reduce your costs is to buy the property with someone else (see Chapter 12). Of course, while this can help you afford a house that you and your co-buyer personally want, it's not a reason for talking someone into an all-around unprofitable investment.

- *Keep your eye on the mortgage market, in case refinancing makes sense.* Provided you've been paying down principal over the years, you may be able to find a more advantageous mortgage. This isn't something you'd do right away, but a few years or more down the road it might be worth it, depending on where interest rates are. If rates are a point or more lower than your current rate, it could be worth the cost to refinance.

In the end, you'll need to determine your own comfort zone when calculating cash flow. Just remember that in the early years, it will most likely be negative. Many investors eventually see a shift, as they pay down their mortgage or learn to maximize their rent and minimize expenses. But the question remains, if you can expect a negative cash flow, why would you possibly buy a second home to rent out? The answer depends on your goals.

If you're anything but a diehard investor—that is, you plan on using your property personally, either for vacation or early retirement—you need not obsess about whether your rental income is enough to make you a profit. It's still income, and nothing to be sneezed at—it's helping you invest in the house. And given that many of your expenses, like your mortgage, insurance, and a certain amount of maintenance, will be fixed and unchangeable, it will be nice to see at least some cash coming in every month.

If you don't plan on using the place personally, but are truly buying for investment, your best bet is to focus on selling it down the road, to capitalize on appreciation. The rent you take in allows you to keep the property and wait for appreciation to occur. With that focus, however, it's extra important that you research appreciation trends, and try to avoid buying just before a major downward price correction.

Appreciation: Will Your House Rise in Value?

One of the reasons second homes have become a favorite among investors—
or any buyers, for that matter—is their recent tendency to rise in value,
sometimes meteorically. These rises are known as "appreciation." In technical
terms, appreciation measures the increase in a house's value, usually year by
year, from the time of purchase until its eventual sale. Of course, appreciation
is simply a paper profit until the day you sell, but most home buyers are
nonetheless delighted to track their house's climb up the appreciation ladder

But wait—there's no guarantee that your house will appreciate. In fact,
some parts of the United States have seen recent dips in property values
(usually in once-overheated markets). But historically, the trend has been for
the housing market to recover from such dips and move steadily upward, as
shown on the chart below. Over the past 20 years, you'll see that U.S. homes
have appreciated, on average, at a rate of 5% per year. The year 1991 was the
only one in which median home prices went down, and then by a mere 2%.

With that bit of reassurance, however, we need to add another dose of
reality. National trends aren't always tracked by local markets. And vacation
markets are the most vulnerable in a downturn, since nobody truly needs a
second home—as demand falls, prices fall.

To get a true picture of whether your prospective house is likely to appreciate in value, you'll need to look at local, historical, median home prices. Ask
your real estate agent to pull this information for the past ten or more years,
or call or visit the town clerk or assessor. The more local the better—one
neighborhood's house values may rise or remain steady while another one's
drops. Next, you might want to create a graph like the chart below.

If the trend looks like it's headed upward, you're probably on safe ground
buying, unless you know of something that will likely change it (the closure
of a major local employer, for example). If the trend is headed downward,
now is a bad time to buy—it's what's called a depressed housing market.
Although it could eventually turn around, that's very speculative investing,
which we don't advise.

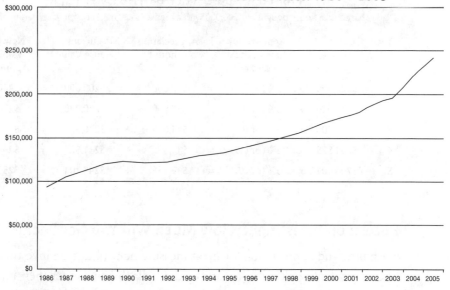

National Median Home Prices: 1986 – 2005

Data source: U. S. Census Bureau

TIP

Heed the words attributed to famed investor Warren Buffet: "Only buy something that you'd be perfectly happy to hold if the market shut down for ten years."

To make your analysis of your prospective house's likely appreciation more scientific, you need to come up with an actual figure—the amount by which the house is likely to go up in value in the coming year (and years). Start with the median, local appreciation rate that you researched above, expressed as a percent. Convert that percentage to decimal form (5% is .05, 10% is .1, and so on). Multiply that by the house's current value in the beginning of the first year (the amount you'll have paid for the house). Then take the resulting figure (which represents the amount the house has appreciated) and add it to the current house value. That gives you the probable new house value based on appreciation. You would repeat these steps for subsequent years. The example below shows the projected appreciation of a $200,000 house over a five-year period.

	Projecting Appreciation on a House: Example								
	(based on a house bought at $200,000 with a median local market appreciation rate of 5%)								
Year	Current House Value		Appreciation Rate in Local Market		Appreciation Amount		Current House Value		New House Value with Appreciation
1	$200,000	x	5% (or 0.5)	=	$10,000	+	$200,000	=	$210,000
2	$210,000	x	5% (or 0.5)	=	$10,500	+	$210,000	=	$220,500
3	$220,500	x	5% (or 0.5)	=	$11,025	+	$220,500	=	$231,525
4	$231,525	x	5% (or 0.5)	=	$11,576	+	$231,525	=	$243,101
5	$243,101	x	5% (or 0.5)	=	$12,155	+	$243,101	=	$255,256

Return on Investment: How Much Will You Get Back?

Cash flow and appreciation are great measurements, but true investors also like to get the big picture—a number that tells them whether their initial investment (the down payment) and subsequent investments (mortgage payments, specifically the principal portions) are worth it once they factor out expenses. The concept they've come up with is called "return on investment" (ROI). It's usually expressed as a percentage. You can calculate ROI on other investments as well, such as stocks, bonds, and certificates of deposit, and see how they're all doing relative to one another.

Before you go any further, you'll need your projected cash flow and appreciation figures. You'll plug them in when using our method of calculating ROI. You'll find a worksheet for this in the Appendix and on the CD-ROM. If you haven't read the relevant sections (above), do so now.

We recommend that you track ROI on an annual, pretax basis (as you did with cash flow). To calculate ROI for your first year, take your estimated annual cash flow and add the dollar amount of your expected home appreciation for the year. You might be adding a negative number to a positive one, or even totaling two negative numbers. Just treat it like an addition problem. For example, if in your first year you had negative cash flow of $7,500 and appreciation of $10,000, the sum would be $2,500 or (−$7,500 + $10,000 = $2,500).

Which Is Better? Using Initial or Total Investment to Calculate ROI?

From an ROI perspective, when you buy a house, your down payment is considered your initial investment. It's no different than putting that same amount of money into another investment vehicle such as a mutual fund. However, as you pay off your mortgage, you'll be paying down the principal on your loan. These principal payments are considered subsequent investments in your house. Again, no different than if, over the years, you put more money into that mutual fund.

Therefore, when calculating ROI, some people will base it on the initial investment only (the down payment), where others will base it on the total investment (the down payment plus subsequent principal payments). The former will yield a much higher ROI figure than the latter, since the investment base is lower and never changes.

We prefer to calculate ROI using the total investment amount, because it shows a more holistic picture, especially over time. This is an important distinction, especially if someone other than you will be calculating the ROI on your house, say your financial planner or even real estate agent.

The resulting figure ($2,500 in our above example) shows your gain or loss on your property for the first year. Remember, these are paper gains or losses unless you sell your property. But we're not done yet.

Next, take your gain or loss and divide by your total investment in the property. This includes your down payment plus any principal you will have paid by the end of the year. You can get this figure at any of hundreds of online mortgage calculators, which will break down principal and interest payments over the life of your loan, such as at www.bankrate.com/brm/mortgage-calculator.asp. The result will be in decimal form—something like .05 or -.05—if one or both of your starting figures were negative. You'll need to turn that into a percentage, by multiplying by 100 (.05 x 100 = 5%) to get your first year's ROI.

So, what does that ROI percent mean? It says that if you sold your home after the first year, you'd get a 5% return on your initial investment. It's similar to a situation in which you invested that same money in a stock, mutual fund, or other investment, then sold it a year later and walked away with a 5% return. To judge whether that's a good return or not, you could compare it to your average bank account or short-term CD—again bearing in mind that you're getting the extra benefit of owning a home, and will probably treat it as a long-term investment.

Let's go back to our example with Ralph, in which he ended year one with a negative cash flow of $7,500. Ralph might be feeling pretty depressed—until he calculates his likely appreciation at 5%, runs the ROI calculation, and sees that he would be earning (on paper, at least), $2,500 off an investment of $41,965. That's a reasonably respectable 6% ROI. (To see how Ralph's situation might develop in subsequent years, see the table below; a blank worksheet has been included in the Appendix and on the CD-ROM in the back of the book so you can do your own.) Ralph shouldn't be too quick to sell, though—that $2,500 and more will be eaten up by the $10,000 he'd have to pay in real estate commissions, resulting in a loss of $7,500.

In Ralph's second year, things would look even better. Despite continued negative cash flow, his ROI for the year would go up to 10%, because of another year's worth of appreciation. And remember, that's just for one year. If Ralph sold after year two, his total ROI would need to factor in both years of appreciation. This would gives him a cumulative ROI of 16%. Here's how we got that figure: Take Ralph's two years of negative cash flow, totaling $13,500, and add his two years of appreciation, totaling $20,500, for a result of $7,000, his gain over the two-year period. Divide that by his cumulative investment of $44,051 (his down payment plus subsequent principal payments). The result is .16 or 16%.

Ralph would end up with $7,500 in his pocket—but only briefly, because he'd need to shell out about $11,000 in real estate commissions (a 5% commission on a $220,500 house). That puts Ralph's cumulative loss at $3,500 (compared with a loss of $7,500 in year one).

If Ralph continued with this analysis, he'd show a cumulative break even in his third year. By year four, if appreciation trends continued, he'd start turning a profit (if he sold) while still showing a negative cash flow. Since Ralph plans on holding onto this house for at least ten years, his analysis shows that it's worth buying.

Ralph's Cumulative Return-On-Investment Example
(based on buying a $200,000 house with 20% down ($40,000)
and carrying a $160,000 mortgage at the fixed rate of 6% over 30 years)

Year	Pretax Cash Flow*		Unrealized Home Appreciation**		Unrealized Gain/(Loss)		Total Investment in Property***		Return on Investment After Sale****
0	n/a		n/a		n/a		$40,000		n/a
1	($7,500)	+	$10,000	=	$2,500	/	$41,965	=	6%
2	($6,000)	+	$10,500	=	$4,500	/	$44,051	=	10%
Total	($13,500)	+	$20,500	=	$7,000	/	$44,051	=	16%

*Cash flow will change over the years based on changes in rents and expenses. For purposes of this example, Ralph has assumed that rents will not rise. Property taxes, which have been calculated at $12 per $1,000 in house value, will also rise based on the current value of the house. Note that "( )" indicates negative cash flow.

**Based on local average of 5% per year

***Down payment of $40,000 + subsequent principal payments made on mortgage

****Not including real estate commissions

As you can see, patience is a virtue when it comes to home investing—and a house may look like a bad deal until you calculate your ROI for the number of years you plan to hang onto the place. As a first-time investor, be cautious. And if you're also planning to use the home for vacation or future retirement, choose a place you'll love for a long time regardless of whether it's earning you a profit.

 INVESTOR

Flippers, beware of real estate commissions upon selling your home. As you saw from Ralph's example, commissions have a tendency to wipe out any gain. This is especially true during the early years of owning the home, when your appreciation will most likely be low. To see how commissions will change your ROI, simply add them (usually 5% of the selling price) to the amount in the Unrealized Gain/(Loss) column for that particular year. Then complete the ROI calculation.

POINTS TO REMEMBER

Looking at houses involves more than finding one that looks good. You'll need to evaluate everything from the condition of the property to whether it's close enough to the beach or will serve you if your health declines. And to make sure you haven't leapt too quickly, your purchase offer should contain contingencies conditioning the closing on your obtaining financing, being happy with the results of home inspections, and more. Finally, you should make some educated calculations about your home's likely profitability, particularly if you're planning to rent it or make money on a quick resale. ●

How Experts Can Save You Time and Money

Buying a home is really too big a deal for anyone to handle alone. That would be like planning a wedding where you bake the cake, sew the dress, and play the music. By using outside professionals, you can save time, money, and your sanity. For example, a real estate agent can help you find, negotiate over, and ultimately buy a reasonably priced house. A mortgage broker can navigate the murky waters of your home-financing options. A home inspector can be your ally in investigating whether the house is structurally sound. And a closing (also called "escrow") agent can make sure the final transfer happens smoothly and on time.

All of these individuals, and a few others, make up your real estate team. Of course, any team is only as good as its leader—namely you, the one plunking down a few hundred thousand dollars.

TIP

Don't fool yourself into thinking that your real estate agent is your team leader. At best, your agent is your second in command. While the agent can and should offer guidance, you're the one who needs to make the final decisions.

This chapter will help you understand the role each team member plays and how best to utilize his or her expertise, by:

- identifying the real estate professionals you might want on your team
- describing exactly what these professionals do, and
- advising you on picking the best of the best.

Working With Real Estate Agents and Brokers

With over two million real estate agents and brokers in the United States, there's no shortage of able bodies eager to help you locate a second home, negotiate the purchase price and terms, and complete the transaction. Although you can theoretically do many of these tasks on your own, an experienced professional can help you cope with surprises and dilemmas; for example, when you're weeks into the purchase and don't understand why the seller is requesting a change to previously agreed-to repairs.

Who Real Estate Agents Are

Agents are not all created equal—they've got different names (broker, agent, Realtor®), different sets of knowledge, and sometimes even conflicting duties to you and the seller.

Agents. The term real estate agent is the most generic of the lot. An agent is always your right-hand person. An agent will show you houses and handle many of the other details required to complete a real estate transaction. All real estate agents must be licensed within the state where they work. For most states, licensing requirements require completing between 30 and 90 hours of classroom instruction, as well as passing a written exam that includes questions on basic real estate transactions and laws affecting the sale of property. Real estate licenses must be renewed every one to two years (depending on the state) and do not require passing another written exam.

Brokers. A real estate broker is one step up from an agent. Although you might work directly with a broker, visiting houses and the like, brokers have more education and experience, and spend some of their time supervising other agents. In larger real estate agencies (also referred to as a brokerages), you'll most likely be dealing with an agent on a daily basis, since they'll have many more agents than brokers. However, it's the broker you would ultimately go to if you had any problems that your agent couldn't resolve. In smaller, independent agencies, which tend to have far fewer agents, the odds are greater that you'll be working directly with a broker who probably owns the agency as well.

Regardless of whether you're working with an agent or a broker, their roles are essentially the same, at least in terms of finding you a house. For the remainder of this book, we'll use the term real estate agent to refer to both agents and brokers.

Realtors®. Over half of all licensed agents are members of the National Association of Realtors® (NAR), a trade association. Agents who are members of the NAR are referred to as Realtors® and must abide by the organization's standards of practice and code of ethics (available at www. realtor.org/mempolweb.nsf/pages/code).

Realtor® Designations/Certifications at a Glance

Through the NAR and its affiliates, a Realtor® can receive advanced education in many specialty areas.

- **The Accredited Buyer Representative® (ABR)** is a Realtor® who focuses on all aspects of buyer representation.

- **The At Home With Diversity (AHWD) Realtor®** is professionally trained in a wide range of cultural issues, and is thus sensitive to the manner in which various cultures impact the home-buying or -selling process.

- **The Counselor of Real Estate (CRE) Realtor®** must demonstrate that he or she has a minimum of ten years of real estate experience (three of which are in counseling on real estate matters). The CRE designation does not require specific continuing education, but is earned by invitation only.

- **The Certified Residential Specialist (CRS)** is a Realtor® who successfully completes advanced training in listing and selling. This designation is of more interest to sellers than to buyers.

- **The Graduate, Realtor® Institute (GRI)** is a Realtor® who has received a minimum of 90 hours of training in major real estate related topics such as business planning, fair housing, and contracts.

- **The Resort and Second-Home Property Specialist (RSPS)** Realtor® specializes in the buying, selling, or management of properties for investment, development, or retirement, or of second homes in resort, recreational, or vacation destinations.

- **The Accredited Buyer Representative® Manager (ABRM)** is the ABR equivalent for brokers, owners, and managers who focus on buyer representation.

- **The Certified Residential Broker (CRB)** indicates management excellence among brokers. This designation means the broker is trained to develop sound financial and marketing programs and provide information on how agents can communicate effectively with their clients.

If you look at the business cards of some Realtors®, you'll see a laundry list of acronyms after their name. These indicate advanced designations/certifications offered through the NAR and its affiliate organizations. Knowing the nature of this advanced education could help you choose a Realtor® who suits your needs. Pay particular attention to the RSPS designation, which denotes a Realtor® who specializes in second-home buying. As of the writing of this book, however, the RSPS designation was relatively new, so many Realtors® didn't have it yet—despite the fact that some of them already specialize in second-home buying.

Who They Represent—You or the Seller?

Believe it or not, your agent isn't necessarily yours alone unless you've signed a written agreement to that effect. The concept of buyer representation—that is, having an agent whose main duty is to serve the buyer, regardless of the seller's interests—is surprisingly new, having been around since only the 1980s. Prior to that, sellers hired real estate agents to market their properties, and the sellers' agents would draw up the paperwork for both parties. That led to unpleasant surprises for buyers, such as discovering that their confessions to an agent that they would willingly pay more had been passed on to, and used by, the seller.

In response to rising concerns that buyers were being taken advantage of, many states passed laws requiring real estate agents to formally disclose in writing their exact role in the process, as well as any potential conflict of interest, to prospective buyers. This agreement is now required in most states, and must be given to you early on, when you meet with a potential agent. Look for it, read it carefully, and don't willingly sign any agreement that says that the agent is simultaneously representing the seller and you.

The majority of agents aren't purists about who they regularly represent—they'll willingly work for buyers one day and sellers the next. Their legal responsibilities and loyalties shift accordingly. Here's how their varying roles are defined:

- *Buyer's agent.* This is an agent who is legally bound to represent the buyer. While the buyer's agent is obligated to be fair and honest with the seller and any other parties to the transaction, this agent's commitment is to getting the buyer the best deal possible. Buyer's agents are usually paid by the seller—receiving half of the total commission paid by the seller when the house is sold (the seller's agent gets the other half). This isn't to say that buyers' agents are completely free of conflicts of interest. In fact, a buyer's agent who helps you negotiate a better deal on a house has just lowered his or her commission. In spite of this, a reputable and ethical buyer's agent will get you the best deal possible.

• *Exclusive buyer agent (EBA).* In the 1990s, a growing number of real estate agents decided to focus solely on buyers' needs for representation. Hence, the exclusive buyer agent, or EBA, was born. An EBA will never represent a seller in any transaction. By default, this means you'll avoid any possibility of a dual or designated agency situation (as described below). EBAs can be paid by either a commission received from the seller or directly by the buyer. And there's no reason to pay a commission if you don't have to. Just make sure to put your financial agreement into writing when the agent begins representing you.

RESOURCES

Looking for an EBA in your area? The National Association of Exclusive Buyer Agents is dedicated to helping buyers plan, locate, and evaluate property, negotiate price and terms, obtain financing and inspections, and more. To find an EBA near you, call 800-986-2322 or visit www.naeba.org/agent/index.htm and complete the short information form.

• *Seller's agent.* Also called the "listing agent," the seller's agent is hired by the seller, and contractually obligated to represent the seller's best interests. The agent focuses on trying to get as much money for the house as possible. While the seller's agent is ethically and even legally bound to be fair and honest towards the buyer, it's ultimately the seller who has this agent's allegiance. That's why you should watch out for seller's agents who claim they can write up a purchase agreement for the two of you without getting a buyer's agent involved. The seller's agent is paid a commission, which is covered by the seller when the house is sold.

- *Dual agent.* This is someone who represents both the buyer and the seller in the same transaction. In virtually every state, being a dual agent is unethical and illegal without written consent from both the buyer and the seller. Dual agent relationships should be avoided at all costs because, no matter what anyone tells you, it's impossible for a dual agent to fairly represent both the buyer and the seller simultaneously.

- *Designated agent.* This is a real estate agent who represents a buyer or a seller while another agent in the same brokerage (real estate office) represents the other party in the transaction. In states where designated agency is allowed, all parties must usually agree it to in writing. This is another area where there is a risk of divided loyalties, so you must decide whether you feel comfortable with this arrangement before agreeing to it.

WARNING

The majority of real estate agents still don't explain to buyers who they're really working for. A study (2005) by the National Association of Realtors® showed that a shocking 70% of agents failed to disclose to buyers who they're representing—despite the fact that most states' laws require them to do just that, in writing, at their first meeting with a prospective client! Hopefully, this problem will have abated by the time you're reading this, but it's a powerful reminder to ask your real estate agent for this information—in writing—as soon as possible.

Tasks Your Real Estate Agent Should Handle

Whether you're using a traditional buyer's agent or an EBA, here is what you can and should expect.

- *Researching neighborhoods.* Picking the right neighborhood is critical, regardless of whether you'll be using your second home for investment, vacation, or future retirement. Particularly if you're unfamiliar with the area, you'll want to learn about local crime rates, cost of living, public transit accessibility, and other factors that define its character. To help, your agent should be intimately familiar with the neighborhoods where you're hoping to buy. Ideally, your agent should have lived in or around the area and provide an insider's perspective. Your agent should also be able to recommend neighborhoods that you hadn't initially considered.

RESOURCES

Want to research neighborhoods on your own? Many websites allow you to check neighborhood statistics, such as crime rates, climate, and cost of living. Two worth visiting are www.homefair.com and www.bestplaces.net. Getting copies of the local newspaper is another good way to find out what's happening around town. And make sure you visit the neighborhood on several occasions, day and night, and talk to local business owners and people you pass on the street.

• *Provide a competitive (or "comparable") market analysis (CMA).* Among the most important tasks your agent can perform is to review recent sales of houses similar in size and type to the one you're looking for, in the neighborhood where you're looking. The purpose is to help you gauge the fair market value of any house that catches your eye. Recent sales, by the way, are those within the past six months, where possible. A super-prepared agent will draft a written report on these comparable properties ("comps") for your use, listing items like asking price, selling price, square footage, year built, number of bedrooms, and the amount of land. Real estate agents have access to this information through the Multiple Listing Services (MLS), a database created and run by real estate professionals. These days, however, anyone with Internet access can view select portions of the MLS by visiting www.realtor.com, the NAR's consumer website. On the home page, click "Home Buyers and Sellers," then "Find a Home at REALTOR.com," then input your prospective house's address in the "What's Your Home Worth?" box. For more results, also try free websites such as www.zillow.com. Even so, a good agent will also have insider knowledge of how to intelligently use the MLS, and of local home sales information that you can't pull from the Internet. For example, your agent should be able to tell you whether or not a house had recent renovations, or why it was sold, perhaps because the seller got divorced or relocated.

- *Accompany you on the initial walk-through of the home.* Your agent should arrange for you to view any home in which you're interested, and accompany you on the walk-through. Depending on the state, the seller's agent may or may not be present. Either way, your agent acts as another set of eyes, hopefully envisioning remodeling potential and spotting such issues as a water stain on the ceiling indicating a possible leaky roof, or a lack of closet space. While by no means a substitute for a thorough inspection by a licensed home inspector, your and the agent's observations may help you realize that the house isn't worth an offer at all, or that you should adjust your price or terms based on your findings. The agent can also coordinate a second and even third showing, if you're interested.

- *Draft a written offer and negotiate the sale.* In the majority of states, your agent will help you decide exactly what you'll offer, including the price (based on the CMA and walk-through) and the contingencies (allowing you to back out of the sale if certain conditions aren't met, without forfeiting your deposit). In some states, a real estate attorney must take on this role instead of your agent. Either way, your offer is usually presented in written form to the seller. Many times, this is done as a purchase and sale agreement using a standard, state-specific legal form that outlines all the offer terms. However, in some states it is dealt with in a slightly different manner. Check with your real estate agent or attorney to find out exactly how the process of drafting an offer and coming to a final sale agreement is handled in your state. You can also consult your local or state real estate association, accessible via www. realtor.org/leadrshp.nsf/webassoc?OpenView.

- *Manage the day-to-day activities leading up to the closing.* Once your offer is accepted, you ordinarily have about 30 days before the closing (depending on how much time you and the seller agreed to) to complete a myriad of activities—schedule a home inspection, line up financing, obtain homeowners' and title insurance, and finally close the sale. Your real estate agent (with help from your escrow or title agent) should guide you through each step, either handling the tasks directly or referring you to the appropriate professionals.

Choosing the Best Real Estate Agent

A good agent can be your greatest ally, while a bad one can be your worst nightmare. We're assuming that you want a buyer's agent, or an EBA, but that's not yet enough to narrow down your choices.

Finding a buyer's agent can be as simple as walking into a real estate agency and telling the person at the front desk that you're interested in buying a house. Finding a good one, however, takes a bit more work. The ideal agent will get to know you personally, and develop a deep understanding about what you want out of a second home besides the lowest price possible.

Start by getting recommendations for a few agents. Your best sources are family members, friends, colleagues, or neighbors who've bought homes—particularly second homes in the same region. If you come up dry on referrals, check out the National Association of Realtors' website at www. realtor.com. There's a "Find a Realtor" search function on the home page. Keep in mind, however, that this is merely a membership listing based on location and doesn't distinguish between good and bad agents.

Most agents have websites with photos of themselves and their skills or philosophies, so if you've gotten several referrals, reading their marketing materials might help you narrow down your list of prospects. Then choose two or three agents to meet in person. During your meeting, try to establish whether the agent has the following traits:

- *Integrity.* Without integrity, none of the other traits matter. Given how much money is on the table, you want an agent who can resist all the temptations to push you into completing a house purchase—perhaps at top dollar—thus guaranteeing the agent a sizable commission.

- *Responsiveness.* An agent should be responsive to your primary goals, whether you're buying for investment, vacation, or future retirement. The agent should also be well tuned to your preferences regarding home style, condition, location, and intended use.

- *Compatibility.* Since you'll be spending blocks of time with your agent over several months, make sure to choose someone with whom you have a personality fit. If an agent is qualified, but say, irritates you a bit by interrupting or making eye contact only with your spouse, it's better to look for someone else.

Real Estate Agent Interview Questionnaire

Ask potential agents the following questions.

❑ Do you work full time as a real estate agent? (Best answer: Yes.)

_____

_____

❑ How long have you been in the real estate business? (The longer the better, but preferably at least three years.)

_____

_____

❑ Do you have additional certification beyond your general real estate license? (More certifications show a commitment by the agent. A REALTOR®'s RSPS certification is particularly appropriate for second-home buyers. However, since this is a relatively new certification, few REALTOR®s may have it.)

_____

_____

_____

❑ How many real estate transactions have you been a part of in the past year? (Should be a minimum of ten.)

_____

_____

❑ In how many of those transactions have you represented the buyer? (Should be at least half; however, an even better answer is "all of them.")

_____

_____

❑ In how many of the transactions where you represented the buyer was it specifically for buying a second home? (Should be at least half; however, an even better answer is "all of them.")

_____

_____

_____

❑ Can you provide at least three names of previous clients who will serve as references, preferably at least one of whom used you to buy a second home? (Only acceptable answer: Yes.)

_____

_____

_____

- *Professionalism.* Be sure to select an agent who acts in a professional and organized manner. Buying a home is a complex process. To make it go as smoothly as possible, you'll want an agent who has learned how to appropriately conduct business, and has the energy to do more than the minimum.

- *Experience.* You want an agent who has been around the block a few times; one who's confident enough to help you with tough situations and decisions, having dealt with plenty of others before. You also want the agent to have experience specific to buying a second home. The needs of a second-home buyer are, after all, unique in many ways.

- *Familiarity.* Choose an agent who's familiar with the area in which you're looking to buy—ideally, an agent who has lived in the area for a number of years. This is especially important if you're looking at areas with which you're less familiar.

To ensure that the agent has these characteristics, use the Real Estate Agent Interview Questionnaire provided in this chapter (also available in the Appendix and on the CD-ROM at the back of this book).

Working With Mortgage Brokers and Bankers

Planning to take out a loan to buy your house? There are two paths you can follow—use a mortgage broker to filter through the options for you, or go directly to a bank, credit union, or other commercial lender. Most buyers go the mortgage broker route. In fact, mortgage brokers are used in an estimated 68% of all mortgage originations (the process through which a mortgage is created).

Who Mortgage Brokers Are

A mortgage broker acts as your agent to "shop lenders" for the best possible loan terms given your financial situation and goals. In many states, mortgage brokers must be licensed, but the type of license, the manner in which the license is obtained, and the degree to which it is regulated varies greatly.

Beyond the licensing, some mortgage brokers seek certification from the National Association of Mortgage Brokers (NAMB), a trade organization that sets a standard of excellence through its nationally available certification program. The two types of NAMB certifications include:

- *Certified Residential Mortgage Specialist (CRMS).* This is given to mortgage brokers with at least two years' work experience in the mortgage industry and at least 50 qualifying points through work experience, education, other professional designations, continuing education activities, and leadership and participation in the industry. The brokers must also pass a written exam.

- *Certified Mortgage Consultant (CMC).* This certification is given to mortgage brokers with at least five years' work experience in the mortgage industry and at least 100 qualifying points through work experience, education, other professional designations, continuing education activities, and leadership and participation in the industry. The brokers must also pass a written exam.

As for compensation, mortgage brokers are paid a commission by the lender, often 1% of the value of the loan. That means the broker's commission is ultimately coming out of your pocket (unlike your real estate agent's commission, which is covered by the seller). Of course, a good mortgage broker should be able to save you the equivalent of his or her commission and then some, by finding you a more affordable mortgage than you could locate on your own.

Tasks Your Mortgage Broker Should Handle

A mortgage broker should work with a range of mortgage lenders in order to find the best loan deal possible. The broker's responsibilities include:

- Conducting an interview with you to understand your financial situation and mortgage needs, then discussing possible ways in which to achieve your second-home financing goals.

- Working with you to get preapproved for a mortgage (a conditional approval), which helps persuade the seller that you can follow through with your offer.

- Contacting the appropriate lender (after your purchase offer is accepted by the seller) and helping you complete and assemble the necessary documentation, such as your loan application, confirmation of employment and wages, financial information, and credit evaluation.

- Reviewing the loan approval with you (assuming you're approved) and explaining the documents in detail so that you understand them before signing. If the lender refuses to approve your loan, your mortgage broker should explain why, and work with you on finding alternative mortgage options.

- Continuing to act as a liaison between you and the lender up to the closing day on your second home.

Choosing the Best Mortgage Broker

Good mortgage brokers possess many of the same traits as good real estate agents—integrity, professionalism, and experience (particularly with second-home financing). In addition, the good brokers stay informed and up-to-date on the policies and requirements of various mortgage lenders, in order to provide you with current and accurate advice.

To find a broker you can count on, interview three or four using the Mortgage Broker Interview Questionnaire provided below (also available in the Appendix and on the CD-ROM at the back of this book). To find the brokers you'll interview, get recommendations from friends, coworkers, and trusted real estate professionals, or use the "search for a mortgage broker" feature on the National Association of Mortgage Broker's website at www. namb.org/assnfe/SearchBroker.asp.

Applying Directly to a Bank or Other Institutional Lender

If you prefer not to shop around for mortgages, perhaps because you have a favorite local bank or credit union, then that institution will be represented by someone called a mortgage banker or loan officer. This person performs the same duties (more or less) as a mortgage broker, except that instead of scouring the entire loan market, the mortgage banker will help you identify which of the bank's own portfolio of loan products best suits your needs.

Mortgage Broker Interview Questionnaire

To make sure you have the best mortgage broker on your team, ask potential brokers
the following questions:

❏ Do you work full time as a residential mortgage broker? (Best answer: Yes.)

_____

_____

_____

❏ How long have you been in the residential mortgage business? (The longer the better, but
should be at least two years.)

_____

_____

_____

❏ Are you certified by the National Association of Mortgage Brokers? (Best answer: Yes.)

_____

_____

_____

❏ How many residential mortgages have you brokered in the past year? (Should be a
minimum of ten.)

_____

_____

_____

❏ How many of those transactions were for second homes? (Should be at least half; however,
an even better answer is "all of them.")

_____

_____

_____

❏ Can you provide at least three names of previous clients who will serve as references, at
least one of whom used you to help finance a second home? (Only acceptable answer: Yes.)

_____

_____

_____

Working With Real Estate Attorneys

In some states, real estate attorneys are a mandatory part of the home-buying process. Even in states where this isn't the case, the complexity of the transaction may sometimes require an attorney's assistance.

RESOURCES
To find out whether your state mandates that an attorney be used in the purchase of residential real estate: Consult your local or state real estate association, which you can find at www.realtor.org/leadrshp.nsf/ webassoc?OpenView.

Who Real Estate Attorneys Are

A real estate attorney is, by definition, an attorney who focuses on real estate transactions. If possible, find a true specialist. While all attorneys have attended law school and passed a bar exam in order to become licensed in their state, that training usually isn't useful for nuts-and-bolts transactions like property sales. Ideally the attorney has worked directly with other, more experienced attorneys to learn the ropes.

Tasks Your Real Estate Attorney May Handle

Depending on your needs and which state you live in, your attorney may become involved in one or more of the following: negotiating the purchase price of the home, creating or reviewing the sales contract, overseeing the home-buying process to check for compliance with all terms and conditions of the contract, reviewing title abstracts (a condensed history of the title that shows any liens or encumbrances on the property) and addressing any title concerns, such as unexpected liens, negotiating or representing you in a contract dispute with the seller, as well as participating in or managing the closing. An attorney can also provide assistance in handling paperwork for complicated transactions, such as those involving cobuyers or loans from family members.

Real Estate Attorney Interview Questionnaire

To make sure you have the best attorney on your team, ask potential attorneys the following questions:

❏ Do you spend most of your time dealing with real estate legal matters? (Best answer: Yes.)

_____

_____

❏ How many years have you been handling real estate legal matters? (The longer the better, but should be at least two years.)

_____

_____

❏ Do you charge hourly rates (if so, at what rate) or flat fees for services? (You'll want to compare fees between attorneys—but try not to base your decision solely on how high or low the fees are.)

_____

_____

❏ Are you a member of the state bar association? (Only acceptable answer: Yes.)

_____

_____

_____

❏ Have you ever been subject to any bar association disciplinary proceedings? (Only acceptable answer: No.)

_____

_____

_____

❏ How many individual home-buying clients have you represented in the past year? (Should be a minimum of ten.)

_____

_____

_____

❏ Can you provide at least three names of previous clients who will serve as references? (Only acceptable answer: Yes.)

_____

_____

_____

Hiring an attorney for one or more of these services may be particularly wise if:

- Your transaction is complex; for example, legal claims have been made against your prospective house that must be satisfied by the time the property is sold.

- You need to structure a private loan (a loan from a relative or friend) that will either be used towards the down payment or to supplement or replace traditional financing from a mortgage lender.

- You are purchasing a property jointly with one or more other buyers and need to structure a cobuyer agreement, as well as determine how title will be held.

Choosing the Best Real Estate Attorney

To find the best attorney for the job, interview three or four using the Attorney Interview Questionnaire provided below (also available in the Appendix and on the CD-ROM at the back of this book). Be clear that you're still making a decision about which attorney to hire—otherwise the attorney may charge you a consultation fee. In fact, some attorneys regard all initial interviews as consultations, since they'll be trying to establish what your case involves in order to explain how they can help you. But some attorneys do offer free consultations, or it may be worth paying the fee to start your case off with a highly regarded attorney. To find the attorneys you'll interview, get recommendations from friends, coworkers, and trusted real estate professionals.

Working With Home Appraisers

When you take out a loan to buy your second home, you can count on your bank, credit union, or other financial institution requiring that the house be appraised—that is, that a professional assess its market value. Why is this necessary? Because your loan will, in turn, be secured by your property so that if you default on your payments your lender can take your house in lieu of you paying back the loan. Your lender's right to foreclose in this manner won't do it much good unless the property you're buying is worth enough to cover the amount of your loan—hence a job for your local appraiser.

Who Home Appraisers Are

A home appraiser is someone (licensed at a state level) who verifies the market value of a property. Because the appraiser is working on behalf of the bank, the bank will choose someone from its approved list. As such, you won't have much input into the process, but it's helpful to understand the appraiser's role and how appraisers arrive at their conclusions.

Home appraisers are licensed by individual states after completing coursework and internship hours that familiarize them with their real estate markets. It usually takes about two years to meet the requirements to become an independent home appraiser.

An appraisal is different from the CMA done by your real estate agent (described in "Tasks Your Real Estate Agent Should Handle," above.) The appraiser should take a more exhaustive approach to determining the current market value of a property, using one of the methods described below. And while your agent's CMA should state a value close to that shown on the appraisal report, a lender will consider only the appraisal when determining whether or not to lend you the purchase money. (That means you can't argue with the lender that the true value of the property is found in the CMA; you're stuck with what the appraiser finds.)

How Appraisers Determine a Home's Value

An appraiser will use one of the following three methods to determine a home's current market value:

- *Sales comparison approach.* This approach is similar to the way in which your real estate agent develops a CMA. The appraiser will look at three to four properties that have recently sold in the neighborhood and compare them to your property. Factors such as square footage, number of bedrooms and bathrooms, the age of the property and its condition, and the size of the lot are taken into account. This is the most commonly used appraisal method.

- *Cost approach.* The appraiser will calculate the estimated cost to recon-struct the property (minus the cost of the land) at the time of the appraisal. The current condition of the property is also factored into this calculation.

- *Income approach.* This approach is based on determining the expected value of a property in investment terms. Therefore, the appraiser uses a calculation to convert anticipated future income into present value. This method is used only for investment properties, and typically in conjunc-tion with one of the other two valuation methods described above.

Most often, the appraiser will sign off on the amount you're paying for the house—and the appraiser is on pretty solid ground doing this, since your willingness to pay the agreed-upon price is a good indication of what the market will bear. However, if your appraisal comes in significantly lower than the amount you want to borrow, your lender could deny your request for a loan. You can always challenge an appraisal if you believe it doesn't reflect the true value of the home. But unless you can prove the appraisal is unusually low compared to those of other, comparable houses, the bank will usually stick to the appraisal.

Working With Home Inspectors

Most buyers make their purchase offers contingent on a satisfactory inspection (or inspections) of the premises—and so should you. A good general home inspector is vital to your real estate team, as he or she can uncover hidden problems that could either reduce the home's current value or later rear their ugly heads. The inspector will give you a solid understanding of what you're buying and possible grounds upon which to negotiate for a better deal.

Commonly found problems after a general home inspection might include leaky plumbing, faulty wiring, basement seepage, or a worn-out furnace or roof. If some of these problems look complex however, your main inspector may recommend that you hire additional, specialized inspectors to take a closer look. Also, a standard home inspection won't cover any unusual home features such as a Jacuzzi or dock—it's often worth hiring additional inspectors to examine these. And you'll probably also need a separate pest inspection, to check for termite, dry rot, and similar damage—most lenders will require this.

Some areas also require point-of-sale inspections for code violations and other health and safety issues. These are usually arranged by the seller in order to make sure no barriers will emerge to properly transferring the title and legal right to occupancy. These inspections are very limited in scope and aren't a substitute for your own inspection.

Who Inspectors Are

A general home inspector visually examines your potential home, inside and out, for mechanical and structural flaws that could impact the value of the home, and produces a written report summarizing the findings. The inspector usually has a background in general contracting, residential home building, or engineering. Some states require home inspectors to pass a test and be licensed, while others do not. The more specialized inspectors obviously have other areas of expertise and backgrounds, and may or may not need state licensing (though licensing is fairly common for pest inspectors). In some states, general inspectors offer a simultaneous pest inspection, but in other states you'll need to hire two different inspectors. We recommend hiring separate inspectors for the two tasks where possible— their respective areas of expertise are quite different.

You'll also want to make sure that your home inspector has proper liability insurance coverage, which is not necessarily mandated. Among other things, this means a home inspector who misses a problem with your property, such as a leaky roof or cracked foundation, is financially covered for the damages you must contend with. You have a better and faster chance of receiving restitution from an inspector who has insurance than from one who doesn't.

Tasks Your Inspector Should Handle

A general home inspection is usually limited to areas that can be seen during one visit without disturbing or damaging the property, such as viewing the condition of the roof, making sure that windows open and shut properly, evaluating the condition of the furnace, visually inspecting the electrical system, examining the integrity of the house's foundation, and more. Even then, these inspections may not uncover all a home's problems. Most inspectors will put a lot of boilerplate into their written report, warning you about all the things they couldn't see.

TIP

What if the inspector misses something? Although the inspector's findings don't represent a guarantee against all potential problems, inspectors do bear some responsibility for things that were listed in their reports as being in good repair but actually weren't. At the time, that is. Don't blame the inspector for normal wear, tear, and decay later on. But if, after moving into your home, you discover that the inspector truly overlooked a problem, the inspector should, at the very least, reimburse you for the inspection fee. If the problem is significant, such as extensive wood rot, you may need to take legal action against the inspector. In this type of situation, consult with an attorney.

A general inspection should take at least two hours. Most good inspectors will encourage you to accompany them. Then they'll produce their written report within a day or two. The report will detail existing as well as potential problems with the property, usually with an assessment of their severity.

The results of the report can be used to negotiate reductions on the price of the home. For example, if the inspection reveals a leaky roof, the seller may agree to have the problem fixed prior to the sale, or to reduce the price by all or a portion of the amount required to fix the problem.

Choosing the Best Home Inspector

Many people put off looking for a home inspector until they're in contract to buy a house. This can be a mistake. Your purchase contract will probably allot a limited amount of time for inspections to take place, which means you could not only be scrambling, but discover that the best inspectors are already booked up. If possible, start your search for an inspector before making an offer.

Home Inspector Interview Questionnaire

Ask potential inspectors the following questions:

❑ Do you work full time as a home inspector? (Best answer: Yes.)

_____

_____

❑ How long have you been in the home inspection business? (The longer the better, but should be at least two years.)

_____

_____

❑ Are you affiliated with any home inspection trade organizations such as the American Society of Home Inspectors, the National Association of Certified Home Inspectors, or the National Association of Home Inspectors? (Best answer: Yes.)

_____

_____

❑ How many home inspections have you done in the past year? (Should be a minimum of fifteen.)

_____

_____

❑ Do you have insurance that is currently active? (Only acceptable answer: Yes. And be sure to ask for a certificate of insurance.)

_____

_____

_____

❑ What did you do before you were a home inspector? (Ideally, should have been a contractor, building inspector, or even on a town planning board involved in issuing building permits and ensuring compliance on home renovations.)

_____

_____

_____

❑ Can you provide at least three names of previous clients who will serve as references? (Only acceptable answer: Yes.)

_____

_____

When choosing a home inspector, look for one who has been in the business for many years and is not only licensed but affiliated with a professional or trade organization. Ideally, you also want someone who has been a residential homebuilder or contractor.

Frequently, buyers use an inspector recommended by their real estate agent. This may work fine, but be aware that inspectors who rely too much on agent referrals for their business may be reluctant to find problems that could end up scuttling the deal, thus disappointing the agent.

To find an inspector who will give the house a thorough going-over, interview three or four using the Inspector Interview Questionnaire provided below (and available in the Appendix and on the CD-ROM at the back of this book). To get the names of the inspectors to interview, talk to your real estate agent, friends, coworkers, and the professional organizations listed below.

RESOURCES

Looking for a home inspector affiliated with a trade organization? Visit one of the following home inspection association websites: American Society of Home Inspectors (www.ashi.org), National Association of Certified Home Inspectors (www.nachi.org), or National Association of Home Inspectors (www.nahi.org).

Working With Closing Agents

The closing is the day on which ownership of the property actually changes hands from seller to buyer. There's a lot at stake here—you don't want to hand the seller your money until you're sure all contingencies have been met or removed and you'll really get title to the house, but the seller doesn't want to give you title before being assured you've met or removed all your contingencies and have truly come up with the money. On top of this, a number of forms and other paperwork need to be reviewed and signed by both you and the seller. What you need, in most states, is an objective third party to coordinate the process: Enter the closing agent. (However, in some states, mostly on the East Coast, these tests are traditionally handled jointly by the buyer's and seller's attorneys.)

Who Closing Agents Are

A closing (also called a settlement or escrow) agent helps you close or complete the real estate transaction in accordance with the terms of your and the seller's purchase agreement. The closing agent usually works for a title or escrow company. Most title companies train closing agents from the ground up, usually starting them off as escrow assistants who work in the office to gain the necessary real estate knowledge before moving into handling actual closings. Additionally, closing agents must usually meet state licensing requirements. Again, however, in some states, a real estate attorney (or combination of attorneys) handles the closing instead.

Tasks Your Closing Agent Should Handle

The closing agent's precise tasks include facilitating the signing of all closing and lender documents, receiving and disbursing funds, and recording the deed and appropriate security documents. Despite being a key member of your real estate team, a closing agent is actually nonpartisan. That is, he or she doesn't specifically represent the interests of either the buyer or the seller (unless he or she is your attorney).

Choosing the Best Closing Agent

Who chooses the closing agent depends on local custom and how strongly you, as the buyer, feel about having a voice in the matter. The choice of a closing agent or title or escrow company is usually made early on and spelled out in the purchase agreement. Often the agent is someone either the buyer or seller's agent works with regularly. If you have a particular company or individual you want to use, mention it at the outset to your agent, so it can be included in your offer.

Some title companies and agents have come under fire in the past for alleging providing kickbacks to real estate agents and lenders. To make sure that you're choosing a reputable title company and closing agent, follow the guidelines below:

- Check with the American Land Title Association (www.alta.org), a trade organization that advocates high standards and ethics among its members. The site has a consumer information section that provides more information about the role of escrow companies. While this won't help you with individual closing agents, it will help you make sure the company your prospective agent works for is legitimate and ethical.

- Get several referrals of closing agents from family members, friends, neighbors, colleagues, or anyone else you trust. Ideally, you want a closing agent who is familiar with the type of second home you're buying, such as a single-family or multifamily home or a condo.

Bringing in Financial and Estate Planners

While not directly related to the home-buying process, you may need a financial professional or estate planner to help you make educated decisions about how a second home fits into your budget and other aspects of your life. If you already use a financial planner or advisor, be sure to schedule a consultation about your plans to buy a second home. Your planner is well placed to advise you on such matters as how much money to pull from your savings for the down payment.

EXAMPLE: Abba is thinking of pulling $20,000 out of a five-year CD yielding 4.5% interest with one year left until maturity. However, she talks to her financial planner, who recommends that, since Abba will have to pay a penalty for early withdrawal on the CD, she should instead take an extra $20,000 out on a mortgage (provided she qualifies to do so). Then, once the CD matures, Abba can use that money to pay down the principal on her mortgage. In the end, she'll have saved enough money to cover the financial planner's fee and then some.

Some financial planners (as well as attorneys and accountants) specialize in estate planning. If you think you'll still own your second home when you die, an estate planner can play a role in how you set up your purchase.

For example, if you have a family limited partnership (an estate planning strategy that uses a partnership set up within a family unit to transfer wealth from one generation to the next) your estate planner may recommend that the family partnership, rather than you as an individual, buy the second home.

RESOURCES

Want to learn more about estate planning? Nolo's *Plan Your Estate*, by Denis Clifford and Cora Jordan, covers everything from the basics of wills and living trusts to sophisticated tax-saving strategies.

Bringing in a Tax Professional

The tax implications of buying another home can range from straightforward to complicated. A lot depends on whether you plan on renting the house out and, if so, how much time you'll use your home personally. While Chapter 14 provides an overview of second-home tax implications to consider before you buy, it's certainly no substitute for professional, personalized advice—most likely from an accountant or other tax pro. And, even after your buy your second home, you should continue to consult your tax professional to make sure you're taking full advantage of the tens of thousands of dollars in tax savings the home could yield.

EXAMPLE: Taddeo plans on partially renting out his vacation home and is considering setting up a separate business entity, such as an LLC, to protect his personal assets from lawsuits. His tax professional tells him that, in that case, Taddeo won't be able to take the federal tax deduction for interest paid on his home loan, which can amount to thousands of dollars in savings each year. The advisor suggests an alternate strategy of purchasing personal umbrella insurance to extend the liability coverage on Taddeo's homeowners' insurance. That way, he can avoid forming an LLC, achieve the same lawsuit protection goal, and still benefit from the federal tax deduction.

POINTS TO REMEMBER

Your real estate team plays a crucial role in helping you find and buy the second home of your dreams. Surround yourself only with knowledgeable, experienced professionals. However, don't lose sight of the fact that you're still leading this team and will live with the outcome of your decisions.

Fixer-Uppers: Finding the Gems and Avoiding the Junk

"Ahh, home, crap home!" That's how Walter Fielding, Jr. (Tom Hanks' character in *The Money Pit*) aptly described dealing with a house in need of repair. Commonly called fixer-uppers, these types of homes can be a nightmare if, like Mr. Fielding, you bite off more than you can chew. On the other hand, if you choose (and chew) wisely, a fixer-upper can provide the dream home you never thought you could afford.

This chapter will help you decide whether or not to take on a fixer-upper. It begins by looking at the state of mind needed to deal with the dust and debris that comes with the territory. It also advises you on how to factor in your level of skill (if you plan on doing most of the work yourself) and patience (if you decide to hire professionals).

Of course, not all fixer-uppers require the same amounts of time and money. A fixer-upper in decent shape may need only low-cost, superficial improvements, like applying a fresh coat of paint or installing new carpets. A serious fixer-upper may need expensive, complex renovations such as gutting entire rooms (ripping them down to the beams) and rebuilding from scratch.

To guide you in balancing time and money, we've included a list of common projects—both inside and outside the house—that you might encounter with a fixer-upper. And, if you find a fixer-upper that interests you, our handy worksheet will help you keep track of your costs so you don't end up blowing your budget before the work is complete.

Are Fixer-Uppers a Good Deal?

A house in disrepair should sell for less (considerably less if the work required is extensive) than a house in good to excellent condition. Then, once you repair and spiff the place up, it will instantly rise in value. At least, that's the theory behind buying a fixer-upper. In reality, it doesn't always work out that way. Not to say you can't get a good deal on a fixer-upper, but you need to be aware of the current condition of the housing market, as well as the seller's possibly rose-colored perception of the house. Both can directly impact the price you're asked to pay.

How the Current Housing Market Influences Price

In a strong housing market, finding a deal on a fixer-upper isn't as easy as you'd think. That's because these houses attract the attention of first-time home buyers who are desperate to break into the market and figure this is their only way. To make matters worse, hordes of experienced real estate investors, especially those with contractor skills or connections, make an ongoing business out of buying fixer-uppers, improving them, and selling them at a healthy markup. These two forces tend to drive up the cost of fixer-uppers to a level that may not be worth your while.

Of course, the inverse is also true. In a flat or falling market, fixer-uppers are perceived as less attractive. That's because first-time buyers can usually get good deals on houses that are in much better condition. As for the investors, turning a buck becomes more difficult because there are more houses on the market from which buyers can choose. Both of these factors, in turn, cause fixer-upper prices to drop, sometimes to considerably less than market value. In that case, they may be more worth your while if you're looking for a place that you'll hold onto for some time, rather than a short-term investment. But don't forget that you might get an equally good deal on a house in good condition that a seller is eager to unload.

How the Seller's Perception May Raise the Price

If you're looking at a house that the current owner has been living or vacationing in for the past 35 years or so, there's a chance the owner has become blind to its problems. Not realizing that the house has become a fixer-upper, such owners tend to overprice them and refuse any lower bids. After such houses languish on the market for many months, the owners usually get the idea and lower their price, but you may not want to wait that long (though you can search for houses that have already been on the market for a long time and use this as a point of negotiation).

In the end, you'll find that fixer-uppers almost always sell below comparable-size houses that are in better condition. Still, that doesn't mean buying one is a good deal for you. It all depends on what's happening in the housing market at the time, how great the discount is, and whether or not the seller is aware that the house is, indeed, a fixer-upper.

Are You Ready for Months of Chaos?

A psychic once told Sarah J. Winchester (the Winchester rifle heiress) that if she ever stopped renovating her home in San Jose, California, she would die. So, the heiress committed the next 38 consecutive years to round-the-clock renovations.

Most of us don't have the patience (or the benefit of a $20 million inheritance) to spend this long fixing up a home. And you probably won't willingly buy a place that needs this many years of work. Still, if you're thinking about buying a fixer-upper, you can plan on the work taking longer than anticipated.

Not convinced? Ask any homeowner who has bought a fixer-upper (be it a first or second home). You'll probably hear that delays and problems are bound to occur. What was expected to take three months drags out to six because the contractor's schedule is full, the work required is more involved than originally thought, or some other unknown factor emerges.

Expecting delays is a necessary part of taking on a fixer-upper. Dealing with constant dust and debris, managing workers (or yourself), continually tracking and adjusting your finances, and schlepping back and forth between your first and second home are all certain to exercise your mental as well as physical muscles. And, if you plan on doing most of the work yourself, you'll need to be sure that you actually possess the requisite skills. Also ask yourself whether you're ready to give up your nights and weekends for an indefinite period of time.

Still not sure whether your head's in the right place? The quiz below (which also appears in the Appendix and on the CD-ROM in the back of the book) may help you more than any crystal ball.

Of course, you may not be the only one signing up for this megaproject. Talk to your spouse, significant other, or cobuyer about the issues involved in buying a fixer-upper. (It's probably not a bad idea to have your fellow buyer complete the quiz, below, too.) If both of you are equally willing and eager, it doesn't mean that problems won't occur, but it will make dealing with them much easier.

Fixer-Upper State-of-Mind Quiz

Rate yourself against the statements below. Total your ratings and see the scorecard at the bottom of this worksheet.

I'm comfortable managing and directing other people.

    (poor condition) 1 2 3 4 5 (good condition)

When things don't go as initially planned, I'm flexible in finding alternative solutions.

    (poor condition) 1 2 3 4 5 (good condition)

I'm a patient person.

    (poor condition) 1 2 3 4 5 (good condition)

When I commit to something, I stick with it until it's complete.
    (poor condition) 1 2 3 4 5 (good condition)

I'm good at tracking how I spend money.

    (poor condition) 1 2 3 4 5 (good condition)

How did you score?

Overall score of 20 or higher: Your head is in the right place.

Overall score of between 15 and 19: You have more or less the right state of mind, but should be aware of areas where you scored low, and plan around them.

Overall score of 14 or less: Think twice about what you're getting yourself into.

REAL-LIFE EXAMPLE: When Tom and Bret Chung of Rockville, New York decided to buy a second home to use as a weekend getaway, their only objective was to find a secluded place in the country with charm and character. When the couple stumbled across an 1820 farmhouse in Red Rock, New York, they were ecstatic. It even came at a reasonable price. There was just one hitch: The house needed a fair amount of work.

    The Chungs then had a dilemma. Having spent the last 12 years renovating their primary residence, a Victorian on Long Island, this "do-it-yourself" couple knew firsthand what was involved in shouldering a fixer-upper. And this one was a 2½ hour drive away. They sat down and discussed what work they thought needed to be done, how they would go about doing it, under what time frame, and how much they would budget to pay for it. In the end, they agreed that the farmhouse was too perfect to pass up and would be well worth the undertaking. A year and a half later, with renovations still going on, the couple had encountered their share of unexpected problems. Instead of lounging on the porch and sipping ice tea all day, visits to their "weekend getaway" meant swinging hammers and brandishing drills. But at the end of each weekend, they knew they were one step closer to completing the second home of their dreams—making all the hard work worthwhile.

Planning for Tenants? No Need for a Luxury Fix Up

Imagine two different people looking at the same fixer-upper. Each one walks through, jotting down what needs to be done in order to bring the house up to par. Both people then give their lists to the same contractor, and solicit a quote. When the quotes are compared, one is for $15,000 and the other for $50,000. How can there be a $35,000 difference on the same house?

The $15,000 quote is for a potential landlord looking to rent out the property full-time. The landlord evaluated the house with the idea of putting in the least possible amount of money—just enough to bring the house up to an acceptable living standard. By going on the cheap, this landlord-to-be is ensuring that the rental income will cover the greatest possible percentage of the property's total costs (including purchase price, repairs, and maintenance).

That's not to say all potential landlords should go for the cheapest possible repairs. At a minimum, you have to make the place habitable, and high-quality upgrades may make it more attractive to renters. But modeling yourself on our cheapskate landlord isn't an entirely bad idea if you'll need to narrow the gap between the rental income and your total costs.

What about the $50,000 quote? This hypothetical person is a future retiree, who plans to use the home as a weekend retreat for five years before retiring there full time. This person created a list of needs based on making the house not only livable, but tasteful and comfortable. Most people will put more money into fixing up a second home that they will use exclusively or that may one day become their permanent residence.

EXAMPLE: Lilly buys a fixer-upper in an up-and-coming suburb of Philadelphia. She plans on renting it out, after the repairs are made, for $1,200 a month (the going rate in the neighborhood). The kitchen, in particular, is in bad shape and needs to be completely renovated. The cost to bring it up to functional, working condition is $10,000. That's based on installing Formica® cabinets and countertops, standard appliances, and a linoleum floor. While shopping for materials at her local building supply store, Lilly comes across a designer kitchen display that, coincidentally, mirrors the size and layout of the kitchen in her fixer-upper. Lilly falls in love with it—especially the solid cherry cabinets, granite countertops, state-of-the-art appliances, and hardwood floor. She inquires about the cost and discovers that it would be $30,000 including labor. Unfortunately, spending three times as much to renovate won't justify increasing the rent by that same amount (from $1,200 to $3,600 a month). At best, Lilly may be able to charge a 10-20% premium. She realizes that, as a potential landlord, it's best to stick to her original plan.

How Much Time and Money Will Different Repairs Require?

Some fixer-uppers can be completed in a matter of weeks at a nominal cost, while others can take months or more and carry a hefty price tag. That's not to say that projects on a short time frame are *always* less expensive than longer ones, but most often they are.

When evaluating the work involved, be sure to distinguish between necessary and preferred repairs. A hole in the roof or a toilet that doesn't flush needs fixing, period. But Formica countertops don't need to be replaced with granite, and carpets don't need to be replaced with hardwood floors, until your own preferences say that they do.

TIP

If your time or budget estimates are mushrooming out of control, scale back to necessary repairs. Focus on things like replacing windows because the wood is rotted out instead of replacing a door that's old and creaky but still functioning.

The list below will tell you what types of repairs are commonly needed in fixer-uppers and approximately how much time and money will be required to deal with them. Read the list now, but more importantly, use it to gain a rough sense of whether a particular fixer-upper is worth making an offer on. (We say "rough" because where your house is located, the type of work you'll need done, the people and materials you use, and other such factors can make a big difference in the amount of time and money required.)

Later, after you've offered to buy a fixer-upper, a professional home inspection will be critical for telling you what type of work needs to be done. After that, you can and should solicit a quote from a contractor, to get a more accurate sense of the costs. If you plan on doing most of the work yourself, a good rule of thumb is that it'll cost you about one-third the cost of using a contractor. That's based on the fact that you'll be paying only for materials.

Common Exterior Repairs

Here's what you'll likely spend, in time and money, for the most common exterior repair projects:

- *Painting.* If the paint on the house is chipped and peeling or the stain is severely weathered, a professional will likely need a week or two to repaint or stain it. Part of this time will usually be spent power washing the house to get rid of dirt and any mildew. The cost varies considerably, but you can expect to pay between $3,500 and $10,000.

- *Replacing windows.* If the current windows are falling out of their frames, you can replace them with windows that are more durable and even energy efficient. A professional handyman or carpenter can usually install a replacement window in a half hour or less. The cost depends on the size and quality of window, but typically ranges from $350 to $700 or more per window, including the window itself and installation.

- *Repairing decks and patios.* Because they're outdoors and people use them, decks and patios get a lot of wear and tear. Repairs could be as simple as replacing some rotted boards or cracked stones, or as major as ripping the whole thing out and starting from scratch. If the latter, expect to pay several thousand dollars depending on the square footage and materials used.

- *Fixing or replacing the roof.* If roof shingles have come loose or leaks are occurring, a simple patch job may suffice. But some leaks are more extensive than they first appear, or the roof may be deteriorating in several spots. You may need an entire new roof. If so, expect the work to take a good week and run anywhere from $5,000 to $11,000. It all depends on whether or not the old roof is being ripped off first, and what materials (tar, wood, terra-cotta, or slate shingles) you'll be using.

Common Interior Repairs

Here's what you'll likely spend, in time and money, for the most common interior repair projects:

- *Painting rooms.* Interior painting is, by far, one of the most inexpensive ways to add value and appeal to a house. A room can be painted within a day or two and you will usually be charged around $800, depending on the size and how much wall and ceiling preparation (removing wallpaper, patching holes) is involved.

- *Replacing carpets.* Dingy, old carpets need to be ripped out and replaced. If you plan on installing new carpet, it can be done in a matter of days (depending on square footage) by a professional. The cost can range from $15 to $60 or more per square yard including installation. The exact amount depends on variables like carpet style (such as plush or Berber), fiber (such as nylon or wool), and the type and thickness of the padding. If you have it in your head to replace the old carpet with other flooring such as hardwood, this can become a complicated and expensive project.

- *Replace lighting and plumbing fixtures.* Switching out old ceiling lights, wall sconces, and other electrical fixtures can update a house in no time. The same is true of bathroom and kitchen faucets. You can have an electrician or plumber do the work in a few hours or less, depending on how many fixtures you're replacing. However, plan to spend a good $80 to $100 an hour for an electrician's services, plus the cost of the fixtures, which can vary considerably depending on quality.

- *Kitchen and bathroom remodel.* You can keep costs down by working within the existing layout or footprint of the old room, as opposed to demolishing, moving, or adding walls between rooms. You'll also save money by keeping the current plumbing and wiring intact instead of running new water lines or electrical circuits. A bathroom remodel, for example, may entail replacing the vanity and toilet. Or a kitchen remodel may involve upgrading the appliances but keeping the existing cabinetry and countertops intact. Unless you're an advanced do-it-yourselfer, remodels are usually best left to professionals. The time and cost involved all depends on the type of room and extent of the remodel. The work could easily take several months to complete and run from $5,000 to $15,000 for bathrooms and $10,000 to $50,000 for kitchens.

Doing Walk-Throughs

Fixer-upper or not, practically everyone does an initial walk-through (a personal inspection of a house's interior, exterior, and surrounding grounds) before making an offer. While a walk-through is an important part of the buying process for any house, for a fixer-upper, it's an absolute must. This is when you'll begin to determine the amount of work required.

You can use the initial walk-through to gauge a general sense of the house (layout, number and size of rooms, general condition, and more). Later, doing a second (and even third) walk-through is a good idea. You'll notice different things each visit, and have more time to fully examine the house.

If you lack the knowledge to fully assess the amount of work involved, it's best to bring along a residential general contractor (someone who oversees all aspects of residential home renovations) on the second walk-through. Admittedly, finding a contractor to do this for free can be difficult unless you have a close connection with one (say, a family member or friend). If not, you may have to pay for the contractor's time, which could easily cost you a few hundred dollars. However, it could be well worth the cost. Otherwise you'll have to wait until after you make an offer on the house, at which point you'll bring in a home inspector.

WARNING

Don't rely on statements by the seller about the house's condition. In most states, sellers must provide you with a written disclosure report, giving you the seller's assessment of the house's various structural and mechanical systems, appliances, hazards, history, and more. However, there are three problems with such reports. One is that they aren't necessarily comprehensive—the report may fail to ask the one question that will bring to light a serious problem. Another is that some sellers simply lie about, or conveniently forget to mention, a repair issue. But the most significant problem is that sellers need only tell you about issues they're aware of. They don't need to commission professional inspections, and may be as blissfully ignorant as you are about cracks in the foundation, holes in the roof, and more.

During your walk-throughs, use the checklist below (also in the Appendix and on the CD-ROM in the back of the book) to gauge the condition of various parts of the property. Be sure to jot down any notes about particular items, such as a fence that's falling over or a hole in a bathroom wall. This checklist will be invaluable in deciding how much to offer on a particular house, or even whether you should make an offer at all.

Also, be sure to take a still or video camera with you so you can record the condition of the property for review later. Just be sure the seller knows in advance that you want to do this, as this is still the seller's personal property and you should respect his or her privacy.

Once you've completed the walk-through, make a few calls to specialty contractors (plumbers, electricians, carpenters) and try to get rough quotes for the work that you'll need to do based on your checklist. For example, if your list shows that an outside deck is dilapidated, call a carpenter and ask what the approximate cost would be to rebuild a deck of similar size. If a contractor is reluctant to give you a quote without actually seeing the house, send the photos or copy of the video. If the contractor is still reluctant, then call another one. At this point, your goal is merely to get a general sense of rough costs.

Fixer-Upper Walk-Through Checklist

Rate the condition of the house based on your own visual inspection during the walk-through. Write down any notes about particular items. Also try to take photos or video of the property.

Exterior

Roof: Reduce the rating for any cracked, missing, or worn down shingles or tiles.

(poor condition) 1 2 3 4 5 (good condition)

Notes:_____

_____

Paint/Stain/Siding: Reduce the rating for any chips or cracks on paint, faded stain, or siding that is buckled and pulling away from the house.

(poor condition) 1 2 3 4 5 (good condition)

Notes:_____

_____

Windows: Reduce the rating for any broken panes and rot around the frames.

(poor condition) 1 2 3 4 5 (good condition)

Notes:_____

_____

Fence: Reduce the rating for any missing slats or sections, unevenness, and loose posts.

(poor condition) 1 2 3 4 5 (good condition)

Notes:_____

_____

Driveway: Reduce the rating for any sagging spots, holes, or cracks.

(poor condition) 1 2 3 4 5 (good condition)

Notes:_____

_____

Walkways: Reduce the rating for any sagging spots, holes, or cracks in slates or bricks.

(poor condition) 1 2 3 4 5 (good condition)

Notes:_____

_____

Landscaping: Reduce the rating for any overgrown or dying shrubs, trees, and grass.

(poor condition) 1 2 3 4 5 (good condition)

Notes:_____

_____

Fixer-Upper Walk-Through Checklist (cont'd.)

Interior

Kitchen: Reduce the rating for any cracked or chipped countertops, poorly working fixtures, or old or worn-down appliances or cabinets.

(poor condition) 1 2 3 4 5 (good condition)

Notes:_____

_____

_____

Living room: Reduce the rating for any cracked or broken windows; chips, cracks, or holes in the walls or ceiling; sagging or squeaky floors; or worn carpets.

(poor condition) 1 2 3 4 5 (good condition)

Notes:_____

_____

_____

Dining room: Reduce the rating for any cracked or broken windows; chips, cracks, or holes in the walls or ceiling; sagging or squeaky floors; or worn carpets.

(poor condition) 1 2 3 4 5 (good condition)

Notes:_____

_____

_____

Bathroom #1: Reduce the rating for any cracked or chipped countertops, or poorly working fixtures, toilet, or tub/shower.

(poor condition) 1 2 3 4 5 (good condition)

Notes:_____

_____

_____

Hallways and stairs: Reduce the rating for any chips, cracks, or holes in the walls or ceiling; sagging or squeaky floors, or worn carpets.

(poor condition) 1 2 3 4 5 (good condition)

Notes:_____

_____

_____

Master bedroom: Reduce the rating for any cracked or broken windows; chips, cracks, or holes in the walls or ceiling; sagging or squeaky floors; or worn carpets.

(poor condition) 1 2 3 4 5 (good condition)

Notes:_____

_____

_____

Fixer-Upper Walk-Through Checklist (cont'd.)

Bedroom #2: Reduce the rating for any cracked or broken windows; chips, cracks, or holes in the walls or ceiling; sagging or squeaky floors; or worn carpets.

(poor condition) 1 2 3 4 5 (good condition)

Notes:_____

_____

_____

Bedroom #3: Reduce the rating for any cracked or broken windows; chips, cracks, or holes in the walls or ceiling; sagging or squeaky floors; or worn carpets.

(poor condition) 1 2 3 4 5 (good condition)

Notes:_____

_____

_____

Bathroom #2: Reduce the rating for any cracked or chipped countertops, or poorly working fixtures, toilet, or tub/shower.

(poor condition) 1 2 3 4 5 (good condition)

Notes:_____

_____

_____

Furnace and Air Conditioning: Reduce the rating for an old, decrepit furnace (listen for rattling or clunky noises) or for an altogether insufficient heating or air conditioning system.

(poor condition) 1 2 3 4 5 (good condition)

Notes:_____

_____

_____

Electrical: Reduce the rating for any old and frayed wires. Also find out how many amps are coming into the house, and reduce the rating for anything less than 100 (depending on the size of the house).

(poor condition) 1 2 3 4 5 (good condition)

Notes:_____

_____

_____

Making Your Purchase Offer

After obtaining price quotes, add them all up to develop a working budget. Now you can make an initial offer on the house. To arrive at your offer price, work with your real estate agent to determine the fair market price of the house if it were in good condition. Subtract the contractor costs from that number to arrive at your initial offer price. (Go a little lower if you think the seller might bite—that will help account for unexpected costs, not to mention your own time and effort.)

When submitting your offer, be sure that your agent (or attorney, depending on the state in which the property is located) stipulates in the offer that the offer is contingent (conditional) on your satisfaction with the results of a professional home inspection. You'll have a limited time within which to complete this inspection, so it's best to have professionals lined up ahead of time. That way you can evaluate all aspects of the property before the deadline comes for making your final decision.

Getting a Second Opinion From a Professional Home Inspector

You certainly don't want to buy a fixer-upper based solely on what you saw during your walk-throughs. Who knows what you may have missed? That's where a professional home inspector comes into the picture.

A home inspector is someone who visually examines your potential home for mechanical and structural flaws that could impact its value. (See Chapter 6 for more on the role of a home inspector.) For a fixer-upper, this is particularly important, because the inspector can uncover hidden problems—ones that you may have missed and that the seller didn't know about to disclose to you.

Upon completion of the inspection, the home inspector will give you a report that details the condition of the property and gives you a better sense of what you are about to take on. That will allow you to perhaps negotiate with the seller over the price, or in case of big surprises, to exercise your contractual right to back out of the sale.

But don't take the inspector's report as the last word—inspectors sometimes miss hidden problems and cannot guarantee that other problems won't develop in the near future. Also, while a home inspection will confirm the type of work that needs to be done to a fixer-upper, it does very little to provide you with a sense of cost. That's why you'll next want to bring in a residential general contractor.

Soliciting a Formal Estimate From a Contractor

Now you need to fine-tune the rough cost estimates that you used to make your purchase offer. Again, a residential general contractor can help, by reviewing the home inspection report as well as your checklist and photos or video (unless the contractor has already seen the house during a walk-through). You'll also want the contractor to walk through the house itself (again, if the contractor hasn't already done this), to see firsthand what's involved. The contractor can then provide you with a detailed cost estimate, which becomes the foundation of your revised budget.

Most contractors provide free estimates. Keep in mind, however, that a contractor who knows that you plan on tackling all the actual work yourself may be reluctant to spend unpaid time giving you an estimate.

Armed with both the home inspection report and a contractor's estimate of what it will take to repair the problems the inspector found, you can validate whether or not your purchase offer price was fair. If the work and cost involved is greater than you had originally thought, you can renegotiate the price with the seller, or ask that the seller separately pay for certain repairs.

 TIP

Add 20% to the contractor's estimate, to give your budget a buffer. Estimates are just that—estimates. To make sure that your budget can absorb the unexpected expenses that are sure to crop up, it's best to add a little extra. Experience has shown that 20% is a safe starting point. However, if the fixer-upper that you're looking at will require extensive work, you may want to bump up your buffer to 25% or even 30%. Just don't expect the seller to pay for this buffer.

How Will You Pay for Repairs?

Whether your repairs will cost $10,000 or $100,000, the money needs to come from somewhere. Before the sale of the house is finalized, make certain that you know exactly how you'll pay for repairs. Three potential resources for funding your renovations include:

- your savings
- a mortgage lender, or
- a gift or loan from family or friends.

Tapping Your Savings

Using money you've saved to pay for renovations is the cheapest route, because you avoid paying interest charges on a loan. Of course, you're probably also tapping your savings to help with the down payment and other costs. If your savings won't cover both, consider reducing the amount you put towards your down payment or delaying your second-home search until you can boost your savings.

Borrowing From a Mortgage Lender

If tapping your savings isn't an option or still won't cover your repair costs, consider borrowing the needed money. You'll probably be in contact with a bank, credit union, or other institutional lender anyway, for your basic home loan. Why not borrow extra to cover the renovation costs? Various national mortgage lenders offer special loan programs that combine these two loan types into one. They go by different names, such as the Purchase & Renovate Program℠ from Wells Fargo, or the Single-Close Renovation Loan from Citibank. The interest rate is typically lower than it would be if you got two separate loans, given that loans for renovation usually charge high interest.

You can usually choose between a fixed-rate loan (with 15- to 30-year terms) or a 30-year adjustable-rate loan in which the rate is fixed at the beginning and then adjusts annually after the third, fifth, seventh, or tenth year.

Before signing up for such a loan program, take a careful look at any restrictions your lender will place on the renovations you can do. For example, you may have to show that the renovations will be a permanent part of the property and will add value to it. You'll also, as part of the loan application process, need to submit a cost estimate for renovating. This allows the bank to take issue with your costs—which isn't all bad, since if the bank thinks your costs don't make financial sense, you may want to reexamine them.

To learn more about this loan program and to find lenders offering it in your state, visit www.fanniemae.com/homebuyers/findamortgage/mortgages/renovation.jhtml?p.

Getting a Gift or Loan From Family

Family and even close friends can be a valuable source of financial and other support. Some may be willing to make you an outright gift. For others, a loan that you pay back with interest is more appropriate. (And if any of them are handy with a hammer, all the better.) Refer to Chapter 10 for more on the mutual benefits of borrowing from family and friends.

Who Will Do the Repair Work?

When it comes to tackling renovations on your second home, you can roll up your sleeves and do the work yourself, or bring in professional help. It all depends on your desire, skill level, budget, and amount of spare time. Most people use some combination of personal and professional labor.

Doing It Yourself

If you have the skill and time to do most of the home renovations on your own, you can save, on average, two-thirds of the total cost. From a budget perspective, doing it yourself certainly looks good. But don't forget to factor in your time. You may be talking years of effort—particularly if the house is located far away from where you live. Still, for some, the time and effort is well worth it—and may even offer a creative outlet.

RESOURCES

Black & Decker's series of home improvement books are a must for any do-it-yourselfer. Covering topics from electrical to carpentry and everything in between, each book contains simple, step-by-step instructions supplemented with photos, illustrations, and diagrams. The books are available from The Home Depot as well as many major booksellers. Another option is to look for the many free or low-cost classes offered at home improvement stores and local adult education centers, on do-it-yourself projects such as tiling, installing light fixtures, and fixing leaks.

Hiring Contractors

A contractor is an expert in a given craft such as electricity, plumbing, carpentry, or tile work. Although this expertise comes with a price tag, a good, experienced contractor can be worth his or her weight in gold.

You've got two choices when working with contractors: to deal with each one individually or to hire a general contractor who handles everything for you, including hiring subcontractors. Either way, be sure to follow these simple steps in selecting a contractor:

- Make certain the contractor is appropriately licensed in your state. Most states have a registered home improvement contractor database where you can not only look this up, but check whether any complaints have been filed against the contractor. Visit your state's website and search under "contractor licensing." Also check with the Better Business Bureau for complaints or search the Internet under "Better Business Bureau [your state]."

- Ensure that the contractor has adequate liability insurance and workers' compensation insurance. (If not, you could end up liable for worksite injuries.) You can usually find this out when confirming the contractor's licensing status. Another approach is to ask to see a copy of the contractor's current insurance policy or ask for the policy number and insurer name so that you can confirm coverage.

- Ask for a written list of the contractor's three most recent projects, including the property owners' names, telephone numbers, and addresses.

- Call the owners and ask about the performance of the contractor and their satisfaction with the end result. For example, did workers clean up each day before leaving, or was the worksite and surrounding area left in disarray? Did the quality of workmanship meet the owner's expectations? Did the contractor complete the work on time? Did any unexpected problems arise, and if so how did the contractor deal with them?

As soon as you choose a contractor, negotiate and sign a written contract covering such important topics as the scope of work to be done, the timeline, and the costs. The contract should also mention that you authorize the contractor to act as your agent in applying for the building permit. Such written contracts aren't legally required, but can save you from misunderstandings and legal disputes down the road. For more information, see the article "Put Your Independent Contractor Agreements in Writing," free on Nolo's website at www.nolo.com (search for the title).

TIP

Looking for a contractor? Referrals are your best source. Ask family, friends, and neighbors which contractors they've used and liked. If you're new to an area and don't have a personal network to tap, you can still ask your neighbors or talk to folks down at your local home center, such as Lowe's Home Improvement or The Home Depot.

Keeping Track of Costs

An extra $50 here, another $75 there—at first, it might not seem like much, but these costs can add up. Maybe you decide at the last minute to go with a higher-quality carpet, or the plumber charges an additional hour because a leaking pipe was hard to access. Whatever the reason, something unexpected always hits. And unless you're keeping tabs on your costs, you'll end up scratching your head as to why you've blown your budget by several hundreds or even thousands of dollars.

Accurate record keeping is not only useful in helping you stay within your budget, but comes in handy around tax time. Clean records make it much easier for you or your accountant to itemize your fix-up costs, many of which will be either tax deductible or depreciable. (Tax deductibility is briefly explained in "Some Fix-Up Costs Are Tax Deductible," below, and explained at greater length in Chapter 14.)

You don't need to be an accountant to accurately track costs and stay on top of your budget. You do, however, need to be somewhat organized and diligent about keeping records. If those qualities just aren't in your genetic makeup, then consider asking your spouse, family member, or friend to play the role of bookkeeper.

Regardless of who does it, keeping accurate records is a relatively easy task to handle. The key is to record costs as you incur them, rather than trying to figure them out months later by digging through a heap of receipts.

To help with your record keeping, we've created a simple, yet effective Fixer-Upper Cost-Tracking Form (see sample below). (A blank version can be found in the Appendix and on the CD-ROM at the back of the book.)

Some Fix-Up Costs Are Tax Deductible

If you plan to rent out your house, or later sell it at a profit, you've got a special interest in tracking your fix-up costs: Some of them are tax deductible. Their deductibility, in turn, lowers your taxable income. If you plan on:

- **renting out your house,** you can deduct certain fix-up costs. However, the manner in which you deduct these costs—realizing the full deduction in a single year versus depreciating it (an income-tax deduction that allows you to recover the cost of a property over a longer period of time)—depends on whether the IRS considers the cost to be a repair or an improvement.

- **selling the house,** you can deduct certain fix-up costs to reduce your taxable capital gains (the profit on the sale of your house). Of course, this assumes that you are actually turning a profit on the sale.

For more on the tax implications of a fixer-upper, refer to Chapter 14.

Fixer-Upper Cost-Tracking Form

Project Description	Expense Description	Labor, Materials, or Both?	Date (Month/ Year)	Budgeted Amount ($)	Actual Amount ($)	Budget Reconciliation (+/_)	Receipt (Yes/No)
Upstairs bedroom	Floor tile	Materials only	1/07	$350	$295	-$55	
Kitchen	New sink	Labor and materials	1/07	$300	$335	+$35	
			Budget Totals	$650	$630	-$20	

POINTS TO REMEMBER

Buying a fixer-upper can get you a second home you might not otherwise be able to afford. Plus, it gives you the opportunity to create a home that suits your needs—whether as an investor, future retiree, or vacationer. But before you don that hardhat and start calling yourself the next Bob Vila, give some serious thought to what you're getting into. A fixer-upper isn't for everyone, but for those who are ready to take on the challenge, the payoff can be rewarding. ●

Buying Straight from the Seller

You're probably assuming that, in the course of your home quest, you'll consider the whole pool of available houses (even if you don't visit them all in person). But what if we told you that there's a whole supply of houses that your real estate agent might not tell you about, and that might not even make it into an MLS database? We're talking about "FSBOs," that is, "For Sale by Owner" homes.

Realistically speaking, your odds of buying a FSBO are slim—FSBOs usually account for only about 13% of the total homes on the market. Still, your perfect second home could be a FSBO, which is why you owe it to yourself to check out these properties.

This chapter covers what you need to know about finding and buying a FSBO—from how they compare pricewise to the different types of sellers you'll encounter and how to deal with them. We'll also look at how you can enlist your real estate agent's help in looking for or buying a FSBO.

Why Some Sellers Go Without a Real Estate Agent

Today, real estate commissions (the fee paid for the services of real estate brokers or agents) run at about 5% of the selling price. Traditionally, the seller pays this commission. If, for example, a house sells for $300,000, the seller has to fork out $15,000 in commissions.

However, there are some sellers who aim to avoid paying commissions by selling their properties themselves. These sellers are looking to cut out the middleperson and deal directly with potential buyers. That means they take on all the tasks of advertising, showing, and negotiating the purchase of their homes.

Watch for Inconsistent Pricing of FSBOs

Pricing a house to sell is an inexact science. Even when real estate agents tell a seller how much a property is likely to sell for, their estimates can vary by thousands (sometimes even tens of thousands) of dollars. If that's happening among professionals who price properties for a living, imagine the difficulty for someone with no or limited experience in selling real estate. Add to this the fact that many FSBO sellers have a personal attachment to their property, which can cloud their objectivity when setting the selling price.

The net result is that most FSBOs are priced at market value, or even above. Then again, you'll find the occasional FSBO seller who has no idea how much the house is worth and has mistakenly priced it below market value.

Shouldn't the Lack of a Commission Lower the Price?

Some buyers hope that FSBO sellers will pass on some of the money they save by not paying a commission, in the form of a reduced market price. Dream on. Although a FSBO seller may circumvent the standard 5% real estate commission, that savings isn't all cash in the pocket. The seller still needs to cover the costs of advertising the property, possibly hiring a real estate attorney to review the sale documents and participate in the closing, and more. Also, depending on market conditions, the seller may need to pay a commission to your agent (see "Getting the Seller to Pay for Your Agent," below). That alone could add up to 2½% of the selling price.

Giving you a below market discount on top of these costs would erase the bulk of the savings the seller was trying to realize by cutting out real estate agents in the first place.

Why You May Encounter Overpriced FSBOs

Some FSBO sellers overprice their houses because they're under the illusion that they're sitting on a gold mine. This phenomenon is particularly common at the tail end of a housing boom, when everyone has heard eye-popping stories about homes selling above their asking prices. The FSBO sellers may not have noticed that prices have begun to flatten or even fall.

When it comes to pricing, emotions can cloud any seller's judgment—but with a FSBO, there's no real estate agent around to correct the seller's misimpressions. For example, a seller may feel that recouping 100% or more of a recent bathroom renovation is reasonable, when a real estate agent would tell the seller that recovering only about 75% of the cost is normal.

The bottom line is that, as a buyer, you shouldn't look to FSBOs as some unique way to save money on a second home. Instead, view these properties as you would any other: Look at their attributes and see whether they satisfy what you want in a second home. If a particular FSBO interests you, have your agent determine whether it is priced reasonably.

Dealing With FSBO Sellers

Not all sellers are created equal—and without the buffer of a real estate agent, you'll come face to face with your FSBO seller's quirks, shortcomings, or misapprehensions. You can create your own buffer by using a buyer's agent. Still, your seller's personality will affect the transaction more than if the seller were getting frank advice from his or her own real estate agent.

Whether you're stepping into the negotiating ring yourself or having an agent do it on your behalf, try to analyze the type of person you'll be sparring with. Three commonly found types of FSBO sellers are:

• the savvy seller

• the uneducated seller, and

• the miserly seller.

The Savvy Seller

From a buyer's perspective, the ideal FSBO seller is a savvy one: someone who understands what's involved in successfully completing a real estate transaction. If you're really lucky, your FSBO seller may be a lawyer or a real estate agent. The savvy seller is usually well versed in the current real estate market and has done extensive research on the value of the home being sold. Such a seller tends to be realistic when negotiating with you, for example basing the final house price on current market data and housing conditions.

The savvy seller has also done some self-education about all of the steps required to sell a home—from initially pricing the property to effectively marketing it to working with potential buyers and completing the sale. The savvy seller tends to spend money where it makes sense, such as to hire a real estate attorney. (The attorney can provide valuable services by drawing up the proper legal documents, reviewing the deal to ensure that federal- and state-mandated disclosure requirements are met, and representing the seller at the closing.)

Below are a few tips on how to work with a savvy FSBO seller:

- *Don't let the seller drive the entire process.* It may be tempting to let an obviously knowledgeable seller dictate everything. Don't! This is a business transaction and the seller is still looking out for you-know-who's best interests. For example, if the seller hires an attorney to handle the closing, make sure that you hire your own attorney as well.

- *Learn enough to make you an equal.* A well-educated seller can easily gain the upper hand. Level the playing field by learning as much about the process as the seller has. Otherwise, the seller may negotiate a better deal at your expense. If you don't have the inclination or time to thoroughly educate yourself, consider using a buyer's agent. (See "Enlisting Your Real Estate Agent's Help," below.)

The Uneducated Seller

The uneducated seller is one who has no clue about what's involved in completing a real estate transaction (even though he or she might have a Ph.D. in an unrelated subject). This type of seller must be approached with extreme caution, not because he or she is malicious, but, rather because this person can wreak havoc on even the simplest parts of the transaction.

A common mistake of the uneducated seller is to unknowingly omit to tell you critical information about the property—for example, that it's located in a designated flood zone. While this particular fact would surface prior to the closing (due to inquiries by your mortgage lender), you would by then have already sunk a fair amount of time and money into the deal. And other nondisclosures might not come back to bite you until the house is yours, such as the seller having remodeled without obtaining the appropriate permits.

Here's how to deal with an uneducated seller:

- *Don't be condescending.* Real estate marketing is complex stuff—if you treat the seller as stupid, it could put the deal at risk. Instead, treat the seller with respect and (since this is a business transaction) try to use the seller's lack of savvy to your advantage. For example, maybe you can convince the seller to cover all or part of the closing costs, which are ordinarily paid for by the buyer. Or, you could negotiate having the seller cover the cost of some repairs on the home as a condition of sale.

• *Expect more responsibility to fall on your shoulders.* The seller's lack of knowledge will, by default, put more pressure on you to make sure there aren't problems in completing the deal. In particular, you'll need to pay extra attention to ensuring that all agreed-upon tasks get done on time, and that necessary documents are prepared. Your title or escrow agent can help with this, too.

The Miserly Seller

The Ebenezer Scrooge of FSBO sellers, the miser's only interest is to drain the house of as much money as can be squeezed from it. By far the most difficult type of seller to deal with, the misers will give up very little while demanding much in return. Negotiations often prove difficult, because the miser doesn't view negotiating as "give and take," but rather as "take, take, take."

The miserly seller is also known for being unrealistic and emotional when dealing with buyers. If you're working with a buyer's agent, the miser will balk at the thought of paying the agent's commission. However, if housing market conditions are in your favor, the miser will usually have no choice but to do so—or risk losing the sale.

Following are some tips on how to deal with a miserly seller:

• *Be professional, and justify everything.* Whether it's the purchase price or a contingency, use data such as current housing figures or reports (such as home inspection or appraisal reports) to support your negotiations. For example, if median house prices have dropped in the area, use this to show the seller that your offer is probably the best that can be expected. If the home inspection report indicates the roof is in need of repair, use this to justify a lower price.

• *Know when to walk away.* At times, the miserly seller can become so selfish and difficult that completing the transaction isn't worth your struggles. Walking away from the deal may be your best bet, regardless of how much you like the house. Your threat to walk may actually shock the miser into being sensible. If not, you'll know that walking away was the right thing to do.

Enlisting Your Real Estate Agent's Help

You'll probably be using a real estate agent in your search for a second home–and that shouldn't change just because you're looking at FSBOs. Of course, you need to make sure someone is willing to pay your agent's commission. In many cases, the FSBO seller will agree to do so. If not, it might be worth paying your agent yourself. But before we tackle that, let's take a look at how to get your agent to show you FSBOs in the first place.

Getting Your Agent to Show You FSBOs

If you want to make most real estate agents cringe, mention that you'd like to see some FSBOs. Seller's agents don't like FSBOs, for the obvious reason that they're cut out of the monetary loop. Buyer's agents often resist FSBOs, because they'd rather deal with an experienced agent than an independent-minded character whose limited real estate experience might throw a wrench into the process. Plus, many buyer's agents act as seller's agents for other clients, so their antipathy toward FSBOs runs deep.

So what's the secret to getting your agent to include FSBOs in the house tour mix? Simply ask. The best time to do so is when you're first interviewing agents (covered in detail in Chapter 6), which means you haven't committed to anyone yet. If an agent says he or she won't consider FSBOs, look for another agent. If the agent says "yes," you're covered.

Even after you have an agent on board, however, it's a good idea to periodically conduct your own FSBO search (see "Finding FSBO Houses," below). Your agent might not be looking as hard as you'd like. It's really no different from continuing to look online or in the newspaper at agent-listed houses at the same time that your agent is searching on your behalf.

Making Sure Your Agent Is Fairly Compensated

Consider how agent compensation works for agent-listed houses. Two real estate agents are usually involved—the seller's (also called the "listing") agent, and the buyer's agent. The commission is paid by the seller and split evenly between both agents. But with a FSBO, the seller has removed his or her agent from the table. So who pays the commission for your agent?

You may have already answered this question, by signing an agreement with your agent. In many states, real estate agents are required by law to provide you with a written contract that explains their relationship to you. It's usually called a "buyer's agency agreement" (covered in detail in Chapter 6). Among other things, this agreement should state how your agent will be paid.

Many such agreements specifically cover FSBOs. The agreement may specify that your agent's commission will be paid by the FSBO seller if the seller has agreed to compensate a buyer's agent, and by you if you choose a property in which the seller refuses to compensate buyers' agents.

If you haven't yet signed a buyer's agency agreement, remember that they're negotiable. You should never sign one unless you're comfortable with its terms. For example, if you have no intention of paying any part of your agent's commission (especially on a FSBO), make sure the agreement specifies that fact. This way, when your agent is looking at FSBOs, he or she will consider only FSBOs in which the seller will pay for the buyer's agent's commission. Keep in mind that if you find a FSBO on your own and the seller refuses to pay the commission, you would most likely need to pay your real estate agent's commission on your own. At the very least, you should clarify with your agent up front how this type of situation would be handled.

Getting the Seller to Pay for Your Agent

FSBO or not, your agent will be looking to pocket up to a 2½% commission (half of 5%) on any home you buy, paid by the seller. It stands to reason that in a FSBO situation, the seller, and not you, should pay your agent's commission. Whether the seller will appreciate this logic depends on what's happening in the real estate market at the time:

- *In a flat or down real estate market, you hold the upper hand.* Use the seller's anxiety about finding a buyer—any buyer at all—to your advantage. In the end, paying 2½% instead of 5% may still seem like a good deal to the seller.
- *During a strong housing market, you'll have a harder time.* FSBO sellers (and all sellers for that matter) are in the driver's seat. You might suggest splitting your agent's commission with the seller (1¼% each, assuming a 2½% commission). But if the housing market is strong enough, you may have no choice but to either cover your agent's entire commission on your own or walk away from the deal.

Finding FSBO Houses

FSBOs aren't always well advertised. You'll need to work harder to find them than you would to find an agent-represented home. In addition to using your agent, other effective search methods include:

- searching the Web
- reading neighborhood classifieds, and
- driving around.

Searching Online

The Internet is your best, if not most convenient, resource for finding FSBOs. Numerous websites give FSBO sellers a place to list their properties for a fee. As a buyer, you won't be charged anything to search the listed properties or to contact prospective sellers. Many of the sites contain photos of the properties and key information such as square footage, number of rooms, and year built.

Some of the more established sites to check out include:

- www.fsbo.com
- www.forsalebyowner.com, and
- www.owners.com.

Combing the Newspaper Classifieds

Look through the real estate classified sections of the major metro as well as local newspapers serving the area where you want to buy. Along with agent-listed properties, you'll find FSBO ads. They're easy to spot—they usually say "for sale by owner" or "FSBO." Note that you don't necessarily have to buy a stack of newspapers—many of the major ones place their classifieds online. And don't forget to look for free local papers at the grocery store.

Driving Neighborhoods

Some FSBO owners don't even get around to advertising. That means that if you really want to know about every FSBO, you'll need to drive around the neighborhoods where you'd like to buy. Keep your eyes peeled for lawn signs that read "For sale by owner." If you happen to know people living in your prospective neighborhoods, also ask them to let you know if they hear of anyone interested in selling.

POINTS TO REMEMBER

While FSBOs aren't necessarily better deals than agent-listed homes, don't cross them off your list without a look. Make sure your real estate agent will tell you about FSBOs that fit your house criteria. If you find one you like, be prepared for the seller's personality to play an unusually large role in the negotiations. When it comes to paying your agent's commission, the seller should accept responsibility. However, in a hot housing market you, as the buyer, may need to pay all or some of the commission.

Raising the Cash You'll Need Up Front

T hink back, perhaps way back, to just before you bought your first home. What was the greatest apparent obstacle to making the purchase? Most likely, it was coming up with the infamous down payment, or as some like to call it, the "down painment." Remember how you scrimped and saved?

Well, it's time to do it all over again—but with a difference. Finding the cash to put down on your second home is often much easier than the first. You now have more resources to tap, such as equity in your current house, and, hopefully, more years of savings.

The exact amount of your intended down payment isn't important yet. For purposes of this chapter, simply estimate the amount, taking 20% of the approximate-priced house you expect to buy. Be generous in your estimate—especially because, although the down payment will command the greatest portion of what you'll need, the sale closing costs (detailed in Chapter 2), can easily add another $10,000 to your up front cash requirements.

Most second-home buyers actually put more than 20% down—the median down payment on vacation homes in 2006 was 27%, and the median on investment homes was 23%. (Source: Survey by National Association of Realtors®, www.narorg.)

If writing a check for 20% of the likely purchase price of your second home is no problem for you, you could skip this chapter—but might want to keep reading anyway, for tips on raising cash for other home-related expenses. If rounding up a 20% down payment will be a challenge, definitely keep reading.

While saving is the most obvious way to muster up the needed cash, borrowing can be an answer too, especially to fill any gaps. This chapter covers unique and effective ways to both build your savings and expand your borrowing capacity.

TIP

Curious where other second-home buyers got their down payments?
A survey by the National Association of Realtors (2005) found that:

- 45% tapped their savings
- 29% used equity from existing homes
- 9% used loans
- 6% used IRA, pension fund, or 401(k) proceeds
- 5% used inheritances
- 5% used proceeds from the sale of securities, and
- the rest used gifts or loans from friends or relatives.

Building Your Savings

Many people think they're already putting as much money into savings as they possibly can or are willing to. The truth is, you can still probably accumulate a nice chunk of change through simple changes in the way you invest your money and manage your spending. Fortunately, these changes need only be temporary.

EXAMPLE: Claire, who hopes to buy a second home as an investment, has a busy job as an associate director. She gets up at 5:30 every morning, and instead of packing a lunch, plans on picking up a sandwich, cookie, and soft drink for about $10. When Claire adds this up, however, she realizes that she's spending approximately $2,500 per year on lunches. By stocking up at the grocery store on weekends, and packing her lunch the night before, Claire can save approximately $2,000 per year (allowing for the cost of her packed lunches). Not bad for a simple lifestyle adjustment.

Don't forget that any amounts you save will earn interest month by month, assuming you don't just leave the money in a no-interest checking account.

Now that you've resolved to pack your own sandwiches, here are four more, potentially bigger-ticket ways to save towards a second home. The first two focus on growing your money, while the latter two look at ways to curb your spending.

Put Your Existing Savings Into CDs

You've probably saved up some money already, or you wouldn't be dreaming about buying a second home. The question is, where is that money being kept, and is it earning as much as interest as it could? One safe, yet potentially high-interest investment vehicle is a certificate of deposit (CD).

CDs are offered by banks or thrift institutions (savings and loans and credit unions). They tend to offer higher rates of return than comparable low-risk investments such as savings accounts or money market accounts. Yet they aren't as volatile or risky as stocks, bonds, or mutual funds.

If you're planning to buy your second home tomorrow (or you have a fear of commitment), stay away from CDs. The higher rates of return require you to lock in your money for a specified period of time, which could range from less than a month to ten or more years. The longer you lock in, the higher the rate of return. And if you withdraw money before the CD matures? You'll be socked with a penalty, usually calculated as a portion of the interest you would have otherwise earned, such as 90 days' worth of interest.

If, on the other hand, you're still some years away from buying your second home, you can take advantage of what's known as a "ladder strategy." This involves spreading your investments among CDs with differing maturity periods. The result is that you maximize your rate of return while retaining access to some of your money on a yearly basis.

For example, suppose you have $9,000 to invest in CDs over a three-year period. Rather than tying up the full amount in one, three-year CD that's paying 4.17%, you could split the amount into even yearly increments, as follows:

- $3,000 into a one-year CD that's paying 3.6%
- $3,000 into a two-year CD that's paying 4%
- $3,000 into a three-year CD that's paying 4.17%.

The result would give you a 3.92% average rate of return while freeing up $3,000 (plus interest) each year. If interest rates climb during one of these years, you can reinvest the freed-up money in another CD at a higher rate. If interest rates fall, you can shift the money to a better paying investment such as a short-term bond.

Reduce the Amount Withheld From Your Paycheck

Do you receive a tax refund each year? If so, you're probably having too much money taken out of your paycheck for income tax purposes. The more personal allowances (married, single, number of dependents) you indicate on your Form W-4, the less money will be withheld from your paycheck.

What's wrong with receiving a tax refund each year? Nothing, if you don't mind giving Uncle Sam an annual interest-free loan. By overpaying throughout the year, you're allowing the government to use your money in any way it wants until you finally claim what's yours in April. You're better off keeping that extra cash and investing it throughout the year, to help grow your down payment.

EXAMPLE: Nick has a gross income of $65,000 per year, including wages and other income from interest and investments. Each year, he receives a tax refund of roughly $1,800. By changing his withholding, Nick will receive an extra $150 per month in his paycheck and neither receive nor owe the IRS money at the end of the year. Each month, Nick can put the $150 into a money market account. After three consecutive years (assuming a 3% return, compounded daily), he'll have $5,658 in his account to put towards a down payment. Of that total, $258 is interest he would have never received had he not changed his withholding.

At any point during the year, you can change how much or how little is withheld from your paycheck by completing a new Form W-4 (pictured below and available at www.irs.gov). Just don't take too many personal allowances, or you may get walloped with a tax bill at the end of the year.

RESOURCES

Need help in determining the appropriate number of personal allowances to claim on your Form W-4? Go to the source: The Internal Revenue Service (IRS) offers an interactive tool to help you, at www.irs.gov/individuals/article/0,,id=96196,00.html.

```
·······················        Cut here and give Form W-4 to your employer. Keep the top part for your records.        ·······················

Form  W-4                     Employee's Withholding Allowance Certificate                    OMB No. 1545-0074
Department of the Treasury       ▶ Whether you are entitled to claim a certain number of allowances or exemption from withholding is
Internal Revenue Service           subject to review by the IRS. Your employer may be required to send a copy of this form to the IRS.        2006

 1  Type or print your first name and middle initial.   Last name                                2  Your social security number

    Home address (number and street or rural route)           3 ☐ Single ☐ Married ☐ Married, but withhold at higher Single rate.
                                                                Note. If married, but legally separated, or spouse is a nonresident alien, check the "Single" box.
    City or town, state, and ZIP code                         4  If your last name differs from that shown on your social security
                                                                 card, check here. You must call 1-800-772-1213 for a new card. ▶ ☐

 5  Total number of allowances you are claiming (from line H above or from the applicable worksheet on page 2)   5
 6  Additional amount, if any, you want withheld from each paycheck  .  .  .  .  .  .  .  .  .  .  .  .  .  .  6 $
 7  I claim exemption from withholding for 2006, and I certify that I meet both of the following conditions for exemption.
    • Last year I had a right to a refund of all federal income tax withheld because I had no tax liability and
    • This year I expect a refund of all federal income tax withheld because I expect to have no tax liability.
    If you meet both conditions, write "Exempt" here  .  .  .  .  .  .  .  .  .  .  .  .  .  .  ▶  7
Under penalties of perjury, I declare that I have examined this certificate and to the best of my knowledge and belief, it is true, correct, and complete.
Employee's signature
(Form is not valid
unless you sign it.) ▶                                        Date ▶
 8  Employer's name and address (Employer: Complete lines 8 and 10 only if sending to the IRS.)   9 Office code   10  Employer identification number (EIN)
                                                                (optional)

For Privacy Act and Paperwork Reduction Act Notice, see page 2.          Cat. No. 10220Q          Form W-4 (2006)
```

Stop Carrying Credit Card Balances

"Put it on the plastic" can seem like such a good idea at the time. But if you habitually carry over credit card balances from month to month, you're spending far too much on interest, and hurting your ability to save up for a second home.

FAST TRACK

If you have no ongoing credit card debt, skip to the next section. However, the Federal Reserve Board's *Survey of Consumer Finances* (SCF) shows that 44 % of households carry credit card balances. That means nearly one out of every two people reading this book may be burdened by credit card debt to one degree or another.

The average U.S. household has more than $8,000 in credit card debt. Assuming an 18% interest rate and no additional charges added, it would take one of these average households 14.8 years to pay off that balance—and cost about $4,716 in interest alone. Ouch! That's $4,716 less to put towards a second home.

One surefire way to save money is to pay off your credit cards in full each month. Consider the following three-step approach to ending your credit card balances:

- *Step 1:* Cut up all but one of your credit cards. Most people carry between three and four credit cards. If you're a multiple-card carrier, your opportunity to charge something is that much higher. Remove the temptation by cutting up all but one of your cards. Which one should you spare? Keep the one with the lowest interest rate or best cash-back plan.

- *Step 2:* Pay with cash or not at all. If you can't pay for something with the cash in your bank account, you can't afford it—at least, not while you're trying to pay off your credit card balances. (You don't have to carry around actual cash—a checkbook or an ATM card will do.) Instead of whipping out the plastic and adding to your ever-growing mound of debt, simply walk away from the item or service you're considering.

- *Step 3:* Pay down high-interest cards first. Even a minor difference in interest rates can make a difference. Pay as much as you can each month on your highest-interest-rate card, and make the minimum payments on your other cards. Once the highest-rate card is paid off, follow the same approach for the next highest card, and so forth until all of your balances are wiped out.

Once your credit card debt is under control, keep your spending habits in check by minimizing use of your credit card (not cards, since you cut up the others in Step 1). Take the money you were using to pay off your balances and squirrel it away in a low-risk investment such as a CD.

RESOURCES

Find out how much your credit card balances are costing you. A simple calculator lets you determine how long it will take and how much interest you'll pay to eliminate your existing balances. Go to www.bankrate.com/brm/calc/MinPayment.asp.

Minimize Nonessential Expenditures

It's amazing how much money you can spend without even thinking about it. Conversely, you can save an impressive amount by putting your brain into gear.

Minimizing, or even eliminating, nonessential expenditures is the quickest way to build up savings. What's a nonessential expenditure? Anything that falls outside the big-three categories of food, shelter, or clothing—and even some of the more expensive or excessive items that fall within them. Regular restaurant visits, for example, are definitely a nonessential expenditure, despite the fact that you receive food there. Buying new slacks for work? A necessity. Buying a new Armani suit because your coworker has one? A nonessential expenditure.

Examples of other nonessential expenditures include:

- vacations and weekend getaways
- movies or renting DVDs
- cultural events (museums, theater, symphony)
- sporting events, and
- luxury shopping—or even compulsive discount shopping.

In the end, it's up to you to determine what you believe to be a nonessential expenditure, as well as the degree to which you want to cut back. Remember, you don't need to go cold turkey here, just turn it back a notch or two. Explore the many ways you can have fun for free—concerts in the park, no-entry-fee days at your local museum, a potluck or game night with friends, or a library book. The more nonessential expenditures you identify and the more you trim back, the faster you'll be able to save.

Use the worksheet below to create your list of nonessential expenditures and see how cutting them can boost your savings. A blank copy of this worksheet can be found in the Appendix and on the CD-ROM at the back of this book.

Annual Nonessential Expenditures Adjustment Worksheet

Instructions:

1. In Column A, list all items and activities you can do without in the short term.

2. In Column B, estimate how much you currently spend annually on each of these nonessentials.

3. In Column C, enter the new, lower amount you plan to spend for each item and activity.

4. Finally, subtract the amount in Column C from the amount in Column B and write that number in Column D. The TOTAL of all your entries in Column D is the annual amount you will be able to put towards your down payment.

(A) Description of expense	(B) Current expense		(C) Reduced expense		(D) Amount allocated toward down payment
Example: Vacation	$3,000	–	$1,000	=	$2,000
	$	–	$	=	$
	$	–	$	=	$
	$	–	$	=	$
	$	–	$	=	$
	$	–	$	=	$
	$	–	$	=	$
	$	–	$	=	$
	$	–	$	=	$
	$	–	$	=	$
	$	–	$	=	$
	$	–	$	=	$
	$	–	$	=	$
	$	–	$	=	$
	$	–	$	=	$
Total	$	–	$	=	$

Borrowing What You Can't Save

Since buying your first home, you've probably gained in years, wisdom, and, hopefully, creditworthiness. How much you should borrow, if at all, to supplement the cash you put into your second home depends on how you plan on using the home.

In particular, if you plan on renting out your property, borrowing 100% of the up front cash might make sense, as you can expect the rental income to help offset the loan payments. But if you won't rent out the property, you may be comfortable borrowing only a smaller amount, because you'll have only your existing income with which to make your monthly payments.

If you do decide to borrow, the traditional way is to take out a loan secured by the equity in your current home. You may also want to consider nontraditional avenues such as borrowing against a life insurance policy or borrowing from friends and family, which can often provide you with a much lower interest rate, or even no interest rate at all. We'll discuss all three of these options below.

Use the Equity in Your Primary Home

Depending on how long you've owned the home in which you now live, and the extent to which it has appreciated in value, you've probably built up equity. (It's calculated as the difference between how much your house is worth and how much you owe on it.) All or part of that equity can be borrowed against for your down payment and closing costs.

There are three popular ways to borrow against the equity in a primary home: a home equity loan, a home equity line of credit, and a cash-out refinance. Many people are confused about the differences between these three. (It doesn't help that the phrases are sometimes mistakenly used interchangeably.) In each case, the loan is secured by your primary home.

- *Home equity loan.* Also called a second mortgage, this is a loan that you take out on top of the existing loan (first mortgage) on your primary home. A home equity loan usually has a fixed interest rate (one that doesn't change over the life of the loan). The loan must be repaid over a set amount of time, typically less time than the loan length on your primary home—about ten, 15, or 20 years. Interest rates on home equity loans tend to be a point or two above the rate available on a loan for a primary residence. Although you can use this loan towards your second home, your primary home (not your second home) will secure the loan.

- *Home equity line of credit.* Commonly referred to as a HLOC (pronounced "he-lock"), this is a revolving line of credit from which you draw. It's not unlike a credit card. Your credit limit (the maximum amount you can borrow at any one time) is set by taking a percentage (usually around 75%) of your primary home's appraised value and subtracting it from the outstanding balance on your mortgage. As with home equity loans, interest rates on HLOCs are usually a point or two above current home mortgage rates. HLOCs are available only as variable-rate loans (the interest rate moves up or down based on an external index). However, you can usually find a HLOC that offers a low introductory fixed rate for the first six or so months, after which the rate becomes variable.

- *Cash-out refinance:* This is a way to physically get cash out of your current house based on the equity you've built up. What you do is refinance your house for more than the amount you owe on it. You then put that extra money towards your second home. For example, let's assume your house is worth $275,000 and you still owe $165,000 on your loan. That means you have $110,000 in equity ($275,000 - $165,000 = $110,000). Suppose you need to come up with $50,000 for a down payment and closing costs on a second house. You can refinance your current home for $215,000, use $165,000 of it to pay off the balance on your current loan, and put the remaining $50,000 towards your second house. Plus, you'll still have $60,000 in equity left in your current house. A cash-out refinance should cost you about the same, in terms of your interest rate and other loan-related costs, as if you had refinanced without taking out any extra cash. Just make sure you don't take out too much—if the loan-to-value (LTV) ratio on your current house hits 80% or higher, you'll have to pay for private mortgage insurance (PMI). (See Chapter 11 to learn more about LTVs and PMI.)

Check on Interest Rates Before Doing a Cash-Out Refinance

Cash-out refinancing makes sense only if interest rates are lower than what you're currently paying on your primary home loan. If so, a cash-out refinance will save you money on your existing loan while providing you with up front money for your second home. However, if interest rates are higher than what you're currently paying, a cash-out refinance will force you to pay more on your existing loan just to get up front money for a second home. It doesn't take a financial planner to tell you that that isn't very smart.

There is one caveat to this advice: If you have an adjustable rate loan for your primary residence, but want to lock in a fixed rate while also pulling money out for your second home, then a cash-out refinance may make sense even if interest rates are higher than you're currently paying on your existing loan.

If you decide to borrow against the equity in your primary home, which of the three ways of doing so (home equity loan, home equity line of credit, or cash-out refinance) is best? You'll need to check the market and see which actual loan product offers the lowest overall cost. Comparing costs (including points, up front fees, and interest over the life of the loan) can unfortunately get quite complex, as an apples-to-apples comparison is all but impossible.

Your best bet is to work with a mortgage broker or loan officer (if you'll be dealing directly with the bank) to pencil out these overall costs. Ask your broker to project how much you'll pay over the life of the loan and what assumptions those projections are based on. Also, if you plan on selling your home prior to paying off the loan, say ten years into a 30-year loan, ask the broker to project how much you'll pay for the limited time that you hold the loan.

If you want to do a rough comparison of prospective loans before meeting with a broker, use the worksheet below (also available in the Appendix and on the CD-ROM). Perhaps a clear winner will emerge—although, if you're looking at an adjustable rate loan, you can't really predict how interest rates may rise.

Borrowing Against Home Equity: Comparison Worksheet					
Type of Loan	Name of Lender	Loan Amount[1]	Points and Loan Fees[2] ($)	Interest Rate[3] (%)	Monthly Payment ($)
Home Equity Loans					
Loan #1		$	$	%	$
Loan #2		$	$	%	$
Loan #3		$	$	%	$
Home Equity Lines of Credit					
Loan #1		$	$	%	$
Loan #2		$	$	%	$
Loan #3		$	$	%	$
Cash-Out Refinances					
Loan #1		$	$	%	$
Loan #2		$	$	%	$
Loan #3		$	$	%	$

[1] For a cash-out refinance, enter only the portion of the loan that applies to the equity being pulled out of your primary home.

[2] Include all costs, such as points, application fee, and credit report fee, that you'll need to pay in connection with the loan.

[3] If the loan will have an adjustable interest rate, don't base your comparison on the lower introductory rate.

Borrow Against a Life Insurance Policy

If you have a life insurance policy, you may be able to borrow money from it for your second home. You don't even have to die first! You do, however, need to make sure you have a "permanent," instead of a "term life" policy.

- *Permanent life insurance* provides coverage for as long as you live (assuming you pay your premiums in a timely manner). It combines the death protection of term life insurance (described below) with an investment component that builds a cash value over time. This is what you can borrow against (interest free, no less). Plus, as long as your loan balance remains less than the cash balance in your life insurance account, you aren't required to pay the loan back. Of course, when you die, the amount you borrowed will be deducted from the payout to your beneficiary.

- *Term life insurance* is meant to provide temporary life insurance to people on a limited budget, for a specific period of time. The time period can be anywhere from one to 30 years. Beneficiaries receive the face amount of the policy upon the insured person's death. You can't borrow against term life insurance.

If reading your life insurance policy materials leaves you unsure about which type of policy you have, contact the company that sold you the policy.

Get a Loan From Family or Friends

You may be able to arrange a private loan from a family member, friend, or someone else you know—preferably in writing, with legal protections for your lender, as fully described in Chapter 10.

A private loan offers potential benefits to everyone involved. For you, it can be very flexible (depending on your relationship with your private lender). For example, you and your family member or friend may decide that you won't start repaying the loan for several years, or your private lender may decide to periodically forgive loan payments throughout the year, perhaps as a means of family wealth transfer. And you can usually take a federal tax deduction for mortgage interest paid on that loan.

For your lender, the benefits may include higher interest than he or she could obtain on a comparable investment such as a CD or money market account, as well as the satisfaction of keeping all interest payments within the family or a circle of friends.

POINTS TO REMEMBER
By using a combination of saving and borrowing, you can amass a nice chunk of change. This will help you to cover your down payment, closing costs, and other up front home-related expenses.

How Family and Friends Can Help (and Why They'll Even Want To)

Bob Hope once said, "A bank is a place that will lend you money if you can prove that you don't need it." His words ring especially true for people hoping to buy a second home.

Banks, credit unions, and other institutional lenders take an extra-hard look at second-home loan requests, because there's more risk involved than with a first-home loan. The finances of second-home buyers are, by default, stretched thinner. Maybe that explains why more and more want-to-be second-home owners are turning to their loved ones, and even-more-distant members of their circle, for help with financing.

But there's more to borrowing from your relatives and friends than simply avoiding loan officers who, as Dr. Seuss said of the Grinch, have a heart that is "two sizes too small." If done right, tapping the "Bank of Family and Friends" offers financial benefits to both you and the person lending you money. You get the cash you need, your friend or family member earns interest at a rate equal to or higher than that available elsewhere—everyone wins.

This chapter will show you how to structure a loan from your relatives or friends so that it makes financial sense for all involved and stands up to legal scrutiny. Equally important, you'll discover how to avoid the feuds that can occur when money and loved ones are inexpertly mixed.

What Is a Private Home Loan?

A private home loan is simply a loan from your family, friend, or other private party that is secured by real estate (the home itself). Commonly called a private mortgage or an intrafamily mortgage—even though your private lender can be someone other than a family member—it's legally speaking no different than a mortgage originated by a bank, credit union, or other institutional lender. As with an institutional loan, you'll normally sign a written contract and establish a schedule of monthly repayments with interest. Your private lender will hold a lien on your property and have the legal right to demand full payment on the outstanding balance if you fall behind in making payments. Your private lender can even foreclose if you default on the loan (though few would go so far).

Rest assured, you have legal rights as well. Your parents can't foreclose on your house just because you arrive late for their 50th wedding anniversary, and your best friend can't demand an early payoff just because he or she wants to buy a new Jaguar.

How Private Home Financing Helps the Family as a Whole

For wealthy Americans, the concept of helping a family member buy a home is nothing new—and that includes second homes. Besides being motivated by love, family lenders may recognize that private home loans serve to:

- transfer wealth (particularly to the younger generation), and
- keep interest payments within the larger family unit.

Transferring Wealth

If the people closest to you are already planning to leave you money in their estate, helping you purchase a second home—with either a gift or a loan—might make perfect sense. In fact, that way your family will gain the satisfaction of seeing you enjoy the money while they're alive. But large gifts may come with tax consequences. You can, by understanding certain tax rules, help your family avoid tax liability. In some cases, a convenient tax strategy is to turn a private home loan into a gift later on.

Why bring loans into the picture at all, if it's possible your family members might gift you money outright? Because you're probably looking for a large amount of cash—large enough that your family members would likely owe gift tax on the transfer. By initially structuring the transfer as a private loan, however, your lenders can, if they later decide to, turn that transfer into a gift without gift tax liability. In terms of logistics, they would forgive your repayments year by year.

Here's more detail on how the IRS gets involved in gift transfers. Normally, if a relative, a friend, or even a total stranger gives you money without any expectation that you'll pay it back, the IRS views that as a gift. A gift may also come in the form of forgone interest on a loan, or because a lender tells you, "Don't bother repaying" (in legal lingo, "forgives" the loan). Oddly enough, the person who makes the gift is responsible for taxes on the amount given—unless it's an amount less than the annual gift tax exclusion.

Receiving Gifts Below the Annual Gift Tax Exclusion

The annual gift tax exclusion allows your family member, friend, or even a total stranger, to give you up to a certain monetary amount without the IRS being overly concerned with it. Currently, the annual exclusion is $12,000, but it increases periodically over the years. There is no limit on the number of people who can give you up to $12,000 without having to file a gift tax return (so your family and friends should feel free to go wild).

EXAMPLE: Samuel plans to buy a small vacation cottage for $124,000. His parents each give him $12,000 outright. He borrows $100,000 from his aunt at 6% interest over 30 years. His repayment plan says he will pay her $599.55 per month in principal and interest, or $7,194.60 annually. His aunt can choose to forgive all or a portion of his payments each year and still be well below her annual exclusion of $12,000.

It gets better. If, for example, you're buying your second home with one or more people (such as a spouse, significant other, or friend), each of you can receive separate gifts from the same person of up to $12,000 without that person having to pay gift tax.

EXAMPLE: Carmen and her husband Cliff are trying to round up a down payment for their second home. If Carmen's parents give the maximum amount, Carmen and Cliff could receive a total of $48,000 (each parent gives $12,000 to Carmen and another $12,000 to Cliff). If Cliff's parents do the same, the couple now has $96,000 to put down on a second home.

WARNING
The IRS takes a "use it or lose it" approach to the annual exclusion. If your gift-giver doesn't take advantage of it in a given tax year, it doesn't carry over as a credit to the next year.

Receiving Gifts Above the Annual Gift Tax Exclusion

Ordinarily, if someone gave you more than $12,000 to buy your home (or gave you and your copurchaser more than $24,000), that person would need to file a gift tax return. The person wouldn't actually have to pay any tax yet (a point we'll get to below), but the IRS would want to know about the gift. However, if the person is instead interested in loaning you the money, but might later forgive some loan payments (thus turning them into gifts), this can help avoid gift tax.

> **EXAMPLE:** Carrie borrows $35,000 from her grandmother to use as a down payment on a vacation home in South Carolina. They sign a loan contract that includes a seven-year repayment plan at a 5% interest rate, with monthly payments of $494.69. After making the first payment every year, Carrie's grandmother evaluates her financial situation, decides she won't need the remaining payments for that year, and sends Carrie a letter forgiving these payments. That makes the grandmother's total annual gifts $5,936.28—well under the annual gift tax exclusion. But if Carrie's grandmother had given her the $35,000 outright, the grandmother would have had to file a gift tax return, because she would have exceeded the $12,000 annual exclusion.

The trouble is, if you launch into a loan forgiveness strategy with everyone knowing at the outset that you're trying to avoid gift tax, you're on shaky legal ground. In fact, the IRS has seen enough people use this strategy that it has become suspicious, and may carefully scrutinize your and your lenders' taxes. Some attorneys recommend that you make some initial loan payments before the lender starts forgiving subsequent payments. It's also important that your financial records show that you had the ability to repay the loan. In addition to documenting the initial loan with a promissory note, the lender should write you a letter whenever he or she forgives any loan repayments, as a further sign that the loan was meant as a serious transaction.

In any case, your gift giver or lender may not need to get too worried about gift tax, for one simple reason: It doesn't actually need to be paid until after death—and then only if it exceeds what's called the "lifetime gift tax exclusion."

Making Use of the Lifetime Gift Tax Exclusion

Everyone is allowed a lifetime gift tax exclusion of $1 million. Practically speaking, that means gift givers can give away up to $1 million during their lifetime without owing any gift tax. If someone makes gifts of more than $12,000 to a single person in a single year, the extra amount counts against the gift giver's lifetime exclusion.

When people file gift tax returns, they're allowing the IRS to keep track of their progress toward the $1 million total. After a person dies, whoever is handling the estate will need to add up the total, lifetime amount of any gifts the person made over the $12,000 annual exclusion (or whatever the applicable limits were in the years the person gave the gifts). If the grand total exceeds $1 million, gift tax will need to be paid out of the person's estate. If not, no tax is owed, even if the person regularly made gifts of more than $12,000 (or whatever the exclusion was then) during a particular year.

Now, the one catch to the lifetime exclusion is that any amount the gift-giver uses up during his or her lifetime simultaneously counts against his or her estate tax exclusion (the amount someone's estate can pass along to heirs tax-free). For people who die in 2006, the estate tax exclusion is $2 million. Unlike the lifetime exclusion, which remains set at $1 million, the estate tax exclusion changes over the years. Under current law, it's set to remain at $2 million through 2008 and increase to $3.5 million in 2009. The entire estate tax will be eliminated (repealed) in 2010. Then in 2011 the estate tax will return to the old rates that were in place prior to the repeal, unless Congress takes action to the contrary, such as extending the repeal.

EXAMPLE: Bill borrows $200,000 from his brother Peter at 6% interest over 30 years. This puts Bill's monthly payments at $1,199 (principal and interest). During the first full year of the loan, Bill will theoretically owe his brother $14,389. However, due to a combination of brotherly love and financial wherewithal, Peter decides to forgive 100% of Bill's payments for that year. For Peter, that means $12,000 counts towards his annual exclusion, and he'll have to file a tax return reporting the additional gift of $2,389 (despite that fact that he doesn't yet owe any gift tax). Furthermore, Peter's lifetime exclusion, as well as his estate tax exclusion, will be reduced by $2,389.

Keeping Wealth Within the Family

In addition to transferring wealth, private home loans can also serve as an investment vehicle. The idea is that, if a family member is taking out a home loan anyway, why pay the interest to a bank instead of a relative? The incentive to keep interest payments within the family is particularly high with loans for second homes, where interest rates from mortgage lenders tend to be one-quarter to one-half a point above those for primary homes.

How a Private Home Loan Helps You, the Borrower

By turning to the bank of mom and dad, your favorite aunt or uncle, your in-laws, a brother or sister, or even your best friend or business colleague for home financing help, you might gain the following:

- *A lower interest rate.* Borrowing from a relative or friend can mean a lower-interest loan than you'd be able to qualify for elsewhere. That's because you and your family-or-friend lender are the ones who determine the interest rate. Most private lenders are, based on their personal relationship with the borrower, willing to accept less interest than any bank would.

- *Flexibility in paying back the money.* Unlike banks and other institutional lenders, how and when you pay back your family or friend is up to you and them. That flexibility can allow you to arrange a loan with an unusual repayment schedule at the outset, or to later temporarily pause payments due to unforeseen circumstances, extend the length of the loan, and more. But be careful: If abused, this very flexibility can cause strained relationships.

- *Federal tax deductions.* Just as with a loan from a bank, private loans allow you to benefit from the federal tax deduction for home loan interest paid. This can add up to tens of thousands of dollars in savings over the life of the loan. For example, suppose you have a $150,000 private home loan from your uncle at 6% interest over 30 years, and you are in the 25% tax bracket. Over the life of that loan, you will save roughly $45,000 through tax deductions (assuming 2006 tax rates, and no changes in your income). That's a nice chunk of change.

How Making a Private Home Loan Helps Your Relative or Friend, the Lender

If the person lending you money is a friend rather than a relative, the arrangement doesn't serve the goal of keeping wealth within the family as a whole. Nevertheless, any person who loans you money stands to gain other benefits, such as:

- *A better return than might be gotten through other investments.* The kind of money you're looking for won't simply be sitting in your lender's checking account. In fact, before loaning you the money, your lender will most likely have to withdraw it from another investment vehicle, such as a money market account or certificate of deposit (CD). But the switch may be worth it, since you can, even without paying as much interest as you'd pay to a bank, probably offer higher interest than the person could get on those other investments.

- *A steady income stream.* Private mortgages are ordinarily repaid over time as opposed to in one lump sum (unless, of course, you sell your house, at which point you'd have to pay off the private mortgage in full). By setting up and following a repayment schedule, for example, with payments due on the first of every month, your payments can actually become a steady income stream for your family or friend lender.

- *Financial liquidity, in case your lender later needs to use the money.* If your private lender happens to need his or her money back before you've finished paying off the loan, the lender can usually sell your mortgage to someone else. (There is a secondary market for the purchase and sale of existing mortgages.) Just knowing that this option exists can tip the scales toward someone saying "yes" to lending you money in the first place.

> **TIP**
>
> **More and more people are turning to relatives and friends for home financing.** According to the U.S. Census, nationally nearly one million houses have been financed with a loan for all or some of the money from relatives, friends, or other private parties.

Your Family and Friends Don't Need to Be Rich

You're now probably thinking, "If only my parents were the Hiltons instead of Mr. and Mrs. Everyday USA" or "Why couldn't my college roommate have been Bill Gates instead of Joe Ordinary?" You're not alone in such thoughts. A belief that your lenders must be rich is the number one misconception surrounding intrafamily mortgages—and the reason that many people miss out on this home-financing opportunity.

The truth is that your family and friends don't need to be in the financial upper echelons to offer a private mortgage. They simply need to have some cash that they can part with for a short time, and the confidence that you will pay the money back without their having to foreclose on your home.

The one caveat to this advice is that the costs required to properly set up a private home loan make it less advantageous for smaller loans. The total transaction costs can range from several hundred dollars to over $1,000, depending on the fees you pay for services from outside professionals, such as an attorney to review the documentation and a licensed home appraiser to verify the home's value. A general rule is that a loan of at least $25,000 justifies the costs of setting up a private mortgage.

EXAMPLE: Samantha plans to borrow $5,000 from her parents to help buy a vacation home in Vermont. However, Samantha discovers that setting up the loan and mortgage will cost around $1,000, or 20% of the amount she plans to borrow (not including the interest she will pay on the loan). Simple math tells Samantha that it's probably not worth paying $1,000 for a $5,000 loan (though a desperate borrower might feel otherwise). However, if that same loan were for $25,000, it would be a much different story. Now the $1,000 setup cost is only 4% of the loan. Paying $1,000 for a $25,000 loan sounds much more reasonable.

While you may be tempted to cut out some of the formalities in order to reduce costs, such measures might be penny-wise and pound-foolish. In structuring and managing a private home loan, fewer formalities usually mean greater risk, because both you and your private lender are forgoing important legal protections.

Combining Private Loans With Other Loans

An intrafamily mortgage doesn't have to be for the full amount of financing needed to buy your home. The actual amount you borrow depends on your lender's financial resources and comfort level. You might either structure a first or second mortgage, as follows:

• *A first mortgage (or "senior mortgage")* is literally the first one filed at the public records office. It gives your lender priority over other lenders in the event of a foreclosure. For example, if you purchase a home for $250,000, put in 10% ($25,000) as a down payment, and your brother lends you the remaining $225,000 and records his mortgage, then your brother would gain a first mortgage, or "first-lien position" on your house. If your brother or another lienholder were to foreclose on the house, proceeds from its sale would go to pay off your brother's loan before any later loans secured by your property, such as a second mortgage or a home equity line of credit. Be warned, however: If you take out two loans simultaneously, for example, from your brother and a bank, the bank may insist that it be allowed to record first.

• *A second mortgage* is when someone lends you an added portion of the financing needed to buy the home. Let's assume you're buying that same $250,000 house, and again put 10% down, but this time you obtain $175,000 from a bank and the remaining $50,000 from your brother. Your brother would have a second-lien position on your house. If either the bank or your brother were to foreclose, proceeds from the sale of your house would be used to pay off the bank before your brother got any money. Thus, a second mortgage would be riskier for your brother. (Note: A second lien can also occur if you fail to pay back debt. For example, if a contractor does work on your home and, for whatever reason, you don't pay your bill, the contractor has the legal right to put a second, or subsequent, lien on your home. This lien would remain in place until you either settled your bill with the contractor, who, in turn, would lift the lien, or you sold your second home, at which point, proceeds from the sale would be used automatically to pay off the contractor.)

The possibilities don't end with first or second mortgages. You can have a third, fourth, and even more mortgages. Mortgages beyond the second one are rare, however, and where they do occur are normally for low amounts of money (such as the cost of a contractor's services).

> **WARNING**
> **The more liens you have against your second home, the more people can foreclose on you.** Any mortgage or lienholder (regardless of position) has the right to initiate foreclosure proceedings if you default on his or her loan, or fail to make contracted-for payments. This is true even if you have been making on-time payments to the lienholders who are first in line. Although the primary lienholders would have their loans paid off first from the foreclosure proceeds, the foreclosing lender might be willing to take a chance on whatever is left over.

Choosing Your Own Interest Rate

One of the biggest advantages of private mortgages is that, in most cases, the borrower actually sets the interest rate. But before you run off and propose low- or no-interest-rate loans to your relatives and friends, consider:

- your lender's competing investment opportunities
- what monthly payment you can afford, and
- the gift tax implications.

Setting an Interest Rate Higher Than the Competition

You're not the only one eager to pay interest for the use of your lender's money. If the interest rate you propose is too low, your lender would be better off keeping the money in its original investment vehicle. Make sure you offer a high enough rate to justify loaning you the money.

It often helps to create an interest rate comparison table for your lender to review. This is easily done by collecting current interest rates and yields on various investment vehicles from sources such as Bankrate.com and Bloomberg.com. Set these forth on a table comparing them with the interest rate you're willing to pay (see "Setting an Interest Rate That You Can Afford," below). Your interest rate comparison table may look something like the one below.

Interest Rate Comparison Table		
Money Market Account	Certificate of Deposit (CD)	Private Home Loan
3.41%	4.66%	4.84%

Sources: www.bankrate.com for money market account and CD yields, and www.irs.gov for AFR.

Setting an Interest Rate That You Can Afford

Calculate your loan at various interest rates and different repayment periods to determine a monthly payment that you can afford. The easiest way to play with the numbers is by using the online calculator mentioned under the resources icon below. If your private home loan will supplement a bank loan, don't forget that you'll have two loan payments to make each month.

RESOURCES

Need help calculating the interest and monthly payments on your loan? MyFico.com, a division of FairIsaac, has two helpful mortgage calculators. They'll even give you an easy-to-read graph illustrating your payments. For fixed-rate mortgages, visit www.myfico.com/CreditEducation/Calculators/MortgageLoan.aspx. For adjustable rate mortgages, visit www.myfico.com/CreditEducation/Calculators/MortgageAdjustable.aspx.

Setting an Interest Rate High Enough to Distinguish the Loan From a Gift

If you receive money from a relative, friend, or other private party, and you pay back the loan without interest or at a rate lower than the minimum rate required by the federal government, the IRS will most likely view the forgone interest as a gift. (The minimum federal rate is called the "Applicable Federal Rate" or AFR.) That's no big deal unless you should have paid your lender a whopping $12,000 or more in interest (the current annual gift tax exclusion). But if your lender was planning to separately give you $12,000 in the same year, this forgone interest might tip the lender over the annual gift tax exclusion. The inconvenient result would be that your lender would have to file a gift tax return, and the gift would be deducted from your lender's lifetime estate and gift tax exclusion.

EXAMPLE: Kathy borrows $125,000 from her mother and sets it up as a private mortgage. The AFR at the time of the loan is 4.24%. The two women decide on an interest rate of 3.24% over 30 years. A full year goes by, with Kathy making all of her payments (both principal and interest). During the same year, Kathy's mom makes her a gift of $12,000. At the end of that year, the forgone interest on the loan is 1% (the difference between the AFR and the actual interest rate paid) or $1,246.32. Kathy's mom will have to file a federal gift tax return reporting that amount, just as if she had physically given the money to her daughter.

In the example above, if Kathy's mom had wanted to avoid gift tax consequences, she should have either set the interest rate at 4.24% (the AFR at the time the loan was set up) or reduced her separate gift so that the forgone interest was within her annual exclusion.

The AFR is set by the U.S. Treasury Department on a monthly basis, and can be viewed at the IRS website at www.irs.gov. Enter "AFR" in the search box. After choosing the appropriate month and year, you'll see a table that looks much like the sample below. The Applicable Federal Rates (AFRs) are listed by the term or length of your loan (in number of years) and the compounding period (i.e., annual, semiannual, quarterly, and monthly).

Applicable Federal Rates (AFRs) – December 2006				
		Period for Compounding		
	Annual	Semi-Annual	Quarterly	Monthly
Short-Term (3 years or less)	4.97%	4.91%	4.88%	4.86%
Mid-Term (more than 3 years and less than 9 years)	4.73%	4.68%	4.65%	4.64%
Long-Term (more than 9 years)	4.90%	4.84%	4.81%	4.79%

Choosing People to Ask for a Loan

Let's assume you're convinced that a private mortgage is the best way to cover all or a portion of the financing needed for your second home. But who do you turn to for the loan? You're certainly never too old to ask your parents for a financial boost. But don't call mom or dad just yet. Instead, follow the four steps below to help choose the most appropriate family or friend lender.

Step 1: Create a List of Potential Private Lenders

Start by jotting down the names of all your relatives and friends. Don't worry yet about how much money you think each has to lend you. That will come later. For now, just get the names down. You can start with your parents and siblings, but be sure to include extended family as well, such as aunts, uncles, cousins, and in-laws. You can—and should—even add close friends and colleagues to your list.

Step 2: Do a Personality Check

The primary difference between getting a loan from a bank and getting one from your family or friends is that, in all likelihood, you do not have an emotional tie to the bank's loan officer. For better or for worse, the loan officer will evaluate your qualifications for a loan—and your subsequent actions concerning the loan—based solely on your financial risk to the bank. There may be times when you wish it were that simple with family and friends.

The people you are close to have personalities. And those personalities can and will play into your private home loan. For example, if you get a home loan from a bank, and you then hop on a plane to vacation in Hawaii, the bank won't care, as long as you're making your loan payments. Do that with a loan from your busybody aunt and you might return to find the following voicemail message:

It's your Aunt Sally. Nice of you to neglect to tell me you were using my money to pay for your vacation, as well as your house. And to think, you didn't even send me a postcard.

To avoid selling your financial soul to an Aunt Sally type, run a personality check on each name on your list. While by no means scientific, try rating each person on a scale of one to five, with one being "difficult to get along with," and five being "easy to get along with." When you're done, cross out anyone who rates a one, two, or three. You've just created your short list of potential private lenders, and are now one step closer to taking a guilt-free trip to Hawaii. Aloha!

Step 3: Determine Financial Compatibility

Using your short list, try to answer the following questions for each person:

- Do I think this person has the amount of money I need?
- Do I think the interest rate I'm willing to pay will be comparable to what this person is currently receiving from other investments?
- Is this person free from any major financial obligations that may arise in the near future, such as college tuition, a wedding, or medical expenses?

If you answered "no" to any of the above questions, cross that name off your list. You now have your short list of potential family lenders.

Step 4: Prioritize Based on Your Comfort Level

Look at the remaining names on your list. Think about how comfortable you feel approaching each person for a loan. Whenever you can, try to be objective in your assessment. For example, if a relative or friend has loaned you money in the past and the experience was positive for both of you, that person should definitely be approached first. Or if someone on your list had mentioned previously that if you ever needed help with anything, count on him or her, you should feel comfortable approaching that person as well.

If it helps, write the number "1" next to the name of the person you feel most comfortable approaching. Then write the number "2" next to the second-most approachable person, and so on until each name has a number next to it.

In the sample box below, notice that Aunt Sally got crossed off at the start due to personality issues, while Best Friend Pete and Uncle Dave dropped off in the following step as a result of upcoming financial obligations. Mom and Dad and Aunt Grace were neck and neck, but Aunt Grace pulled ahead in the end. For whatever reason, the borrower in this example just felt a bit more comfortable asking Aunt Grace for money. Of course, if Aunt Grace says "no," Mom and Dad are backup possibilities. There's even the possibility that if Aunt Grace says "yes" but can't cover the full amount of the loan, Mom and Dad can make up the difference.

Potential Private Lender	Personality Rating	Financial Compatibility	Comfort Level Ranking
Mom & Dad	5	Yes	2
Aunt Sally	3		
Uncle Dave	4	No	
Aunt Grace	5	Yes	1
Best friend Pete	4	No	

Requesting the Loan

Here's a loan request script that's no doubt been tried:

Hi, Aunt Grace. It's Jenny. How are you? Tom and I are doing fine. Yes, the house hunting is going well. Actually, we just saw one we really like. Ah, but we're coming up a bit short on cash. So, we got to thinking. Well, you know, how about you making up the difference? We'll pay you back, honest. . . Aunt Grace? Hello? Aunt Grace, are you there?...

What did Jenny do wrong? She flat out asked for the money, having put almost no thought into her request, and having given her Aunt Grace no good reason to say yes. Such a sloppy approach practically guarantees that you'll be turned down.

Also beware of approaches that imply or say, "If you love me, you'll loan me the money." No one would ever try that with a bank. A better approach is to demonstrate that you've given the matter serious thought and are looking out for the lender's interests as well as your own. Ideally, that means putting your request down in writing, in the form of a loan proposal.

If creating a loan proposal sounds excessive or too formal, think about it this way: Not only are you proving to your potential lender that you've given the matter serious thought, you yourself are accomplishing that very thought process by the act of creating the loan proposal. You will force yourself to work out the details of your intrafamily mortgage, right down to interest rate and repayment terms that will satisfy both you and your lender.

Fortunately, unlike the lengthy loan applications that banks require, loan proposals to private lenders do not have a standard format or required elements. Most can take the form of a one- or two-page letter, and be written in a way that is both friendly and businesslike. You can decide the exact format of your loan proposal, but it should communicate at least three things:

- *The amount of money you need to borrow.* While this may seem obvious, it's surprising how many people are unclear about how much they need. Usually, that's because they go for the old "I'll borrow as much as my relative is willing to give me" approach. Bad idea. Instead, your proposal should provide a rationale for how much you need, and not request a penny more. But don't underestimate your needs, either: Add up all the expenses you'll incur in your home purchase. These will likely include closing costs on the sale, moving expenses, and even money needed for necessary home improvements, especially if you're buying a fixer-upper.

- *The terms of the loan.* Name the interest rate you're willing to pay, the start date of your first payment, the frequency of each payment (monthly, quarterly, or as you specify), whether you are willing to pay a late fee and how much, and your payment schedule. Widely used payment schedules include "amortized," in which each payment consists of principal and interest, and "interest-only," in which initial payments cover only the interest owed, while later payments or one huge final payment incorporate the principal debt.

- *How the loan offers a solid investment opportunity.* While the first two sections of your loan proposal focus on you (the amount you need and the terms you're willing to follow), the next section emphasizes what's in it for your family-or-friend lender. Explain how this loan competes with or outdoes other investment vehicles in which your prospective lender may be keeping his or her money. You may be able to offer an interest rate higher than your relatives or friends could get on comparable short-term uses of their money.

Now let's take a look at how Jenny could have improved her phone conversation with her Aunt Grace:

Hi Aunt Grace. It's Jenny. How are you? Tom and I are doing fine. Yes, the house hunting is going well. Actually, we just saw one we really like. Ah, but we're coming up a bit short on cash. So, we got to thinking. Last week at dinner you mentioned that you were disappointed with how some of your investments were doing. Well, Tom and I may have a solution to your problem. How would you like to invest in us? That's right. If you loan us the money we need, we'll pay you back with interest, and at a rate that could be higher than your current investments. It would help us out, and wouldn't it be better to keep the interest within the family, instead of us giving it to a bank? As a matter of fact, we've created a loan proposal that details everything. We'd love to review it with you. Oh, that's great. We'll come by tomorrow to go over everything.

Don't be put off by the fact that Jenny and Tom had the perfect opening in asking for a private home loan, since her aunt had already mentioned disappointment her current investments. You might handle this part of your opening request as follows:

You know, I've recently read how more and more people are borrowing money from family and friends to buy homes. It's an interesting approach because both the person borrowing and the person lending stand to gain from the deal.

The rest could track Jenny's opening pretty closely, or you could offer your prospective lender some additional reading material, such as relevant sections from this book. Also, your financial advisor might be willing to speak to your potential lender about the benefits of private lending.

Preparing the Loan Paperwork

Once your private lender has agreed to loan you money to finance all or a portion of your second home, you'll want to handle the transaction almost as a bank would. This includes:

- drafting and signing a written loan agreement, complete with supporting mortgage documents

- protecting the value of your new property by buying insurance and appraisal reports, and

- possibly paying professionals to prepare the paperwork and other reports.

Such attention to detail serves both your private lender's and your interests. For example, the discussions required in order to put your loan agreement into written form will help iron out any possible misunderstandings between you and your lender. Also, by not treating these opening stages of the transaction casually, you demonstrate your commitment to professionally handling and ultimately repaying the loan.

The Loan Agreement and Supporting Documents

To formalize your agreement with your family or other lender, you'll need to prepare the following three documents:

- *Promissory note.* Also referred to as a mortgage note, this is a legally binding document signed by you, the borrower, saying that you promise to repay the loan under agreed-upon terms. These terms should be spelled out in the note, and cover the interest rate, payment dates, and frequency of payment. The note should also describe any penalties that the lender can assess if you fall behind in repaying the loan, including requiring full payment prior to the end of the loan term. See the sample promissory note below, a blank version of which can be found in the Appendix and on the CD-ROM at the back of this book.

- *Repayment schedule.* You'd never think of telling a lending bank, "I'll pay you back when I have the cash." Yet a surprising number of borrowers try this on their friends and family members—or assume it's okay without even asking! In fact, the main source of friction between private borrowers and lenders usually occurs over miscommunications about when payments should be made. Although a written repayment schedule is not legally required, it's both a convenient and important way to avoid straining the relationship with your family-or-friend lender. You can generate a repayment schedule using the online calculator at www.myfico.com.

- *Mortgage or deed of trust (depending on which state the property is located in).* This is a legal document that secures (provides collateral for) the promissory note. It says if you don't pay back the loan, plus all fees and interest, then your private lender can foreclose on your property and use the proceeds to pay off the loan. Depending on your state, it will either be called a "mortgage" or a "deed of trust." The difference is that a mortgage involves two parties (you as the borrower and your family member or friend as the lender), while a deed of trust involves three (you, your family member or friend, and a trustee—usually an attorney or title company—to act as a neutral third party holding temporary title to the property until you pay off the loan). The mortgage or deed of trust lists the currently recognized owner and legal property description, and describes the borrower's responsibility to: a) pay principal, interest, taxes, and insurance in a timely manner; b) maintain hazard insurance on the property; and c) adequately maintain the property. If you fail to comply with these requirements, your private lender can demand immediate, full payment of the loan balance. A sample mortgage and deed of trust can be found in the Appendix to this book. These samples are, however, for your general information. You'll want to find a version that's commonly used in the state where the property is located, for example by visiting: www.freddiemac.com/uniform/unifsecurity.html.

> **TIP**
>
> **Why take the trouble to prepare a mortgage if your family lender would never foreclose on you?** Because if someone else decides to foreclose on your house—for example, a bank from which you took out a second mortgage, or someone else who placed a lien on your property—you want your family lender to remain first in line for the proceeds.

Over half of all states use mortgages, and the remainder use deeds of trust. The chart below indicates which document each state uses:

Mortgage States		Deed of Trust States	
Alabama	Minnesota	Alaska	Oregon
Arkansas	New Hampshire	Arizona	Tennessee
Connecticut	New Jersey	California	Texas
Delaware	New Mexico	Colorado	Utah
Florida	New York	District of Columbia (DC)	Virginia
Hawaii	North Dakota	Georgia (though they	Washington
Illinois	Ohio	call it a "security deed")	West Virginia
Indiana	Oklahoma	Idaho	
Iowa	Pennsylvania	Maryland	
Kansas	Rhode Island	Mississippi	
Kentucky	South Carolina	Missouri	
Louisiana	South Dakota	Montana	
Maine	Vermont	Nebraska	
Massachusetts	Wisconsin	Nevada	
Michigan	Wyoming	North Carolina	

Drafting the Loan and Mortgage Paperwork

Given that you're simply borrowing some cash from someone who knows and trusts you, bringing other people into the picture might seem counterintuitive. You can, if you're careful, detail oriented, and comfortable working with legal forms, draft all the paperwork yourself. However, since even the most basic mortgage contains technical and legal language—and a lot is at stake—it's always best to have a real estate attorney review your documents before you finalize them. The degree to which you use an attorney will depend on your comfort level and the complexity of your transaction. Expect to pay around $200 an hour.

Doing most of the work yourself. Everything you need to structure your private mortgage is readily available. First off, you can use the promissory note contained in this book. Second, you can get a free, standard form mortgage/deed of trust from your own state at www.freddiemac.com/uniform/unifsecurity .html. To fill it out, you'll need a legal description of the property, which you can get by visiting your local registrar of deeds or county clerk.

Once you have everything in hand, review the documents with a real estate attorney to make sure you understand them completely and they will work for your situation.

Sample Promissory Note (amortized loan)

1. **Identity of Borrower and Lender**

   Borrower's name: Joe Borrowguy

   Lender's name: John Lenderman

   The term "Borrower" may refer to more than one person, in which case they agree to be jointly and severally liable under this note. The term "Lender" may refer to any person who legally holds this note, including a buyer in due course.

2. **Promise to Pay**

   For value received, Borrower promises to pay Lender $100,000 plus interest at the yearly rate of 6% on the unpaid balance as specified below. Payments will be made to Lender at 123 Main Street, San Mateo, CA 12345, or such other place as Lender may designate.

3. **Payment Schedule**

   Borrower agrees that this note will be paid in monthly installments of principal and interest. Accordingly, Borrower will pay 360 installments of $599.55 each.

4. **Payment Due Dates**

   Borrower will make installment payments on the 1st day of each month beginning May 2006, until the principal and interest have been paid in full, which will be no later than May 2036. If Borrower fails to make a payment until the 10th day of the month or later, Borrower will owe a late fee of $15.

5. **Prepayment**

   Borrower may prepay all or any part of the principal without penalty.

6. **Loan Acceleration**

   If Borrower is more than 15 days late in making any payment, Lender may declare that the entire balance of unpaid principal is due immediately, together with any interest that has accrued.

7. **Security**

   Borrower agrees that until the principal and interest owed under this promissory are paid in full, this note will be secured by a mortgage covering the real estate commonly known as 456 Main Street, City of Swampscott, County of Essex, State of Massachusetts.

8. **Attorney's Fees**

   If Lender prevails in a lawsuit to collect on this note, Borrower will pay Lender's costs and attorney's fees in an amount the court finds to be reasonable.

9. **Governing Law**

   This note will be governed by and construed in accordance with the laws of the state of Massachusetts.

BORROWER:

Signature: *Joe Borrowguy*

Printed name: Joe Borrowguy

Address: 789 Main Street, Marblehead, MA 12345

Dated: April 3, 2007

Sample Mortgage

After Recording Return To:

_____

_____

_____

_____

_____[Space Above This Line For Recording Data]_____

MORTGAGE

DEFINITIONS

Words used in multiple sections of this document are defined below and other words are defined in Sections 3, 11, 13, 18, 20 and 21. Certain rules regarding the usage of words used in this document are also provided in Section 16.

(A) **"Security Instrument"** means this document, which is dated _____, _____, together with all Riders to this document.
(B) **"Borrower"** is _____.
Borrower is the mortgagor under this Security Instrument.
(C) **"Lender"** is _____.
Lender is a _____ organized and existing under the laws of _____. Lender's address is _____ _____. Lender is the mortgagee under this Security Instrument.
(D) **"Note"** means the promissory note signed by Borrower and dated _____, _____. The Note states that Borrower owes Lender _____ Dollars (U.S. $_____) plus interest. Borrower has promised to pay this debt in regular Periodic Payments and to pay the debt in full not later than _____.
(E) **"Property"** means the property that is described below under the heading "Transfer of Rights in the Property."
(F) **"Loan"** means the debt evidenced by the Note, plus interest, any prepayment charges and late charges due under the Note, and all sums due under this Security Instrument, plus interest.

Note: Only the first page is shown. A mortgage is typically 16 pages long. See the CD-ROM for a full sample.

Sample Deed of Trust

After Recording Return To:

_____

_____

_____

_____

_____[Space Above This Line For Recording Data]_____

DEED OF TRUST

DEFINITIONS

Words used in multiple sections of this document are defined below and other words are defined in Sections 3, 11, 13, 18, 20 and 21. Certain rules regarding the usage of words used in this document are also provided in Section 16.

(A)   **"Security Instrument"** means this document, which is dated _____, _____, together with all Riders to this document.
(B)   **"Borrower"** is _____.
Borrower is the trustor under this Security Instrument.
(C)   **"Lender"** is _____.
Lender is a _____ organized and existing under the laws of_____. Lender's address is _____ _____. Lender is the beneficiary under this Security Instrument.
(D)   **"Trustee"** is _____.
(E)   **"Note"** means the promissory note signed by Borrower and dated _____, _____. The Note states that Borrower owes Lender _____ Dollars (U.S. $_____) plus interest. Borrower has promised to pay this debt in regular Periodic Payments and to pay the debt in full not later than _____.
(F)   **"Property"** means the property that is described below under the heading "Transfer of Rights in the Property."
(G)   **"Loan"** means the debt evidenced by the Note, plus interest, any prepayment charges and late charges due under the Note, and all sums due under this Security Instrument, plus interest.

Note: Only the first page is shown. A deed of trust is typically 16 pages long. See the CD-ROM for a full sample.

When you've completed the documents and are ready to sign them, find a licensed notary public—at your attorney's office, your bank, or in your local Yellow Pages. The mortgage must be notarized. The promissory note doesn't legally require notarization, but your lender may feel more comfortable if you also do this. Since a notary's role is to confirm the identity of the signer, this helps assure that you can't later claim the note was a forgery.

Finally, see "What to Do With the Finished Documents," below, for information on filing with the appropriate public records offices.

Doing this amount of work by yourself makes the most sense if:

- both you and your private lender are comfortable handling standard legal forms
- the terms of the loan will be straightforward, meaning you won't need to insert any special language or conditions into the existing documents, such as prepayment penalties or a requirement to carry private mortgage insurance (PMI), and
- you have the time to pull all the paperwork together and you are looking for the lowest-cost way to do so. Costs for the core components of a private mortgage (which consists of the mortgage document and promissory note), as well as one hour's worth of an attorney's time are normally under $300 (depending on your state).

Using an attorney to handle most or all of the work. Any experienced real estate lawyer can prepare your promissory note and mortgage. An attorney is particularly helpful if your transaction will involve special requirements such as a prepayment penalty, a PMI requirement, or a family trust acting as the lender. A real estate lawyer can also help you with negotiating your home purchase, as well as title searches, obtaining title insurance, and closing tasks. You'll gain peace of mind—but potentially spend a pretty penny. Most experienced attorneys start at $200 an hour, although some offer flat rates for standard work such as this. Hiring an attorney for these tasks is particularly worthwhile, however, if:

- you need a resource to answer your legal questions and advise you about the best way to structure the transaction based on your state's real estate laws, or

- you live in a state that requires a local real estate attorney to be involved in real estate transactions. These states currently include: Connecticut, Delaware, Georgia, Massachusetts, New Jersey, and West Virginia.

What to Do With the Finished Documents

Here's what to do with the promissory note and mortgage or deed of trust after you've filled them out and signed them:

- Give the original promissory note to your lender, and keep a copy for your records.

- Take a copy of the notarized mortgage or deed of trust to whichever registry of deeds or county clerk serves the area where the property is located. They will "record" it, that is, turn it into a public record. The purpose of recording is to advise the rest of the world that your family-or-friend lender holds a lien on the property, and that any other lienholders will have to get in line. Recording also provides evidence that you, the borrower, will need in order to show the IRS that you're eligible to take a federal deduction for interest paid on the loan.

- Keep a copy of the mortgage or deed of trust with your own records, and advise your private lender to do the same.

Protecting Your Property: Appraisals and Insurance

A bank or other mortgage lender wouldn't be content to know that it can foreclose on your house if you failed to repay the loan—quite justifiably, it would also try to make sure that the house will not have dropped in value, or been burnt to the ground in an uninsured fire, by the time the bank gets around to foreclosing. Banks therefore impose various requirements before lending you money, such as your obtaining a home appraisal and various forms of insurance.

But what if an intrafamily mortgage will cover 100% of your financing? Technically speaking, these appraisal and insurance requirements disappear. Nevertheless, both you and your private lender might also appreciate the information and protection offered by the following:

- *Home appraisal:* As you probably remember from buying your first home, the main function of a professional home appraisal is to help establish a property's current market value. If you're overpaying for a house, then the right to foreclose doesn't do much good to anyone loaning you money—the lender must be able to sell the property for at least the amount of money it is lending. A bank would look particularly hard at the appraisal of your second home, knowing that the loan places an additional financial burden on top of your primary home—and your private lender will be similarly happy to see that the home's value is sufficient. Of course, an appraisal isn't just for the lender. It also helps you feel comfortable about the amount you are paying for the home.

- *Title search:* This is a close examination, typically done by an attorney or title company (depending on your state), of all public records that involve title to (that is, ownership and use of) the property. It's not unheard of for someone to buy a property only to discover that its real owner is someone else, that it's already mortgaged to the hilt, or that someone else has the right to use the driveway. The search is conducted to avoid such disasters, by verifying that there are no liens or other claims against the property other than those scheduled to be erased at closing. Title searches typically involve examinations of documents filed during the previous 30 years, but can go back much further. The person conducting the search looks at past deeds, wills, trusts, mortgages, judgments, and other liens. Furthermore, the title search will look for any rights other parties may hold, such as rights of way, view easements, power line easements, or mineral rights. The title search usually acts as a precursor to title insurance.

- *Title insurance:* While most forms of insurance (for example, automobile insurance or life insurance) are meant to protect someone against events that may occur in the future, title insurance is the opposite. Its purpose is to protect you against past events that have happened to the property you're buying—events that not even the title search revealed. Title insurers take the results of the title search, find out whether anyone can eliminate any known existing claims on the property, and if not, normally issue a title policy excluding those claims from coverage. If you choose to purchase title insurance (remember, it's not mandatory), you'll pay a one-time premium when the real estate is transferred.

• *Homeowners' insurance:* Most standard homeowner's insurance policies will provide hazard coverage, which includes damage to your home and many of the items within it, where that damage is caused by theft, fire, lightning, smoke, or similar unexpected events. Some of the coverage you need will be regionally dictated—earthquake insurance is important in California, for example, while coverage of damage from frozen pipes and ice or snow is a higher priority in the northern states. Homeowners' insurance can also provide coverage for liability claims, medical payments to third parties, and legal costs if a lawsuit is brought against you. If you were getting a bank loan, the bank would ordinarily ask to see a receipt proving that you paid the entire first year's premium for homeowners' insurance (the hazard, not the liability portion) prior to the sale closing. But even without a bank looking over your shoulder, you'll probably want to protect your investment with homeowners' insurance.

After You Receive the Loan

After the loan is made (that is, the documents are completed and the money is in your hands), your obligations should be pretty clear: Send the lender regular repayments, at the time and in the manner set out in your promissory note. Also comply with any other requirements set out in the note, such as maintaining your homeowners' insurance.

Of course, unforeseen circumstances may arise. Maybe you run short on cash because you can't find renters as quickly as you'd expected, or a tropical storm causes significant water damage at your vacation home.

Whatever the problem, if it's a legitimate cause for you to be late with your payment, discuss it with your lender. Get in touch as soon as possible, and by all means before the next payment comes due. Your lender will likely appreciate your honesty, and help by lowering your payments, temporarily freezing them, or even forgiving some payments altogether.

That's the beauty of an intrafamily mortgage. Repayment is much more flexible than with a bank. Just make sure not to abuse your lender's trust—be organized about making your payments, and save special requests for the true emergencies.

POINTS TO REMEMBER

Intrafamily or private mortgages can be a great way to supplement or replace home financing that comes from a bank or other institutional lender. They can create a "win-win" situation for both borrower and lender. Most people can and even should consider tapping relatives or close friends for financial help. Just make certain that the arrangement is formalized in writing so that miscommunications or legal tangles don't occur later, leading to strained or broken relationships.

Finding Your Way Through the Mortgage Maze

U nless you have a stash of cash tucked away that needs investing, you'll probably decide to get a loan to help finance your second home. As with your current home, your most likely sources of loan money are banks, credit unions, and other institutional lenders. (But see Chapter 10 for when and how to borrow from friends and family.)

There are literally thousands of different loan programs available, and new varieties seem to surface every day. Each loan program has its own pros and cons, depending on your financial situation and what you're trying to achieve. This book can't possibly cover the multitude of options available. What we can do, however, is to help you understand how to find the best mortgage for your own needs and comfort level. And if you're using a mortgage broker, we'll help you confirm that the broker is alerting you to all your options.

> **WARNING**
> **Many people are unwittingly overpaying on their home mortgages.** Maybe they're paying an extra quarter to half point in interest. Or maybe their monthly payments, which started off low, have slowly crept up. Whatever the reason, we're not just talking about a few hundred extra dollars. Overpaying on a mortgage can add up to thousands or even tens of thousands of dollars in wasted money. Most of the affected homebuyers don't even realize this is happening and could have avoided these mistakes by paying closer attention when shopping for a loan.

To make sure that you find an appropriate and affordable mortgage, this chapter will:

- explain the key differences between a first- and second-home mortgage
- provide you with a refresher course on mortgages (purely optional), and
- show you ways to save money on your second-home mortgage.

Unique Features of Second-Home Mortgages

At its core, a mortgage on a second home is structured no differently than the one you have (or had) on your primary home. You still borrow a set amount of money and pay it back with interest over a predefined period of time. Still, there are some important differences.

You'll Probably Pay More Interest

Second-home owners default on their mortgages more than first-home owners do. That's not lender prejudice talking, it's a statistical fact. And it's no surprise when you consider that, if you get into financial trouble, you'll probably stop making mortgage payments on your second home before you stop on your primary home, too. A second home, by its very nature, adds to your financial burden.

This doesn't mean the banks won't lend you money (provided you qualify). Your loan will, however, come at a cost, in the form of a higher interest rate (about one to two percentage points more). These percentage points aren't insignificant.

For example, suppose you have a $200,000 mortgage at 7% interest to be repaid over 30 years. Paying just one additional percentage point more in interest will cost you an extra $49,288 in total interest over the life of the loan. Two additional points will cost you $100,299 more in interest.

You May Need a Higher Down Payment

You may have been able to get away with a 0% down payment on your current home, but don't expect that to happen with your second home. Most, if not all, mortgage lenders require a minimum of 5% down (10% if it's an investment property) because of the higher risk of default.

As with your first home, if your down payment is less than 20% of the home's value, your lender will likely require you to carry private mortgage insurance (PMI). How much your PMI will cost depends on the size of your down payment, as well as the terms of your particular loan and the amount of PMI insurance necessary. Regardless of cost, PMI payments are money down the drain because they don't help pay down your loan and they're not even tax deductible.

But there are ways to circumvent PMI if you can't come up with a 20% down payment. A good mortgage broker can help: According to

Karen Toms-Brown, mortgage broker with Adamarc Financial Company, Inc. in Menlo Park, California (www.adamarc.com), "Loans can be structured these days with less than 20% down and no PMI. That's because lenders have developed second-mortgage products to go behind a maximum 80% first mortgage. By breaking the loan in two, the requirement for PMI is nullified and the client is spared having to pay for a costly insurance that is not tax deductible and can be difficult to have removed."

Ms. Toms-Brown is referring to the "piggyback" or "combo" loan, which is really two loans—a first mortgage (usually for 80% of the house value) with a second mortgage (usually for 10% to 15% of the house value). That means you can put 5% or 10% down on your second home and still avoid PMI.

You'll Face a More Stringent Approval Process

Because second-home mortgages are riskier, your lender will want some assurance that your home is worth enough to cover the amount of your loan. On its face, the approval process and benchmarks for a second-home mortgage are no different than those for a first home. However, lenders tend to scrutinize second-home mortgage applications harder than those for primary residences.

In particular, your lender will look at:

- *The appraised value of your second home.* Your lender will send out a licensed home appraiser to give an objective opinion as to the home's market value. Then your lender will likely require that your loan amount not exceed 95% of the appraised value or 95% of the purchase price, whichever is less.

- *Your income.* Lenders want to know how much money you have coming in on a regular basis. This includes not just your gross salary and wages, but other income as well, such as alimony/palimony and interest/dividend income. For the self-employed, you'll need to prove that you have a viable business that is generating income. Most lenders require you to show at least two years' worth of tax returns. Also, if you plan on renting out your property, lenders will factor in the projected rental income. However, the projections will be discounted to allow for likely vacancy periods.

- *Your current debt.* The more money you owe to other creditors, the less money you'll have available to pay back your second home loan. Your lender will review your current debt load, which may include automobile and other loans, credit card balances, and more. By far your largest debt burden, and the one a lender will be most interested in, is the outstanding balance on the loan for your current home.

- *Your credit score.* This is a measure of your credit risk, calculated by using a standard formula. To a lender, your credit score is one of the main considerations in deciding whether or not you qualify for a second-home loan. As such, we've dedicated an entire section to this. (See "Got a High Credit Score? Get a Low Interest Rate," below.)

Mortgage Basics: A Refresher Course

> **FAST TRACK**
>
> **Have you bought or refinanced a home within the last few years?**
> If so, or if you feel comfortable in your knowledge of how mortgages are structured, feel free to skip this section. If not, read on for a crash course in mortgage principles. For more comprehensive information, consider reading *Mortgages for Dummies*, (For Dummies) by Eric Tyson and Ray Brown.

The Big Three: Principal, Interest, and Loan Term

In its simplest form, a mortgage consists of three components, which together determine how much you will ultimately pay:

- *Principal* is the amount of money that you initially borrow from a bank, credit union, or other institutional lender. Many times, this amount includes not only the purchase price of the house (minus your down payment), but also any closing costs (which run, on average, between $2,000 and $11,000, depending partly on the state where the property is located). If you're buying a home that needs repairs, you may decide to borrow even more money, to cover the cost of renovations.

• *Interest* is the amount (expressed as a percent) that your lender charges you to make the loan. Interest rates can be fixed (never change) for the life of the loan, or adjustable (also called "variable"). Adjustable rate mortgages are tied to a pre-identified financial index such as the prime rate, which will fluctuate over the life of the loan. Your payments will rise and fall along with the prime rate or other index, with a few extra percentage points added on (called a margin) to profit the lender.

• *Loan term* is the amount of time within which you agree to pay back the loan. The most common home loan terms are 15 and 30 years. The longer you take to pay back your loan, the more it'll cost you in the end. The chart below compares the total cost of interest on 15- and 30-year fixed rate mortgages. As you can see, taking twice as long to pay back your loan will cost you more than double the amount of total interest.

Comparative Interest Payments for Different Loan Terms				
Loan Term	Loan Amount	Interest Rate	Monthly Payment	Total Interest
15-year	$150,000	6%	$1,266	$77,841
30-year	$150,000	6%	$899	$173,755

Comparing Fixed and Adjustable Rate Mortgages

Broadly speaking, there are two types of mortgages from which to choose—fixed-rate mortgages (FRMs) and adjustable rate mortgages (ARMs). Each has its own advantages and disadvantages. Which one is right for you depends not only on your situation, but also on your tolerance for risk and change.

Fixed Rate Mortgages: Lower Risk, But Higher Cost

You know what you're getting with a fixed rate mortgage: Its interest rate remains constant or fixed over the life of the loan. You'll probably make the same payment every month, although variations on this payment plan do exist. And, your lender will probably allocate more of your payment toward interest rather than principal in the early years.

The main disadvantage of an FRM is that it tends to carry a higher initial interest rate than an ARM. And if interest rates fall and you don't qualify for refinancing (which can happen if your property loses value or your financial situation declines), you may regret being locked into a fixed rate.

FUTURE RETIREE

Lock in a low interest rate if possible. Future retirees have the benefit of knowing that they will, with any luck, hold onto their second home for the rest of their lives. If interest rates are low when you're ready to buy, an FRM is worth latching onto. Sure, the interest rate on a fixed-rate mortgage may be higher than that offered by other loan types, but over the long haul, you'll win.

FRMs are available for 40-, 30-, 25-, 20-, 15-, and ten-year terms, with the most common being the 15- and 30-year FRM. The longer the term, the lower the monthly payment (usually), but the higher the total interest paid. You can always pay down your principal early to save on interest payments, on one condition: that there's no prepayment penalty clause hiding in your mortgage documents. (Read them carefully before signing to make sure you can pay off your mortgage early without a financial penalty.)

One strategy for lowering the interest rate on your FRM is to pay for points. Points are really prepaid interest.

How Paying for Points May Save You Money

Certain mortgages (almost always fixed rate) come with what are known as "points." These are up-front fees charged by the lenders to process your loan. One point equals one percent of the loan amount. So, if you chose a $100,000 loan with three points, you would be required to pay $3,000. In general, the more points you pay, the lower your interest rate. Not all mortgages come with points—but you'll pretty much always end up paying for them anyway, in the form of a higher interest rate on a no-point mortgage.

Unfortunately, no standards exist to determine how much a point can lower your interest rate. For some lenders, one point could lower your interest rate by one half percent, while for others, that same point will get you a reduction of only a quarter percent.

Regardless, in many cases, the amount you pay for points is tax deductible, again since points are equivalent to prepaid interest. (See Chapter 14 for more on what mortgage costs are tax deductible.)

The FRMs that don't have points are, cleverly enough, called "no-point" or "zero-point" loans. They'll save you cash at closing, but the trade-off is that you'll pay a slightly higher interest rate. So you're faced with a quandary. Do you go for the loan with a lower interest rate, but shell out an up-front fee, or do you sidestep that fee but take on a higher interest rate? The answer to that question is a definite "it depends"—on how long you'll hold onto your second home, that is.

Paying for points to gain a lower interest rate can be advantageous— especially if you plan on holding onto your second home for a relatively long period of time. How long? Long enough that the lower interest rate you gain will more than offset the up-front cost of the points.

EXAMPLE: Lelia is shopping for a $200,000, 30-year fixed rate mortgage, and has a choice between a zero-point loan at 6.5% interest or a one-point loan at 6% interest. To find out which one is most advantageous, she'll need to do a little math. First, she'll figure out the monthly payment on each loan. Payments on the zero-point loan at 6.5% interest will run $1,264 per month. Payments on the one-point loan at 6% will, by contrast, be $1,199 per month, but will cost $2,000 (1% of $200,000) up front. Now she simply divides the total cost of her points, in this case $2,000, by the difference between the two monthly payments, which is $65. The result is 31 (rounded), which reflects the number of months it will take Lelia to recoup the up-front cost of paying for that one point. Therefore, if she plans to hold onto her second home for more than 31 months, the one-point loan is probably the way to go, even though it costs an extra $2,000 up front.

 FUTURE RETIREE

Future retirees should always look at paying points as an option.
Since the intent of future retirees is to hold onto their property for the remainder of their lives, they stand to gain some significant interest savings down the road.

Adjustable Rate Mortgages: Lower Payments, Higher Risk

Adjustable rate mortgages (also called ARMs or "variable rate mortgages") involve a little more gambling. Their interest rate fluctuates up or down over the life of the loan. When this fluctuation occurs, and how often, depends on what you agree to with your lender. However, your lender should always inform you in writing at least a month or more in advance of your rate change so you'll know the new amount you'll need to pay each month. The lender doesn't have totally free rein, but will tie the rate to one of the various indices described in "Major ARM Indices," below.

Although your ARM's interest rate will be tied to an index, it won't use the exact same percentage as the index. For one thing, your lender wants to make a profit—which it will do by adding a certain fixed percentage to your interest rate every month. This percentage is called a "margin." It's set at the beginning of your loan and will not change for the loan's duration.

The most common adjustment periods (the amount of time that passes before the interest rate changes) on ARMs are six months and one year. However, for some ARMs it can be more, for others less.

Major ARM Indices

Below are some common indices to which ARMs are tied. Which one is right for you depends on your tolerance for risk.

11th District Cost of Funds Index (COFI): The Federal Home Loan Banks (FHLB) system is sort of a bank of banks. It comprises 12 regional banks that lend money to over 8,000 members (including other financial institutions such as commercial banks, credits unions, and insurance companies). This index is based on a monthly weighted average of interest paid by members of the FHLB of San Francisco (the 11th District), which includes members in Arizona, California, and Nevada. COFI is a slow-moving index compared to some others. This works to your advantage when interest rates rise, because the COFI index doesn't just jump upwards in tandem—it's slow to respond. But when interest rates drop, it works against you, because the COFI index is again slower to react.

Major ARM Indices (cont'd.)

One-Year Constant Maturity Treasury Index (CMT): This index is based on the weekly or monthly average yields on U.S. Treasury securities (a debt obligation issued by the U.S. government) that have one year remaining until maturity. This index tends to respond rather quickly to changes in interest rates. If you don't have the stomach for a rapidly changing interest rate, avoid the CMT.

12-Month Treasury Average (MTA): This index is based on the average of the 12 most recent rates of the Constant Maturity Treasury index (see above). The MTA is a bit more steady than the CMT, but still responds quickly to changes in interest rates.

Certificate of Deposit Index (CODI): This index is based on the average interest rate that banks are paying on three-month certificates of deposit. The average is determined by looking at the interest rates over the last 12 months. This, too, is a quickly moving index, but not quite as fast as the CMT or MTA.

Cost of Savings Index (COSI): This index is based on the average interest rate that banks pay their common customers (everyday people) on checking, savings, and CD accounts. This index is highly stable: A mortgage tied to it will change interest rates at a snail's pace.

London Interbank Offered Rate (LIBOR): This index is based on the interest rate at which international banks lend money to each other in the London wholesale money market. There are several LIBOR maturities (the amount of time that must pass for the interest to be paid out in full), namely: 1-, 3-, 6-, and 12-month deposits. The LIBOR is yet another fast-moving index.

Prime Rate: This index is based on the interest rate charged by banks to their best (as in most creditworthy) customers, usually large corporations. The most widely accepted measure of the prime rate is the one quoted in *The Wall Street Journal* (WSJ), which surveys the 30 largest banks. The WSJ will adjust the prime rate only when at least 75% of these banks change their rates. Although the prime rate is not highly volatile, it does rise faster than it declines.

The advantage of an ARM is that it usually has a lower initial interest rate than an FRM. And that means your initial payments are lower too. Plus, because of these lower initial payments, you may, in fact, qualify for a larger mortgage amount compared to an FRM. But all of this comes at a price, in the form of higher risk. As long as interest rates remain low, you win. But when interest rates rise, ARMs pull a Jekyll and Hyde, and your payments may far exceed what they would have been with an FRM.

Your ARM will probably contain certain buffers against the possibility of interest rates rising dramatically (in which case you're the loser) or falling dramatically (in which case your lender is the loser). The ARM will contain a so-called rate cap, that is, a limit on the degree to which the loan's interest rate can increase or decrease. This overall rate cap is broken down into two parts, including the:

- *periodic cap,* usually around 1% to 3%, which limits the interest rate at each adjustment period, and the
- *lifetime cap,* generally around 5% to 6%, which limits the rate change over the life of the loan.

Options for Scheduling Your Repayments

Regardless of whether you're getting a FRM or an ARM, you may have choices about how you pay back the loan. The payment structure you choose can impact the size of your monthly payments, as well as how quickly you're able to pay down your loan principal. Below are the two most common payment structures.

- *Amortized payments* consist of principal and interest payments. While each payment is the same amount throughout the life of the loan, the allocation is frontloaded in favor of interest. For example, on a $125,000, 30-year fixed-rate loan at 6% interest, amortized payments would come out to about $750 per payment. Of the first payment, the lender would apply only $125 towards the loan principal and the remaining $625 towards interest. However, over the course of the loan, that allocation will shift, so that by the last payment roughly $746 would count towards the principal and $4 towards interest. The advantage of an amortized schedule is that your payments are consistent throughout the life of the loan and you start building equity in your home (the difference between the fair market value of your home and the unpaid portion of your mortgage and any other debt that is attached to the house) beginning with the first payment. The disadvantage is that monthly payments

Different Types of ARMs

Not all ARMs work the same way. While they all have adjustable interest rates, you may have a choice of how and when they adjust, how much you pay each month, and more. Here are some of the most popular ARM variations:

Hybrid ARMs. These start off with a fixed interest rate for a period (anywhere from three to ten years), after which the rate adjusts at periodic intervals. For example, a so-called "3/1 hybrid ARM" starts with three years of fixed interest. Beginning in the fourth year, the interest rate adjusts once each year, based on an outside index such as the LIBOR. By comparison, a 5/1 hybrid ARM starts with five years of fixed interest, after which the rate adjusts once each year. Other types of hybrid ARMs include 3/3, 7/1, and 10/1. The appeal of a hybrid ARM is the relatively low fixed interest rate (at least at the beginning of the loan). This is called the starter or introductory rate. Sometimes mortgage lenders will offer very low starter rates, known as teaser or introductory rates, as a means of seducing borrowers. However, once a hybrid ARM switches to the adjustable rate, you'll be at the mercy of the index upon which it's based.

Option ARMs. These ARMs allow you to actually choose how much you'd like to pay each month, at least during the early years of the loan. You can make monthly payments that cover only the interest (interest-only payments). Or you can pay according to a so-called "deferred interest option," allowing you pay no principal and very little interest. Your lender simply adds this unpaid interest to the outstanding balance of your loan (this is known as "negative amortization"). But be careful: If you take the deferred interest option too many times, your outstanding loan balance will grow instead of shrink and you'll end up owing more than you initially borrowed.

Conversion ARMs. Some ARMs allow the borrower to convert to a fixed-rate loan after a specified period of time. For example, a borrower may have the option to convert to a fixed-rate loan once yearly during the first five years of the loan. Of course, you pay a price for this privilege: a slightly higher initial interest rate. The interest you pay once your ARM is converted is usually determined by an index, the most common being the Fannie Mae Required Net Yield (RNY), which is based on when lenders deliver 30-year mortgages to Fannie Mae for sale.

tend to be higher than other loan payment structures. At any point throughout your loan, you can choose to make extra payments against your principal (unless you agreed to a prepayment penalty, which would appear in your mortgage documents). As you pay down more of your principal, the amount of interest you pay will also decrease, as interest is constantly recalculated based on the current principal balance.

- *Interest-only payments* mean you pay down only the interest portion (no principal) of the loan each month. Usually, this is for a predetermined period of time (three, five, seven, or ten years). At the end of the interest-only period, your loan converts to an amortized payment schedule. For example, on a ten-year interest-only loan of $125,000 at 6% interest, you would pay $625 each month for the first ten years. These payments would cover all interest and no principal, so you wouldn't build up any equity in your home during this period. At the conclusion of the ten years, the loan would shift to an amortized payment schedule and your payments would increase to $896 per month, covering both interest and principal. Certainly, the lower up-front payments are an advantage to interest-only loans. However, the trade-off is that those lower payments don't build equity in your home. It's not until the loan switches to an amortization schedule (and you start paying down the principal) that you begin to build equity. Some interest-only structures remain in place throughout the life of the loan. It's not until the end that you are hit with a massive, lump-sum payment equal to the initial amount you borrowed. This is known as a "balloon" payment. Unless you plan on selling your property before the end of the loan, avoid this structure like the plague.

INVESTOR

If you're looking to profit in real estate by flipping properties, consider an interest-only payment structure. Investors who flip make their money by pocketing the difference between the purchase price (including expenses) and the sale price. They aim for the sale to occur in a very short period of time, say one year or less. Building equity is not on the flipper's mind, but having the lowest possible loan payment is. As such, interest-only payment structures are an attractive option, whether using an ARM or FRM (though ARMs usually offer the lowest interest rates).

How Conforming Loans Can Lower Your Interest Rate

Very few people know what a conforming loan is. At least, that's what we discovered when we did a quick, random survey of 100 homeowners. Only 8% could tell us whether they had a conforming loan or not.

Now you may be saying, "So what?" We'll give you the answer in dollars: Qualifying for a conforming loan could yield a good half-point difference or more on the interest rate you pay. For example, on a $150,000, 30-year loan, paying 6.5% instead of 6% interest would mean shelling out an additional $17,564.

What Do Conforming Loans Conform To?

Conforming (also called "conventional") loans are offered by banks, credit unions, and other institutional lenders. They are not guaranteed or insured by the U.S. government. However, as the name suggests, conforming loans must conform or adhere to something—that something being guidelines set by "Fannie and Freddie."

Not to be confused with your eccentric aunt wearing bunched-up stockings and her cigar-wielding husband, "Fannie and Freddie" are short for Fannie Mae (also called the Federal National Mortgage Association) and Freddie Mac (also called the Federal Home Loan Mortgage Corporation). These are federally chartered corporations, established in the late 1960s and early 1970s to support home ownership and rental housing.

Fannie and Freddie don't lend money. Rather, they buy mortgaged loans from banks, credit unions, and other institutional lenders, then package the loans and sell them to investors. This all happens behind the scenes and doesn't change the terms of the loans these organizations buy. From the borrower's perspective, all it usually means is a switch in the name that goes on the loan payment check.

The reason that conforming loans ordinarily carry lower interest rates than nonconforming loans is twofold. One, the borrowers tend to be lower credit risks. Two, conforming loans are easier for lenders to sell, allowing them to turn around and make additional loans. Why are they interested in doing that? Because when interest rates rise, banks and other lenders like to know that they can sell off their loans with lower interest rates in favor of making newer loans at higher interest rates.

What Guidelines Must Conforming Loans Follow?

Before Fannie and Freddie will buy a loan, they must be assured that the selling lender followed certain guidelines. Let's briefly review these, so that you understand why your bank is, in turn, imposing them on you:

- *Maximum loan amount.* This is the maximum amount a lender can loan to a homebuyer. It's calculated based on the type of property (one-, two-, three-, or four-family unit) being purchased, as well as whether the loan is secured by a first or second mortgage. For example, see the table below for the maximum loan amounts for 2006 (it changes every January).

2006 Single-Family Mortgage Loan Limits		
First Mortgages	One-family loan*	$417,000
	Two-family loan*	$533,850
	Three-family loan*	$645,300
	Four-family loan*	$801,950
Second Mortgages	One- to four-family loan**	$208,500

*One- to four-family mortgages in Alaska, Hawaii, Guam, and the U.S. Virgin Islands are 50% higher than the limits for the rest of the country.

**In Alaska, Hawaii, Guam, and the U.S. Virgin Islands: $312,750.

Source: Adapted with minor modifications from the Fannie Mae website; the original table is available at: www.fanniemae.com/aboutfm/loanlimits.jhtml?p=About+Fannie+Mae&am

- *Borrower credit requirements.* Conforming loans require borrowers to have a credit score of 620 or higher. Credit scores are discussed in detail under "Got a High Credit Score? Get a Low Interest Rate," below.

- *Borrower income requirements.* How much income a borrower needs to show is calculated by evaluating the person's debt-to-income ratios. Specifically, the lender will calculate the following two ratios: 1) the "front ratio," determined by dividing your proposed mortgage payment (principal, interest, taxes, and insurance) by your gross monthly income, and 2) the "back ratio," which adds other debt (such as your mortgage on your primary home, car loans, and credit card balances) to your proposed mortgage payment before dividing by your gross income. For conforming loans, your front ratio can't exceed 28% debt to income, while your back ratio can't be over 36%.

- *Down payment amount.* Your down payment must be at least high enough to keep your loan amount within the maximum conforming loan limits. For example, if you're buying a $450,000 house, you'll need to put down at least $33,000 to keep your loan from going over the maximum limit of $417,000. The exact percentage required for your down payment will vary based on the type of mortgage and your lender.

- *Suitable properties.* Not all properties qualify for conforming loans. For example, multiunit dwellings of more than four families don't fall within Fannie and Freddie's standards. So, if you're an investor, or even a vacationer, who's looking to buy a multiunit property with a conforming loan, you'll want to limit your search to dwellings that hold no more than four families.

Your loan will fall into the nonconforming category if you need a loan higher than Fannie or Freddie's maximum loan amount (called a jumbo loan) or if your credit history is tainted (called a subprime loan). If a nonconforming loan is your only option, consider supplementing bank financing with a family and friend loan (see Chapter 10) or taking on a co-owner to help defray costs (see Chapter 12). By lowering the amount you need to borrow from an institutional lender, or teaming up with someone who has a strong credit score, you might qualify for a conforming loan after all.

Got a High Credit Score? Get a Low Interest Rate

If you've always paid your debts on time, banks, credit unions, and other institutional lenders will be happy to lend you more money. But if your track record of paying back debts is poor, you either won't be approved for a loan, or the loan will be offered at less favorable terms, such as a relatively high interest rate.

To determine your credit history, your prospective lender will obtain a copy of your credit report. These days, the industry standard for lenders is to use a credit-scoring system called the "FICO score," which was developed decades ago by a company called Fair Isaac. Your FICO score is determined by pulling your credit history from the three leading credit reporting agencies: Equifax, Experian, and TransUnion. You actually have three FICO scores, one for each agency. The credit-reporting agencies collect data about people on an ongoing basis. Your credit file will contain:

- *Personal information.* This usually includes your name (including former names, such as maiden names), Social Security number, date of birth, current and former home addresses, and current and former employers.

- *Credit history.* This is the heart of your credit report. It contains detailed information about all your credit accounts, whether active, inactive, or closed—the latter two going back approximately ten years from the date of last activity. An account doesn't have to be directly in your name to be considered yours—one in which you appear as an authorized user counts too, such as your spouse's credit card account. For each account, the report will usually mention the open date, credit limit or loan amount, outstanding balance, and payment history.

- *Credit inquiries.* Whenever you apply for credit, such as with a lender, credit card company, landlord, or insurer, that potential creditor will usually inquire about your creditworthiness, by obtaining a copy of your credit report. Any inquiries made during the last two or so years are listed on your credit report. If a high number of those inquiries actually represent your own applications for new credit, it may raise a red flag for a lender, suggesting that you're stretching yourself too thin.

- *Public records.* Other debts of yours that have made it into the public record (usually within the past seven to ten years), such as liens on your primary residences, bankruptcies, overdue child support, and alimony payments, may also appear on your credit report.

RESOURCES

Get a free copy of your credit report from all three credit reporting agencies. Federal law requires Equifax, Experian, and TransUnion to provide you (at your request) with one free copy of your credit report every 12 months. The easiest way to obtain your free copy is via the three companies' centralized website, www.annualcreditreport.com.

Once your credit history has been pulled, it is run through an algorithm (a mathematical calculation) that spits out your actual FICO score. Your score can range from 350 (poor) to 850 (excellent). The median score in the U.S. is 723. A score of 700 or higher is usually deemed "good" from the bank's perspective, qualifying you for the lowest interest rates.

RESOURCES

If your credit isn't in great shape, take steps to improve it. The myFICO website, www.myfico.com, contains useful information about improving your credit score. Check out its calculators, allowing you to run "what if" scenarios specific to your financial situation. You may also want to read:

- *Credit Repair*, by Robin Leonard (Nolo), which includes not only a wealth of suggestions, but 30 forms and letters for your use.
- *Your Credit Score: How to Fix, Improve, and Protect the 3-Digit Number that Shapes Your Financial Future*, by Liz Pulliam Weston (Prentice Hall), which offers concise information, great examples and follow-up reference material on the poorly understood system used to calculate your credit score.
- *Rich Dad's Advisors: The ABC's of Getting Out of Debt : Turn Bad Debt into Good Debt and Bad Credit into Good Credit*, by Garrett Sutton (Warner Business Books), which covers credit and debit in a thorough and objective manner, provides simple, yet practical steps to get out of debt, and even addresses the health effects of debt.

How Your Credit Score Can Impact Your Interest Rate		
For a $216,000, 30-year, fixed-rate mortgage:		
If your FICO score is:	You qualify for an interest rate of:	In which case your monthly payment will be:
760–850	5.75%	$1,260
700–759	5.97%	$1,291
660–699	6.25%	$1,330
620–659	7.06%	$1,446
580–619	8.27%	$1,626
500–579	9.17%	$1,764

Source: myFICO, a division of Fair Isaac. The information above is valid as of 7/4/05. Please visit: www.myfico.com to view updates based on the current, average national interest rates.

Where to Start Shopping for a Mortgage

As with most everything in life, finding a good deal on your second-home mortgage, requires shopping around. Even if the first mortgage you come across proves to be the best, you'll never know for sure until you investigate other options. Here are the most productive ways to start your quest:

- *Enlist the services of a mortgage broker or banker.* If you've used a good mortgage broker before, there's no reason not to return to the person. If you have an established relationship with a lender, that might be another good place to start. Sometimes (but not always), it's possible to get a better deal if you get your second-home mortgage from the same lender that gave you the mortgage on your current home. Nevertheless, if you go directly to one lender, it's worth speaking with loan officers from at least two other institutions, to help assure that you get the best deal. (See Chapter 6 for a full discussion of the role of mortgage brokers and lending bank representatives, and how to find good ones.)

- *Comparison shop online.* When it comes to comparison shopping, the Internet is an excellent resource. In a matter of minutes, you can find out the average rates on different types of mortgages. At the very least, you can use this information to assess whether your mortgage broker or bank is presenting you with competitive offerings. If you find better rates, ask them to explain the discrepancy. Don't take the online rates at face value, however. Many of them don't tell you about hidden or unnecessary fees, commonly called junk fees, you've already applied for the loan. Even at an established lender's sites, the loan terms aren't always adequately explained until you talk to someone in person. Nevertheless, the Internet can be useful for learning more about mortgages.

Top Online Mortgage Resources and Lenders		
Comparison Shopping Websites	Online-Only Lenders	Lenders with Physical Branches
www.bankrate.com	www.ditech.com	www.bankofamerica.com
www.interest.com	www.eloan.com	www.citibank.com
www.lendingtree.com	www.quickenloans.com	www.countrywide.com
		www.washingtonmutual.com
		www.wellsfargo.com

- *Flip through the newspaper.* The Sunday real estate sections of local newspapers usually list the various types of available mortgages along with their current interest rates. This is a great way to see the rates in specific geographic locations—important, since rates can vary based on where your house will be. (Don't forget to look in the newspaper that's local to where you're thinking about buying a second home if that's not the same area where you currently live.)

POINTS TO REMEMBER

When choosing a mortgage for a second home expect to pay more in interest than you did for your first. You'll get the best second-home mortgage rate if you have a high credit score and qualify for a conforming loan. Having a clear picture of what impacts interest rates before you start looking for a mortgage can save you thousands, even tens of thousands, of dollars down the road.

You Don't Have to Go It Alone: Buying With Others

W hat you learned in kindergarten about sharing could help in your quest for a second home. But this time around, rather than sharing your Lincoln Logs, you'll be sharing your second home with a cobuyer. (By the way, the son of famed architect Frank Lloyd Wright was, ironically enough, the creator of Lincoln Logs.)

Once the domain of married or committed couples, more and more second-home buyers are discovering the advantages of teaming up with a relative, friend, or someone else to buy a house for investment, vacation, or even future retirement. In some cases, sets of married couples have even teamed up. And why not, given that over the past five years, median home prices have skyrocketed by 37% nationally, while household incomes have grown by a sluggish 4%? You'll probably need to take on far more debt than your parents or grandparents would have in order to buy a second house.

Although house prices have been stabilizing since the mid-2000s, few experts believe they will drop significantly any time soon. Worse, the disparity between house prices and household incomes is even greater in regions where real estate prices have gone up the most—many of the very same regions that attract second-home buyers like you. (See Chapter 3 to learn more about the hottest second-home markets.)

Rather than shoulder this debt burden on your own, you can partner financially with someone similarly interested in owning a second home. If done right, the shared-purchase approach can get you a second home you might not otherwise have been able to afford. On the other hand, if you don't fully think through the arrangement and set it up correctly, it could lead to financial and legal chaos, not to mention a strained or broken relationship.

This chapter looks at the pros and cons of buying and owning a second home with someone besides a spouse or significant other. Furthermore, it digs into what's involved in structuring the deal so that each party is protected—both now and in the future.

The Pros and Cons of a Shared Purchase

The chart below will help you make an informed decision about whether or not a shared purchase is right for you.

Pros	Cons
Allows you to buy a second home that you might not otherwise have been able to afford	Can sometimes lead to strained and even broken relationship
Lowers your debt burden by 50% or more, depending on how you and your cobuyer agree to split the costs	Introduces a layer of complexity that requires additional paperwork and expense
Depending on your cobuyer's background, may round out your own knowledge and expertise in areas such as financing, home improvement, and property management	Requires you to have foresight and give extra thought to issues and areas of disagreement that could arise in the future
Saves time, since you and your cobuyer can split property management responsibilities; particularly advantageous if you plan on renting out the property	Forces you to relinquish some control and get "buy in" on key decisions from your cobuyer

Finding a Shared-Purchase Partner

If you've decided the pros of a shared purchase outweigh the cons, the next step is to find a potential cobuyer. And that doesn't mean sitting at home and waiting for the phone to ring. Rather, you need to:

- tell people you know about your plans, and
- ask a real estate professional to hook you up with others.

Announcing Your Plans

Most people can't read your mind. If you don't tell your relatives, friends, coworkers, and acquaintances that you're interested in partnering with someone to buy a second home, they'll never know. And don't be shy about who you tell. The more people who know, the better your chances of finding someone who might be interested.

When you tell people about your plans, you're likely to receive one of three responses:

- *Response #1:* "I have no interest whatsoever in buying a second home." No need to argue. Nothing you say is likely to change the person's entire outlook. But make sure to ask whether this person knows someone who may be considering a second-home purchase.

- *Response #2:* "I hadn't really considered buying a second home, but I'm intrigued by the notion of doing it with you." This response is most likely to come from someone with whom you have a close tie, such as a family member, good friend, or longtime business partner. In marketing circles, this person is called a "warm lead." Next, you need to help the person understand what's really involved in such an arrangement. You might start by giving him or her a copy of this book.

- *Response #3:* "I've been considering buying a second home as well." A marketer would call this person a "hot lead." The person is already in the market to buy a second home, so you can skip some of the preliminaries. The key will be to determine whether buying a house together makes sense. See "How to Determine Cobuyer Compatibility," below, for more on this.

Getting Leads From Real Estate Professionals

While it's common to team up with people you know to buy a second home, in certain situations (such as pure investments) a shared purchase with a stranger might make sense.

Your local real estate professionals—in particular, real estate agents, attorneys, and mortgage brokers—can play a dating-service sort of role. They are often in long-term contact with real estate investors, past clients, and colleagues who are always looking for the right opportunity. Ask these professionals to connect you with clients who might entertain the thought of joint ownership.

For that matter, many real estate professionals themselves buy second homes. You might need to look no further for a cobuyer—and a plenty experienced one, at that.

How to Determine Cobuyer Compatibility

Buying a home with someone who isn't your significant other is still a marriage of sorts, at least in the financial sense. And, like any marriage, it takes commitment to make it work. But before you say, "I do" to your second-home soulmate, make sure that both of you agree on what you want out of the relationship. Start by establishing whether your reasons for wanting a second home are similar. While this may seem like a no-brainer, things aren't always as they appear.

> EXAMPLE: Tanisha and her best friend Sadie decide to invest equally in a fixer-upper in Philadelphia. They plan to sell it at a profit when the work is complete. Before moving forward, the two calculate how much they're ready to pay for the house and the repairs. Sounds like they're both on the same page, right? Don't be too sure. In fact, the two of them buy an old Victorian and fix it up according to plan. But when it comes time to sell, Sadie keeps rejecting what Tanisha feels are reasonable offers. When Tanisha confronts her friend, she discovers that Sadie was hoping for a higher profit margin—one that Tanisha thinks is unrealistic. What's more, Sadie says she would just as soon hold onto the property and rent it out rather than take a lower profit. Tanisha, on the other hand, doesn't want anything to do with becoming a landlord. Now what?

Unexpected disagreements can be avoided if you and your real estate buddy talk out various contingencies in advance. To start, each of you should complete (on your own) the compatibility questionnaire below. Then compare your answers.

Wherever answers don't match, discuss why. This will prompt conversations that could reveal whether or not a partnership between the two of you makes sense. Keep in mind that this questionnaire is meant to gauge basic compatibility, not solve detailed partnership issues (which will be addressed in our discussion of creating the co-ownership agreement, below).

Cobuyer Compatibility Questionnaire

1. What is your <u>primary</u> reason for buying a second home?

   ❑ Investment

   ❑ Vacation

   ❑ Future retirement

2. How long do you plan on keeping the property?

   ❑ Less than one year

   ❑ One to five years

   ❑ Six to ten years

   ❑ Indefinitely

3. How do you plan to handle maintenance and repairs on the property?

   ❑ In conjunction with your cobuyer, without a management company

   ❑ By hiring a property management company

   ❑ Haven't thought about it

4. Do you intend to rent out the property?

   ❑ Yes

   ❑ No

5. Do you plan on using the second home personally?

   ❑ Yes

   ❑ No [Skip to Question #7]

6. In which months do you plan on using the second home for personal use (check all that apply)?

❑ January	❑ July
❑ February	❑ August
❑ March	❑ September
❑ April	❑ October
❑ May	❑ November
❑ June	❑ December

7. Would you mind if your cobuyer used the second home for personal use?

   ❑ Yes

   ❑ No

Co-Ownership Options for Holding Title

Any time you buy a home, you receive what's called "title," evidenced by a piece of paper called a deed. The deed will contain a legal description of the property, identify who is transferring an interest in the property (the grantor) and who is accepting it (you and your cobuyer, the grantees), and explain how the grantees are sharing the title.

Your main options for sharing title include:

• as tenants in common (TIC), and

• as joint tenants with right of survivorship (JTWROS).

Married couples may also take title as "tenants by the entirety" or in the form of community property—however, those topics aren't discussed further in this chapter, on the assumption that your cobuyer is someone more distant.

Legally, many similarities exist between a tenancy in common and a joint tenancy. Both give each of you what's called an "undivided interest" in the property, meaning you can both use and enjoy the entire property (not, say, only up to the fence you build down the middle) and you're both entitled to income from the entire property in proportion to your ownership share. In either case, if one of you wanted to sell, that person couldn't simply divide the property in half and sell it—your cobuyer would instead have to sell his or her tenancy or interest in the property. The new buyer would gain the same rights as the seller had.

> **TIP**
>
> **Just between the two of you:** You may be able to separately agree to divide the usage of the property. For example, if you and your cobuyer purchase a duplex, you'll probably want to put into writing who is going to use which half. A lawyer should be able to help you with this task. But be warned, local zoning ordinances and state laws may limit the contents of such agreements.

Another similarity between TIC and JTWROS forms of title is that both give each owner the so-called "right to partition." This means that if one co-owner wants out, but can't reach an agreement with the other co-owner or can't find a third party willing to buy a partial interest in the property, then the one who wants out can go to court and force the tenancy to be dissolved. The assets are then distributed to each co-owner.

A partition action, which usually involves an attorney, can drain your time and money. Therefore, it should be used only as a last resort. You can help avoid the need for a partition action by creating a co-ownership agreement, covered below.

There are also some important differences between a tenancy in common and joint tenancy, particularly when it comes time to sell or dispose of one person's ownership interest.

Unique Features of Holding Title as Tenants in Common (TIC)

A tenancy in common (TIC) is by far the most common way for unrelated cobuyers to take title. Despite the unlimited rights of access and usage, you and your cobuyer are allowed to own unequal interests (also called shares) of the property. Each of you can sell or transfer your ownership interest without getting consent from the other owner. Also, if one co-owner dies, his or her share is transferred to the beneficiaries of the estate.

> **EXAMPLE:** Thelma and Louise are best friends who buy an investment home together for $200,000. Thelma covers 65% of the purchase price, with Louise making up the rest. They agree that Thelma will take a 65% ownership interest in the property and Louise a 35% interest. Thelma dies when her car goes over a cliff. According to Thelma's will, her young beau Brad is her beneficiary. That means Brad gains a 65% ownership interest in the property.

Unique Features of Holding Title as Joint Tenants with Right of Survivorship (JTWROS)

Cobuyers who are related often choose to take title as joint tenants with right of survivorship (JTWROS). With this form of ownership, you and your cobuyer have no choice but to own equal interests in the property, 50/50. If you buy a home with two other partners, you each own a one-third interest, and so forth.

Unlike with a tenancy in common, upon the death of one joint tenant, the remaining owners gain the deceased owner's interest in the property. This happens automatically—no need for a court or probate proceeding. In fact, even if the deceased owner wrote a will specifying that the property was to pass to some other person, that request would not usually be allowed.

EXAMPLE: Using the same example as above, if Thelma and Louise had taken title as a JTWROS, each would have had a 50% ownership interest in the property, regardless of the amount each had contributed towards the purchase. After Thelma's death, her half would automatically transfer to Louise, who would now own 100% of the property, while Thelma's young beau Brad would be out of luck.

RESOURCES

Buying a second home in California? You'll find lots more useful information on taking title in *Deeds for California Real Estate*, by Mary Randolph (Nolo).

Co-Ownership Agreements

Talk is cheap—and what's worse, easily forgotten later. That's why you need to draft and sign a co-ownership agreement. This document will explain how you and your cobuyer plan to deal with various potential issues, thereby helping head off confusion or misinterpretation down the road.

The most challenging part of drafting a co-ownership agreement is anticipating issues while everything looks rosy. Most people enter into a partnership with the friendliest of intentions, thinking they can work out any unforeseen questions later. But with big dollars and possibly your leisure or retirement time at stake, fundamental disagreements can arise—and be tough to work out.

EXPERT

Work with an attorney experienced in drafting co-ownership agreements for real estate transactions. Sure, it'll cost you, but not as much as the lawsuit that could result from not agreeing on important points in advance.

Co-ownership agreements can range from short to lengthy. The advantage of a longer agreement is that it allows for more potential issues to be covered, which can make the agreement more effective should a problem arise. However, regardless of length, the agreement should at least address the issues discussed below.

Who Owns What Percentage

You don't need to draw a line down the center of the house, but you do need to clarify what percentage of it each of you will own. This is especially important in case one of you later dies or decides to sell his or her interest. This decision is easy if you take title as joint tenants with right of survivorship (JTWROS)—you divide your interest in equal parts, such as 50/50 if there are two of you.

If you take title as tenants in common (TIC), however, you don't need to divide your interests 50/50, nor even on the basis of how much money each of you puts in. For example, the two of you might decide that one will receive a greater percentage based on having agreed to manage renting the property. Or, one of you could agree to a lesser percentage of ownership in return for spending more time at the property during the year.

Another possibility is that one co-owner contributes less for the down payment, but shares equally in paying ongoing expenses such as mortgage payments, property taxes, and utilities. The owner who contributed less towards the down payment might agree to a lesser percentage of ownership (or, you could come to some other arrangement, such as a long-term loan). It's all up to the two of you to negotiate according to what you think is fair.

Real-Life Example: Couple Learns Value of Co-Ownership Agreements the Hard Way

Stacey and her husband, Al, had always dreamed of owning a second home—a place to escape the hustle and bustle of the San Francisco Bay Area. One evening, while dining with two long time friends, Stacey and Al mentioned their dream. It turned out the other couple had thought about the same thing. "What if," both couples thought, "we buy a second home together?"

Within months, the two couples bought a vacation home in Auburn, California, a 2½ hour drive away. They took title as tenants in common, but didn't bother to create a co-ownership agreement. They agreed verbally to split expenses and responsibilities proportionally to each couple's contribution to the down payment.

Everything went smoothly for the first eight months. Both couples spent weekends and holidays at their new home, sometimes together, sometimes separately. But then one day, the other couple dropped a bomb. They said that, due to some personal issues (nothing to do with Stacey and Al), they wanted out of the deal. They asked Stacey and Al to buy them out.

There was just one problem. The house had appreciated 22.3% since the couples had bought it, so Stacey and Al would need to come up with more money than what the other couple had initially contributed to buy them out at current market rates. Plus, interest rates had crept up during that time, so refinancing (which is what Stacey and Al would have had to do to come up with the necessary cash) would have also cost them more.

Still, Stacey and Al hoped somehow to hold onto the home. Because of the tenancy in common, the other couple could have legally sold their ownership interest to another party (if they had found one) without Stacey and Al's permission. Or, they could have exercised their right to partition, and forced both couples to sell. Fortunately, they did neither of those things.

Instead, the departing couple agreed that it was in everyone's best interest for Stacey and Al to buy them out at the original value of the home. This way, the couple got out of the deal (while getting back their initial investment), Stacey and Al got to keep the vacation home, and, most important of all, the two couples remained friends. So, would Stacey and Al do it again? Absolutely. But if they did, they'd be sure to create a co-ownership agreement.

How Co-Owners Allocate Ongoing Expenses

Expenses may include mortgage payments, property taxes, insurance premiums, utilities, and other costs associated with maintaining and operating your second home. Your co-ownership agreement is one of the few, if not the only, places in which you can specify how to allocate these expenses between you and your co-owners. Here are several allocation options:

- *Mirror ownership allocation.* Many co-owners simply allocate costs at the same percentage as ownership. For example, if you own 60% of the home and your co-owner owns 40%, then you would cover 60% of the expenses and your co-owner would cover 40%. This approach works particularly well for TIC titles, since ownership can legally be allocated unequally. However, anything other than a 50/50 split won't work for JTWROS titles, in which ownership can only be allocated equally, regardless of time and money contributions.

- *Based on down payment allocation.* This approach uses the down payment contribution of each co-owner as the foundation for determining expense allocation. For example, if the total down payment on a second home is $100,000, and you contributed $55,000 while your co-owner contributed $45,000, then you would cover 55% of the expenses and your co-owner would cover 45%. Because ownership allocation isn't an issue, this approach works well for either TIC or JTWROS titles.

- *Apply an allocation based on personal usage.* If you and your co-owner plan to use the home personally, then another approach could be to allocate expenses based on the amount of time each co-owner uses the home. For example, if the home is used a total of 13 weeks out of the year, eight by you and five by your co-owner, then you would cover 62% of the expenses and your co-owner would cover 48%.

What Happens If One Co-Owner Later Wants Out

If you own a house by yourself, you can of course sell it whenever you choose, without consulting anyone. But if you co-own it, getting out of the deal may not be so simple. Neither of you probably wants the other one to be able to sell his or her interest to any old third party (assuming there's even a market for a partial interest in a house). But that's exactly what can happen, because, regardless of whether title is held as TIC or JTWROS, each co-owner does not legally need the other's approval to sell his or her interest in the property.

One way around this issue is to have a provision in the co-ownership agreement that gives the co-owner who's staying a right of first refusal to purchase the selling co-owner's interest. However, even with this provision, there are still several questions the co-ownership agreement will need to address:

- *How will you fairly assess the property's value?* In a buyout situation, the co-owner purchasing the departing co-owner's interest wants to make sure he or she isn't paying too much. The selling co-owner, on the other hand, wants to make sure he or she is receiving fair market value for the interest. To minimize potential problems, the agreement should stipulate how the property will be valued. The most common and least expensive way is to use a licensed home appraiser to determine the current market value of the property. The actual buyout amount could then be determined based on percentages of ownership interests.

- *Does the selling co-owner have to accept the buyout offer?* In most cases, the answer is "no." Allowances are usually made for the selling co-owner to have a change of heart. For example, he or she may realize that the interest in the property isn't worth as much as expected. The co-ownership agreement should leave room for this.

- *What if the remaining co-owner can't come up with sufficient funds?* The co-ownership agreement could contain language that would allow him or her to find a replacement co-owner who would purchase either 100% of the seller's interest or a fractional amount in conjunction with the remaining co-owner. Most agreements will specify a maximum amount of time to find a new co-owner.

What Happens If a Co-Owner Buys the Farm

Not to be confused with the actual purchase of a farm, we're talking about the arrival of the Grim Reaper here. You and your cobuyer need to decide who would get the remainder of the property if one of you died. Would it go to the surviving co-owner, to the deceased person's heirs, or to someone else? While the type of ownership structure you choose in your title deed will largely take care of this, it's not a bad idea to discuss your wishes now and reinforce your choice in the co-ownership agreement. Heirs have been known to contest deeds and win a court ruling in their favor.

> **TIP**
> **Not sure when to begin drafting a co-ownership agreement?** The best time is usually after you and your cobuyer have decided on a particular house but before the two of you have financially committed to the property. This allows you to address issues that may be unique to the property, while you still have time to walk away from the deal if you can't reach a consensus.

Whether to Form a Separate Business Entity Before Buying

Rather than taking title as co-owners, you and your cobuyer might choose to form a separate business entity, such as a limited liability company (LLC) or an S corporation. You would then have the business entity take title. You and your cobuyer would, in turn, own shares of or a membership interest in the business, depending upon its structure. (Note that we don't recommend forming a regular, or C corporation, due to the possibility of double taxation, discussed below.)

Why set up a separate business entity? Primarily to cover your assets, so to speak, against becoming fodder for your or your cobuyer's creditors (including those who successfully file lawsuits against you). We're talking here about your personal assets, such as your savings accounts, cars, stocks, bonds, and even the houses in which each of you separately live.

Creditors can always come after property owned by the business entity, but what you're worried about is that some debt or liability having to do with the newly purchased second property—such as an injured worker or an angry tenant—results in loss of your personal assets as well. Certain business structures allow you and your cobuyer to in effect divorce yourselves from the purchased property.

Of course, forming a separate business entity takes some effort. For starters, there's filing with the state, and paying fees. Forming a business also means you won't be able to take the federal tax deduction for the mortgage interest you pay, because the business will be paying the interest, as opposed to you or your cobuyer. To avoid these issues, many buyers protect themselves against liability by simply buying extra insurance. Nevertheless, forming a separate entity may still be worth your while if the second home will be:

- *rented out over time* to generate rental income while realizing longer-term appreciation in value. Being a landlord means opening yourself up to the possibility of lawsuits initiated by your tenants (or even their family members and visitors) should an accident occur on your property; or

- *sold in the short term* (typically 12 months or less) with the intention of making a profit (called flipping). These types of houses usually require some degree of repair or updating and are not usually rented out. Accidents can happen during construction. Maybe a worker falls off a ladder or a passerby gets hurt on your property. If so, you and your co-owner could face a lawsuit.

EXAMPLE: Martin and Luther are repairing the roof on their jointly owned rental property when Martin drops his hammer, striking a passerby (Hildegaard) on the head. After release from the hospital, Hildegaard sues both owners, claiming millions of dollars in damages as a result of her concussion, loss of memory, broken elbow, and more. Martin and Luther's insurance isn't enough to cover the settlement. So, in addition to trying to force the sale of Martin and Luther's second home in order to cover damages, Hildegaard also goes after their personal assets. Martin and Luther now wish they'd formed an appropriate business entity in advance to make their personal assets legally untouchable.

In addition to accidents, forming an LLC or an S corporation will shield your personal assets from creditors who may come knocking if your business falls behind in making payments (for example, to contractors or suppliers). While that shouldn't give you carte blanche to shrug off your financial obligations, it's nice to know that your second-home creditors can't touch your personal assets and possessions.

> ⚠ **WARNING**
>
> **Your bank won't let you off the hook.** Many mortgage lenders will have you and your cobuyer cosign your second-home loan. By doing so, you personally agree to take full responsibility for the loan if the business entity defaults (fails to make its payments or meet its other obligations under the loan). If you cosign, your personal assets will not be protected.

Forming a Limited Liability Company (LLC)

Forming an LLC is a good option if you and your cobuyer plan to buy *and* hold the property, renting it out for all or a portion of the time. Why? Because the LLC structure allows each of you to protect your personal assets while utilizing tax benefits such as favorable capital gains tax rates and depreciation deductions (addressed in further detail in Chapter 14).

An LLC is a fairly recent type of U.S. business structure, combining features of corporations and partnerships. It is recognized in all 50 states plus the District of Columbia (Washington, DC). An LLC is made up of so-called members (as opposed to owners or shareholders), with each member owning a percentage interest or stake in the company. In small LLCs, the members usually share management responsibilities equally (referred to, conveniently enough, as member management).

The major advantages of an LLC are:

- *Limited liability.* Only the LLC's assets—as opposed to its members' personal assets—can be used to satisfy business debts, including claims or judgments brought against it. That means the most each member can lose is the amount of money invested into the LLC. The shielding power of an LLC is not, however, absolute. Under certain circumstances, such as if a member has deliberately hurt someone or committed a fraudulent act, that member can be held personally liable.

- *No double taxation.* Regular or C corporations and their shareholders are subject to a double tax (both the corporation and the shareholders are taxed) on the increased value of the property when the property is sold. By contrast, LLC owners avoid this double taxation, because the business's tax liabilities are passed straight through to them. The LLC itself does not pay a tax on its income. As Jim Gaudreau, CPA for the accounting firm of Green & Green LLC in Norwood, Massachusetts, explains, "If a C corporation sells a second home, it is required to pay taxes on any profit from that sale. Subsequently, the owners of the corporation would also be required to pay personal capital gains tax on the remaining amount. Whereas with an LLC, the profit on the sale passes through to the owners without having to pay taxes at the corporate level. However, the owners must pay personal capital gains tax."

Forming an LLC can be a time-consuming process. It requires you, for example, to file articles of organization with your state and draft an operating agreement defining the rights and responsibilities of your LLC's members.

INVESTOR

Forming an LLC with your cobuyer may prohibit you from carrying out what's called a "1031 Exchange" (or "like-kind exchange"). This useful tax concept allows owners of investment homes to defer capital gains tax (which can be as high as 28%) when the property is sold, so long as they purchase another investment property of equal or greater value within 180 days. Unfortunately, partnerships (such as LLCs) do not qualify for a like-kind exchange. However, if you and your cobuyer each set up your own LLCs and have the two entities purchase the property as tenants in common, then both of you will qualify for a like-kind exchange. See Chapter 13 to learn more about these exchanges.

In situations where the cobuyers are family (in particular, parent and child or grandparent and grandchild), setting up a family limited liability company (FLLC) may be the best route. An FLLC is a common estate-planning tool, used to transfer wealth (including real estate investments such as a second home) from one generation to the next while minimizing tax consequences.

RESOURCES
Want more information on LLCs? See the free Business & Human Resources articles on Nolo's website at www.nolo.com. In addition, *Nolo's Quick LLC,* by Anthony Mancuso, details the advantages and drawbacks of forming an LLC; and Nolo's *LLC Maker* software will help you do the paperwork. The Company Corporation also offers useful information on how to set up an LLC or corporation in all 50 states. Visit www.corporate.com.

Forming an S Corporation

An S corporation is a good option if you and your cobuyer plan to *flip* the property (resell soon, to make money). That's because the IRS will likely consider you a real estate dealer (someone engaged in the business of selling real estate to customers with the purpose of profiting). As such, you and your co-owner will each owe self-employment tax—currently 15.3%—on your respective shares of the proceeds after you sell. However, by forming an S corporation, you avoid the self-employment tax liability you'd face if you set up an LLC.

The term S corporation comes from the fact that you file under Subchapter S of the Internal Revenue Code. An S corporation consists of shareholders, capped at 100, all of whom must be U.S. residents. Compared with an LLC, management of an S corporation is more formal. For example, you will need to create a board of directors and hold annual meetings of shareholders and directors, and take minutes of the meetings for filing with your corporate records.

The advantages of an S corporation are:

- *Limited liability.* Just as with an LLC, shareholders are shielded against personal liability for business debt, claims, and judgments.
- *No double taxation.* Also like an LLC, an S corporation is a *pass-through* or *flow-through* entity, whose profits and losses are passed through the business and taxed solely to each member at the person's individual tax rate.

- *Shareholders are not subject to self-employment tax.* If you're in the business of selling real estate for profit purposes, you'll have to pay self-employment tax on your share of the proceeds. An S corporation, however, is exempt from self-employment tax.

WARNING

If your rental income exceeds 25% of your S corporation's total income for more than three consecutive years, the IRS can terminate your S status. That means your business entity would be taxed as a C corporation, causing you and your partner to take a double tax—once as a corporation and again as individuals.

Forming an S corporation is more complicated than an LLC. You'll need to create and complete a host of documents and forms—not just articles of incorporation, but bylaws, organizational board resolutions, a stock ledger, and more.

See the chart below for a comparative overview of LLCs and S corporations. Which one makes sense for you and your cobuyer will depend on your reasons for buying a second home in the first place.

POINTS TO REMEMBER

Sharing the purchase of a second home can significantly reduce your debt burden. It might also, depending on the background of your cobuyer, enhance your collective knowledge of home improvement, financing, property management, and other relevant matters. However, you should thoughtfully and carefully decide whether sharing homeownership makes sense for you as well as your potential cobuyer.

Comparing LLCs and S Corporations		
Entity Characteristics	**Limited Liability Company (LLC)**	**S Corporation**
Ownership limitations	Unlimited number of members allowed	Up to 100 shareholders; only one class of stock allowed
Personal liability of the owners	Generally, no personal liability of the members	Generally, no personal liability of the shareholders
Tax treatment	No taxation of the LLC itself (unless it chooses to be taxed); profits and losses are passed through to its members	Profits and losses are passed through to the shareholders
Key documents needed for formation	Articles of incorporation; operating agreement	Articles of incorporation; bylaws; organizational board resolutions; stock certificates; stock ledger; IRS and state S corporation election (if applicable) since not all states require or permit a separate election
Management of the business	The operating agreement sets forth how the business is to be managed; a manager can be designated to manage the business	Board of directors has overall management responsibility; officers have day-to-day responsibility
Capital contributions	The members typically contribute money or services to the LLC and receive an interest in profits and losses	Shareholders typically purchase stock in the corporation, but only one class of stock is allowed

Source: Comparison table provided by The Company Corporation (www.corporate.com).

Being a Landlord:
What You Need to Know

Many people buying a second home end up being landlords. An investor buys in order to rent out the property and generate a steady income stream, all the while striving for long-term appreciation. Other buyers might head towards the rental business, at least on an occasional or short-term basis, because they need the rental income (either from the get-go or at some point down the road) to help cover mortgage and other costs.

The allure of using other people's money to eventually turn a profit or simply help pay off some of your mortgage and other house-related expenses is strong for many landlords-to-be. But if you think renting out your second home involves kicking back and watching the rent checks roll in, think again. When you rent out your house, be it for a few weeks each season or year-round, you're a landlord, plain and simple. As a landlord, you'll need to deal with a host of issues, such as how to choose tenants without violating fair housing laws, and whether to handle every aspect of the rental yourself or use a property management company.

Before you purchase a home you intend to rent out, you'd be wise to learn what's involved with being a rental property owner, and whether it makes sense given your goals for your house, available time, skill set, and comfort levels. (For example, how do you feel about strangers living in your house?) Being a landlord is not for everyone, but for those who have the time and are ready to take on the challenges, the financial benefits can be worthwhile.

FAST TRACK

If you selected one of the boxes under the "Renting out your home does not make sense" column, skip the remainder of this chapter. Those who selected any of the boxes under the other column should keep reading, since it looks like being a landlord is in your future. But don't stick that "For Rent" sign in the window just yet! First, figure out whether you have what it takes to be an effective landlord.

Should You Rent Out Your Second Home?		
Your motive for purchasing a second home is...	Renting out your home makes sense if...	Renting out your home does not make sense if...
Investment	You plan to hold on to your property and use it to generate steady cash flow while achieving long-term appreciation.	You want to make a profit by selling the property within a short period of time ("flip" it).
Vacation	You want to offset expenses when you're not using the place for yourself.	You want free rein to use the place for yourself whenever you want, which probably includes impromptu visits.
Future retirement	You want to offset expenses until you're ready to move into the place permanently (you may or may not use it yourself during the interim).	You want free rein to use the place as a vacation getaway until you move in permanently.

Should You Be a Landlord?

Being a successful landlord involves more than simply looking at dollars and cents—it also takes time, effort, commitment, and patience. (Of course, the dollars need to add up, too—see Chapter 5 for how to run the numbers.) And if you'll be using your property yourself from time to time, you'll need to be comfortable with the idea of strangers in your home and all that entails. Still, it can be an exciting and profitable venture if you're ready to take on the responsibility. How much spare time you have, and what your existing skills are, top the list of important issues to consider. That doesn't mean you'll be working round the clock to manage and maintain your property or that you need to have the skills of a general contractor, but it does mean that you'll need to know what you're getting into.

Do You Have Time to Be a Landlord?

If you work a job with long hours or lots of travel, you need to think about your ability to find and screen tenants, deal with property repairs and maintenance, and handle all the other demands of being a landlord. While offloading some of the work may seem to be the obvious solution, it's amazing how many people don't want to pay for some support, yet really don't want to deal with being a landlord on their own, either.

The physical condition of the property, the demands of your tenants (including the turnover rate), and the type of rental (long-term or vacation) will all affect the time you'll need to spend on renting out your second home. The next variable is whether you plan to handle every aspect of the rental yourself or hire some outside help. While you can hire a property management company to do much of the work, you'll still need to keep on top of them. Plus, you'll need to make sure the added cost still makes it worthwhile to rent out your place. (See the analysis of cash flow in Chapter 5.) In some cases, a property management company can actually pay for itself—particularly if they keep your house packed with rent-paying occupants.

EXAMPLE: Lydia buys a house in Charleston, South Carolina, for future retirement. In the meantime, she rents it out for $800 per month. However, because she works long hours as a math professor, she has trouble finding time to place ads and follow up on tenant inquiries. Her first year, the place sits empty 20% of the time, or 2.4 months. Lydia runs the numbers (in her head of course), and realizes that she's lost $1,920 in rental income over the year. She hires a property management company, which charges her $80 a month (10% of her monthly rental rate, totaling $960 per year) to take care of advertising, tenant screening, and other issues. They're able to cut the annual vacancy rate in half. Now, Lydia can add $960 per year to her rental income, use the savings to cover the cost of the property management company, and spend her free time grading papers or enjoying life.

How a Property Management Company Can Pay for Itself					
	On Your Own			Using a Property Management Company		
	Example A	Example B	Example C	Example A	Example B	Example C
Monthly Rent	$600	$800	$1,000	$600	$800	$1,000
Annual Vacancy Rate	20%	20%	20%	10%	10%	10%
Annual Rental Income	$5,760	$7,680	$9,600	$6,480	$8,640	$10,800
Annual Cost of Property Management Company	$0	$0	$0	$720 ($60 per month)	$960 ($80 per month)	$1,200 ($100 per month)
Your Annual Profit	$5,760	$7,680	$9,600	$5,760	$7,680	$9,600

Do You Have the Skills to Be a Landlord?

Successful landlords are detail oriented and persistent. They timely and accurate provide information to renters, and conscientiously follow through on chores such as checking tenant references and returning deposits. They also have a good head for business, and are able to maximize rental profits by taking advantage of tax deductions or determining the highest amount of rent they can charge without lowering their occupancy rate. The most successful are handy with tools and repairs, too, and can save time and money by handling everything from basic upkeep to extensive repairs.

Is Your Home Appropriate for a Long- or Short-Term Rental?

When it comes to renting out your property, there are two routes you can take. You can rent it out continuously to the same tenant for many months or even years (known as a long-term rental). Or you can rent to a series of tenants for short blocks of time, such as a few days or weeks (these are typically called vacation or short-term rentals). The route you choose depends primarily on the location of your second home—very few tenants will be interested in a two-week rental of a house in a quiet, boring suburb with access to great schools and attractive jobs, but this rental might be just the ticket for a family who wants to stay for a year or more.

Each rental type has financial and practical pros and cons. You'd be smart to appreciate them before buying a home that you know will become a rental—the last thing you want is to get yourself into a business that won't support your costs.

- *Long-term rentals.* These tenancies can be for a set term (typically a year) and are based on a lease that expires at the end of the term. Or, you may prefer a month-to-month arrangement, based on a rental agreement, which continues indefinitely until terminated by the landlord or tenant with proper notice (typically 30 days). Either way, your place becomes someone else's primary home for an extended period of time. The key benefit of this type of rental is the low turnover rate (and lower turnover expenses). Plus, long-term rentals are more resistant to economic downturns than short-term rentals. And with the right tenants, the amount of wear and tear tends to be lower than for short-term rentals, because you don't have different people traipsing through your place every week. However, a major downside is that you won't be able to use your property personally.

REAL-LIFE EXAMPLE: Laura Robins, of Piedmont, California, was looking for a long-term investment that would grow steadily over the next 20 or so years. Rather than traditional investment vehicles such as stocks, bonds, or treasury bills, she decided to purchase a second home in Bellingham, Washington. Laura felt that over the long haul, the appreciation on that home would be a better investment than dumping money into a volatile stock market or low-yielding bonds. She picked Bellingham (a short plane ride away) because she was looking for a housing market that had strong appreciation, but was more affordable than where her primary residence was located. Plus, Laura felt it diversified her portfolio by not having both homes located in the same market. To offset monthly expenses, Laura rents out the property. Currently, the rent covers about 85% of her total monthly expenses (including mortgage payment, property taxes, insurance premium, and property management fees). What's more, maintenance on the house promises to be low, because Laura opted to buy a new build instead of an older home. So far, her strategy seems to be working.

• *Short-term rentals.* These arrangements are also called vacation or seasonal rentals, with many renters using your place for a period of days, weeks, or a few months at a time. Such rentals tend to be located in vacation-oriented areas or major metropolitan markets (people visit cities for vacations or weekend getaways as often as they flock to the mountains or the beaches). The key benefit of a short-term rental is that you can use your place personally while also taking in higher rental rates (at least during the peak season). However, a big downside is that your rental window may be limited, especially if your place is located where the peak rental season is short, such as Cape May, New Jersey, where the high season lasts just three months. That means you'll have the highest demand from renters during the same period that you'll want to use the place.

REAL-LIFE EXAMPLE: Masha and Leo Malkenson of Swampscott, Massachusetts, are not just fond of Cape Cod, they're downright junkies. For the past ten years, they have spent their available time renting various vacation homes in what they describe as their ideal getaway destination. From May through September, virtually once a month, Masha and Leo used to pack up the car and drive south for two hours to enjoy a weekend escape. Finally, this past year, the Malkensons had an epiphany. Since they spend so much time on the Cape, why not buy a place of their own? After several months of looking, they purchased a three-bedroom cottage in Harwich, Massachusetts. Situated in a quiet neighborhood that's a stone's throw from a long, sandy beach, the Malkensons knew they made the right choice. To help offset the added debt burden that comes with owning another house, the Malkensons decided to rent out their property for half the season. This way, they still get to enjoy their Cape Cod home, yet have enough money coming in to pay about a third of their annual mortgage payments.

Long-Term Rentals: What You Need to Know

If you've decided that a long-term rental is for you, you'll be looking for tenants who will be renting for extended periods of time. In many ways, it's like dating. You're trying to find the perfect match and then hold onto him or her indefinitely. And since you probably won't be using your property personally, you can maximize your tax deductions (see Chapter 14 to learn more about tax strategies for landlords).

To get a sense of what landlords of long-term rentals need to deal with, take a quick look at the following discussion. By no means exhaustive, it's meant to give you a flavor of the landlord's role and responsibilities specific to long-term rentals.

Learn About Landlord Law

Before you jump into landlording, educate yourself about the laws (federal, state, and local) that you'll need to comply with. Some of the common landlord laws are listed below (many states, and some localities, are even more specific and restrictive on some issues).

- *Discrimination.* Federal fair housing laws prohibit you from discriminating based on religion, race, gender, age (unless in a designated adult community), family status, or disability. Some states prohibit discrimination based on sexual orientation or marital status as well. You may reject tenants based on business reasons, such as bad credit, inability to put down a deposit, and negative references. You can find more information about fair housing laws by visiting the U.S. Department of Housing and Urban Development's website at www.hud.gov/groups/fairhousing.cfm.

- *Amount charged for rent.* In most states, landlords can charge as much as they want for rent, although in practice you'll need to choose a competitive rent (at or near that charged for comparable rentals in your area). However, some cities in five states (California, the District of Columbia, Maryland, New Jersey, and New York) have rent control or rent stabilization laws that limit how much a landlord can charge. Also, be sure you understand the history of rent increases in the area, to provide a benchmark for how much you'll be able to raise the rent over the years, which will help with your cash flow on the property. (See Chapter 5 for more on this.)

- *Late fees.* Landlords commonly use a late fee policy to encourage on-time payment. But it's a mistake to choose an unreasonable amount (one that is much higher than the real damage you suffer when the rent is late). In some states, late fee amounts are regulated; and in every state, an unreasonable fee may be uncollectible if your tenant refuses to pay and you try to evict based on nonpayment (judges are increasingly leery of fees that exceed your real damages).

- *Security deposit amounts.* The purpose of the security deposit is to give you a cushion in case the tenant takes off owing unpaid rent or leaves your property in disrepair (damage beyond normal wear and tear). In most states, the amount you can charge for a security deposit, as well as when and how you return it to the tenant, is controlled by state laws.

- *How you use a security deposit.* When a tenant vacates the premises, you should return the deposit in full. If you return less, in many states you will need to itemize the costs. A handful of states exempt certain landlords (usually those with small or single properties) from some aspects of the state security deposit law, such as a requirement to pay interest or keep deposits in separate accounts.

- *Repair and maintenance.* In virtually every state, you are required to keep your rental property in a condition that is considered "fit to live." (Colorado and Arkansas don't have a statewide requirement, but many cities within those states have local ordinances that impose substantially the same duties.) That means you can't let the inside or outside fall into disrepair, especially to the point where it poses a safety hazard to your tenants.

- *Maintaining a safe property.* You have a duty to take reasonable steps towards keeping your tenants safe from foreseeable criminal acts. That's not to say that you need to hire security guards to patrol round the clock, but you do need to act responsibly. For example, if you procrastinate in fixing a broken lock on the front door of your property and an intruder uses that easy pathway to enter and assault your tenant, you might be held liable for the tenant injuries.

- *Environmental health hazards.* You may need to address a variety of issues that can affect the health of your tenants. These range from asbestos and lead paint to radon, carbon monoxide, and mold. Generally speaking, once you are aware of a situation that poses a health risk, you have some responsibility to attempt to fix it.

- *Access to premises.* Although you legally own the property, in most states you don't have the right to barge in on a whim, or even for a good reason (such as wanting to check for needed repairs). Rather, you need to provide your tenant with sufficient notice (typically 24 hours', but this varies by state) and have a legally recognizable reason to enter, such as showing the property to a prospective renter or buyer or making a repair.

- *Tenants' privacy.* You may be in violation of your tenants' privacy if you inappropriately reveal information about them, such as their credit or employment histories. Even when you have reason to think that a tenant wants you to share the information—for example, because the tenant is moving away and lists you as a reference—it's wise to insist on written proof (a "release") signed by the tenant, allowing you to answer the queries.

RESOURCES

Want to learn more about landlord law? Pick up a copy of *Every Landlord's Legal Guide*, by Marcia Stewart, Ralph Warner, and Janet Portman (Nolo). This comprehensive 50-state book with CD-ROM provides all the information and forms you need, from move-in to move-out, including rental applications, leases, repair forms, and security deposit itemizations.

Choose Between a Lease or a Rental Agreement

Written rental agreements that are understandable and conform to federal, state, and local laws are powerful tools. They educate both landlords and tenants about their rights and responsibilities, making it less likely that someone will inadvertently or purposely make a mistake. Landlords of long-term rentals may choose one of two types of written agreements:

- *Rental agreement.* This is an agreement that covers a short period of time, most commonly 30 days. The agreement automatically renews at the end of that period unless you or your tenants submit written notice to terminate (in most states, the termination notice period is 30 days). A month-to-month arrangement gives you flexibility to change the terms of the lease (such as increasing the rent) after very short periods of time (usually 30 days). On the down side, these types of agreements usually mean a higher turnover rate for tenants, since they, too, have more flexibility and can give notice that they're leaving, usually with the same notice period that the landlord has.

- *Lease.* This agreement commits you and your tenant to your agreed-upon arrangement for a set period of time, most commonly one year. During that time, you can't change the terms of the lease, unless the lease contains a clause that gives you that right. Also, you can't terminate the lease prior to the expiration date unless the tenant violates a condition of the lease, such as not paying the rent. Tenants must also abide by the one-year lease term (or whatever amount of time you agreed on), which results in fewer turnovers for you.

The rental method that will work for you depends on your analysis of the market. For example, if rents are trending down, it might be good to lock in your rental rate for an extended period with a year's lease. You'll also want to think about your own preferences. If, for example, you have little time to spend on being a landlord, then good, long-term tenants will serve you best. On the other hand, if your property is in an area that sees a lot of turnover, you may have to settle for month-to-month tenants.

Decide on Your Key Rental Terms

Regardless of which type of rental arrangement you choose, you'll need to choose and define key terms, such as the amount of rent and when it's due. Many of these terms are standard, while others are based on your personal preference, such as whether to allow pets. Here are some of the common terms in a comprehensive lease or rental agreement (they're usually presented in clauses or paragraphs).

- *Names of tenants.* In this clause, you list who can live in the rental (the tenants you've approved and their children). You may want to add that guests can stay for a certain period of time without your consent. This clause prohibits your tenants from moving in others whom you haven't approved.

- *Term or length of the tenancy.* You'll want to spell out how long the tenant can stay in your place. A lease will define the beginning and end date, while a rental agreement will stipulate a beginning date along with the number of days' notice required to terminate by either the landlord or the tenant.

- *Pets.* While you can't discriminate against people, it's perfectly legal to be choosy about pets, as long as you understand that you must allow service animals that are needed by disabled persons. That said, if you don't want to allow pets in your house for fear of additional wear and tear, or for any other reason, you can prohibit them in the lease or rental agreement. Your rule can be absolute (no pets, period), or selective, such as allowing only cats or dogs that are under a certain weight.

- *Sublets.* You won't want your tenant to sublet the rental to another tenant, either permanently or temporarily, without your consent. For example, suppose your tenant is three months into a year long lease and suddenly gets transferred to another state. The last thing you want is to have the tenant's friend move in unannounced. This friend may well be a good tenant, but you won't know that until you've done proper tenant screening.

- *Tenants' maintenance responsibilities.* All states require tenants to keep rental property in a reasonable state of cleanliness and repair, but it doesn't hurt to restate this responsibility in the rental document. You can get into specifics if you like, such as requiring maintenance on the hot tub or gardening.

- *Disturbances or violating laws.* It's a good idea to remind your tenants that you won't tolerate activities that unreasonably disturb neighbors, such as all-night parties, loud music, or whatever else may disturb the peace. A thorough clause will also advise tenants that they cannot use your property for criminal activity.

- *Repairs and alterations by tenant.* You want to prevent tenants from doing work to your property that damages it or that you may have to undo when they leave. For example, painting, changing locks, or putting holes in walls should be off-limits without your written consent.

- *Disclosures.* A disclosure clause is an acknowledgment by the tenant that you have provided the necessary state and federal disclosures regarding the premises, such as the presence of lead-based paint.

Establish a Good System for Finding and Screening Tenants

Good tenants can make your life as a landlord a profitable enterprise, but bad tenants can make it a disaster. You must effectively screen tenants so that you end up with only the former.

Here are some ways to find the right tenants:

- *Word-of-mouth from a trusted source.* This is often a reliable way to find good tenants, since the recommendations come from a network of people who you know. Of course, to make sure that you won't end up with your cousin Vinny's rocker-wannabe son who practices his drums at two in the morning, follow up with calls to the son's current landlord and employer.

- *Print advertising.* This is the traditional way of attracting potential tenants. It could be as simple as putting a "For Rent" sign in your window, placing a notice on a bulletin board at your local coffee shop, or placing an ad in your local newspaper. The most successful ads are written with your target market in mind—emphasize the good schools if you have a home in the 'burbs, but if you've got a condo downtown, its proximity to good restaurants, shops, and entertainment should be your hook.

- *Rental websites.* Post your property on websites such as www.craigslist.org (no connection to this author) or www.rent.com. There may also be some local agencies or community services that list available rentals.

Once you've found potential tenants who are interested in your place, you'll want to narrow down your candidates through an effective screening process.

- *Check references.* Call employers, current and past landlords, and personal references to check tenants' income and personal reliability. Questions include: Did they pay their rent on time? How much was their rent at the time? Did they leave their rental in good condition? Were they responsible tenants—did they adhere to the rules of occupancy? How long did they live there?

- *Run a credit check.* With the potential tenant's written consent, you can order a credit report on a prospective tenant. Since going directly to one of the major credit bureaus is not feasible for landlords who own single properties, you can instead use a reseller who will purchase the report on your behalf. For example, www.intelius.com sells credit reports in blocks of ten for $99.95. The report should corroborate the answers you've gotten already (from an interview or rental application) regarding the applicant's job, current address, and past residences. You'll also see whether the person has a credit history, has made timely payments, and whether there are any red flags such as bankruptcy or criminal convictions. If you reject someone based on information in the credit report, you need to give that person specific, written information about the basis of your rejection and the applicant's right to see the report.

You should now have a better idea of what to think about when renting out a property for the long-term. Unless you're interested in comparing this to short-term rentals, you can skip the following section.

RESOURCES
For a thorough guide on screening tenants, see *Every Landlord's Guide to Finding Great Tenants*, by Janet Portman (Nolo). It includes over 40 forms, letters, and checklists, including rejection letters that comply with federal requirements.

Seasonal or Short-Term Rentals: What You Need to Know

If you've decided that a short-term (also called vacation or seasonal) rental is for you, then you're in the market for tenants or "guests" who will stay at your place for short blocks of time, anywhere from a night or two to a week, several weeks, or more. Unlike the landlord of a long-term rental, you're on a constant search for new renters in an effort to maximize your occupancy rate.

Most landlords of short-term rentals also use their places personally, unless they're investors focused on turning a profit while maximizing tax deductions. If you plan on using your home personally, consider how often you want to stay at your place, what time of year you'll use it, and whether you want certain times to be available for friends or extended family.

Reserving certain times for yourself or friends or family can eat into your profits, however. For example, if you own in a resort area, you may want to enjoy the peak season yourself, but the tradeoff is forgoing rents that are often the highest of the year. One month's rent in the high season can often pay off a couple months of your mortgage. How much you are relying on rental monies to contribute to paying for your second home is also part of your decision as to how often to rent and when.

Learn About Laws Affecting Vacation Rentals

In general, landlords of short-term rentals must follow many of the same laws that govern landlords of longer-term rentals. However, there are exceptions that vary on a state-to-state basis. For example, landlords who rent units for less than 100 days need not produce the federally-required lead paint disclosure form. In Massachusetts, landlords with tenancy agreements of less than 100 days can use part of the renter's security deposit to cover basic cleaning costs, whereas landlords with longer-term tenancies can use it only if the tenant leaves the place unreasonably dirty. A few states exempt short-term rentals from their requirement that the landlord place security deposits in interest-bearing accounts, or establish separate accounts for them. One state that has a substantial number of vacation rentals—North Carolina—has passed a law designed particularly for short-term rentals (North Carolina Vacation Rental Act, NC Stat. Sec. 42A-39 and following). Check your state's laws to see how they affect short-term vacation rentals.

You will also be required to keep your rental property in a condition that is considered "fit to live in." That means you can't let the inside or outside fall into disrepair, especially to the point where it poses a safety hazard to your tenants.

Do Antidiscrimination Laws Apply to Short-Term Rentals?

It's not uncommon to see vacation rental ads that rule out children, or guests under a certain age. Owners with homes near the ocean or other bodies of water may be worried that children will wander off and be hurt. Or, a particular house may simply not be suited for children, with inadequately fenced decks, unfenced swimming pools, and steep stairs. These owners are rightfully concerned—but can they *legally* refuse to rent to guests with children?

As far as we can tell, the answer is no. The widespread practice of excluding children from some vacation rentals would probably not pass muster if challenged in court. If you decide that you do not want children in your vacation rental, understand that you're taking a risk—and if challenged by a family of potential renters, you might want to rethink your position (it will be cheaper to fence the pool than pay your lawyer, their lawyer, and the judgment against you).

You may also need to make your short-term vacation rental accessible to disabled persons, just as you would if you were renting it out for a longer period of time. If your rental can't be used by a person in a wheelchair, for example, and it would be a simple matter to install a ramp, a judge may find that fair housing laws require you to do so. If a disabled renter (and his or her lawyer) demand an accommodation like this, be sure to get competent legal help.

Use Written Agreements for Short-Term Rentals

Making a written vacation rental agreement with your renters (even if they are family or friends) is always a good idea. No matter how clear you may think your oral understanding is, you'll invariably end up with problems unless it's written down. Send the agreement to your renters in advance of their arrival (or send it as a PDF attachment to an email and have them mail a signed version back). Here are some of the common terms that the agreement may include:

- *Period of stay.* This lists the date of arrival and the date of departure.

- *Pricing.* Typically, pricing for vacation rentals fluctuates depending on the time of year and the location of the property. For example, a ski cabin in Vail, Colorado, will command higher rates in the winter months during ski season than in the summer when the slopes are naked. Check out competitive rentals at key points throughout the years (spring, summer, winter, and fall) to determine what rates are being charged so you can set yours accordingly. A good rule of thumb is to stay within approximately 10% of your competition. Pricing that is too high will knock you out of the market, unless you can justify the higher rate based on how your place is furnished or extra amenities. Pricing that is too low may make potential guests suspect something is amiss—that it's "too good to be true." Also, be sure you understand the history of rent increases in the area, to provide a benchmark for how much you'll be able to raise the rent over the years, which will help with your cash flow on the property. (See Chapter 5 for more on this.)

- *Advance payment.* Careful landlords of vacation rentals require full payment before they hand over the keys. Some owners divide the rent in half, requiring the first payment 60 to 90 days in advance, and the second 30 days in advance. Whether these time periods will work for you will depend on the nature of your property and the time most tenants stay (it may be unreasonable to require a full three months' rent from tenants who rent for two or three months). The point is, get your money up front.

- *Security deposit.* A security deposit is money you'll return as long as the tenants leave your place in good shape. You can collect it at check-in time, or add it to the rent and require its payment in advance, as explained just above. When the tenant leaves and you're satisfied that the property is in good condition, you'll return the check or cash (or tear up the credit card charge slip without processing it). You need to follow your state's laws on returning deposits, which set time limits and often require you to itemize deductions.

- *Occupancy rules.* Detail any occupancy limitations such as the number of people your place can accommodate, whether pets are allowed, additional charges for extra guests or pets (when allowed), and what kind of cleaning service is provided, if any. Also, you many want to prohibit or restrict large gatherings or parties in your place, say if you're renting out your condo in Fort Lauderdale during Spring Break.

- *Cancellation and refund policy.* Your written agreement should clearly spell out your policy on cancellations and refunds. Contrary to popular belief, you cannot simply keep the full rent if someone cancels, no matter how last-minute or flaky the reason. Instead, you're legally obligated to use reasonable efforts to find replacement tenants. If, despite your efforts, you cannot secure new tenants (sometimes you'll have to drop the price a bit), then you'll be on solid ground keeping the original tenants' rent (and if you've rented for a lower amount, you can keep the difference). If storms, hurricanes, or other intense weather is common in your area, specify how these affect your cancellation policy. Many landlords will recommend that renters purchase trip insurance that will reimburse them for monetary losses due to weather, medical, or other reasons.

- *Furnishings and equipment.* In addition to standard furniture (couches, tables, beds), vacation rentals furnished for normal use have dishes, cookware, flatware, glasses, linens, bath towels, and other items that you should specify in the agreement.

Decide on Your Rental Policies

Whether you're lending your place to people you know, renting to potential strangers, or a combination of the two, you'll want to establish policies that are consistent with how you want other people to use your home. You may want to include these policies in your vacation rental agreement, or you may want to attach a "rental policies" sheet to the agreement (and refer to it). Below is a list of policies to consider. If you have any question whether a particular policy is legal, check your state law.

- *Minimum stays.* Outline the amount of time required for a rental. Owners often set minimums in resort areas; otherwise it isn't worth the landlord's time and resources to turn over the rental.

- *Pets.* You can decide whether to allow pets. Not allowing them can reduce the wear and tear on your place. However, allowing them can mean broadening your pool of potential renters. If you choose, you can put in restrictions, such as "cats only," or "dogs that weigh less than 75 pounds."

- *Smoking or nonsmoking.* It's up to you to decide whether to prohibit smoking in your second home. If you're a nonsmoker and intend to use the home too, the decision will be clear. But if you're not using the home, you'll have to decide which approach will generate the most profit. To do so, consider which policy will attract the most interested renters, but be sure to factor in the money you'll spend in added cleaning and refurbishing if you allow smoking, not to mention the increased risk of fire.

- *Check-in/-out times.* Identify the times for check-in (usually a range, such as "after 4 p.m.") and check-out (usually a set time, such as "by 11 a.m."). Many owners offer an extended check-out (though you may want to charge more for this privilege). Just make sure you leave enough time in between guests for the place to be cleaned.

TIP

Give your guests practical information. No matter how fastidiously you maintain your property, things can go wrong. And even the handiest of renters may have trouble figuring out your appliances. Help your guests by providing instructions for appliances, electronics, and the heating and cooling system—as well as a list of emergency phone numbers for the police, fire department, hospital, and yourself or the property management company in charge. It's also a good idea to include other kinds of useful local information, such as recommended restaurants, places to hike, and grocery stores.

Establish a Good System for Finding and Screening Guests

With a vacation rental, you want to advertise in the area where your vacation home is physically located and in "source" areas, which are the cities and regions where vacationers come from. For example, if you have a place in South Beach, Florida, you'll want to advertise in and around that area, as well as in other geographies, such as New York City that sees its share of residents going to South Beach for some fun in the sun.

To learn the source areas for a particular destination, talk to other vacation home landlords in the area, local real estate agents, and property management companies, as well as local businesses, hotels, and chambers of commerce.

Once you determine which geographies you'll be targeting for your marketing efforts, consider the following ways in which to advertise your vacation property:

- *Word of mouth.* Your social network is often a reliable way to find good guests, especially if they are referred by people who you know and trust. To encourage business, you could offer a discount on your rental to people who refer friends, family, neighbors, or colleagues to you.

- *Print advertising.* The written word is the traditional way of attracting tenants, through the use of "For Rent" signs in your window, a notice on a bulletin board at your local coffee shop, or an ad in the newspaper. With a vacation home, you can think broadly. For example, many major metropolitan papers have ad sections for vacation homes in resort destinations popular with their readers. You can also advertise in local lifestyle magazines such as *Palm Springs Life* or *Hawaii Magazine*.

- *Online options.* The Internet is becoming the standard way for people to plan their vacations. Most online vacation sites allow you to write a detailed description of your property and include photos. These sites normally charge a listing fee, starting at around $99 and going as high as several hundred dollars or more. The fee depends in part on the services you select, such as premium placement of your listing, and how long you want your listing to run. Examples of these sites include: www. vacationrentals.com, www.vrbo.com (vacation rentals by owner), www. cyberrentals.com, and www.vacationhomerentals.com, to name a few. You may also be able to advertise on special-interest websites. For example, if you have a vacation home in Monterey, California, which is a popular scuba diving destination in Northern California, you could advertise on a local scuba diving website such as www.montereyscubadiving.com.

As people reply to your marketing efforts, you'll want to screen them to make sure they're decent people who won't trash your place. If you're working with a property management company, it will handle this for you. If you're managing the whole process on your own, the more time you put into talking with and screening people, the more likely you'll end up with satisfactory renters.

Even though email is efficient for communicating and sending information back and forth, try to speak with your potential guests on the phone at least once. That will give you a better sense of who they are and whether your home will meet their needs—for example, a family with small children may not be keen on a house that is perched on a rocky bluff without a fence. You want to be honest on your side as well, because you want your guest to have a positive experience and speak well of your home to potential customers.

Detailed financial screening is not possible with vacation renters (though you'd be wise to do it with those staying for two to three months). Instead, minimize your financial risk by taking full payment up front. Some owners insist on checks or money orders; others are willing to handle credit card payments. Understand that with credit cards, you'll have to pay the issuing company a fee (usually 2% of the total charge) and your bank may charge a fee as well. However, credit cards are more secure than personal checks, and potential guests may prefer using them. If you process a credit card payment for the reservation deposit, and you receive the authorization code (a confirmation from the credit card company) you know the payments are solid. You may also want to consider using PayPal (www.paypal.com), which is a fast, secure, and cheap alternative to traditional credit card collection. This service acts as an intermediary, allowing your guests to send you money online without your having to process their credit card.

If you accept personal checks, you have to wait to make sure the check clears. That can take, on average, up to ten business days. Of course, this shouldn't be a problem if you insist on full payment 30 to 60 days in advance. However, if the check does bounce, you'll have wasted that time waiting for it to clear. Also, your bank will most likely hit you with a bounced check fee, often as high as $20.

Manage Your Property Without Breaking Your Back or Your Wallet

For most potential landlords, the mere mention of the phrase "property management" prompts the question: Do I handle it on my own or use a property management company? There's no right or wrong answer—what will work for you will depend on your available time, skills, and the profit margin you need from your rental. Also, it's not an all-or-nothing situation. As we'll discuss below, sometimes it makes sense to split the responsibilities between you and the property management company.

No matter who does the work, or whether it's a short- or long-term rental, managing your property will involve advertising, finding and screening tenants, preparing leases or rental agreements and other paperwork, keeping files on applicants as well as tenants, plus managing deposits, payments, and late fees. It also means handling general upkeep of the property and managing repairs and improvements in a timely manner and in accordance with local housing codes. You'll also need to address ongoing tenant issues or complaints.

Just imagining what's involved in property management may seem exhausting, let alone actually doing the work. A property management company will typically charge 6% to 10% of the monthly rental amount for long-term rentals, and upwards of 30% or more for short-term rentals. Plug these numbers into your cash flow formula discussed in Chapter 5 to see how using a property management company affects your financials.

WARNING

Planned-unit developments may have on-site property management. If your property will be part of a planned-unit development, such as a condominium complex or townhouse community, be sure to read the homeowners' association rules carefully. They may require you to use the services of an on-site property management company. On a related note, some associations may restrict your tenants' use of common areas such as fitness centers, pools, or other amenities, which could be problematic for your renters and make your place less desirable.

Do It Yourself Activities

If you have the time, inclination, and skill set, handling property management yourself can save you a boatload of money. Not only will you save on the property management company's fees, but if you're handy with a hammer, you can save a significant amount on general upkeep, repairs, and improvements as well. It's certainly easier to handle this on your own if you live within a few hours' drive or less of your property. That's not to say that you can't do it from afar. For example, if your tenant calls and says the kitchen faucet is leaking, there's no reason why you can't call a local plumber to fix the problem. Simply ask your tenant to let the plumber in and have the plumber bill you. After the work is complete, call your tenant to find out if the problem was satisfactorily dealt with.

TIP

If you don't live near your property, it's a good idea to have someone in the area to act as your eyes and ears. Your pal could be a friend, relative, neighbor, or anyone else you trust. Simply having someone to report back on the condition of your property or be around for simple matters such as giving repair people access to the premises can help you in managing your property from afar.

Hire a Property Management Company

If you decide to use a property management company, start by identifying companies that are known and visible in the area, by viewing ads, doing an online search, or getting referrals from real estate agents, other real estate professionals, or fellow landlords. While you may be able to handle property management from a distance, don't trust a property management company to do so. Part of the reason you're paying them is to have someone in your backyard.

Once you've targeted several prospective companies, it's time to interview the candidates to find one that is reliable, familiar with local rentals, and communicates well. Use the questionnaire below to ferret out the best one.

Property Management Company Interview Questionnaire

Ask potential property management companies the following questions:

❏ How long has your company been around? (Best answer: Ten or more years.)

_____

_____

_____

❏ What is the percentage breakdown of the types of properties (single-family, condo, etc.) your company handles? (At least half should be the same type of property as yours.)

_____

_____

_____

❏ What is the average vacancy rate of all the properties you handle? (Should be less than 20%; ideally, under 10%.)

_____

_____

_____

❏ Are you licensed or affiliated with any trade organizations? (Best answer: Yes, such as with the National Association of Residential Property Managers or the Property Management Association.)

_____

_____

_____

❏ Can you provide me with a list and explanation of all the services you offer? (Best answer: Yes.)

_____

_____

_____

❏ How do you typically communicate (both with the landlord and the renter)? (Should be by phone as well as email to allow for more personal communication.)

_____

_____

_____

❏ How and where will you advertise my property? (Best answer: At the very least, it should be listed in the local newspapers, appear online in rental and other relevant websites, and have a "for rent" sign in the window.)

_____

_____

_____

Property Management Company Interview Questionnaire (cont'd.)

❏ Do you provide documentation of any charges, bids, repairs, etc.? (Best answer: Yes.)

_____

_____

_____

❏ What fees do you charge? (Normal fees range from 5% to 10% for long-term rentals and 30% plus for short-term rentals.)

_____

_____

_____

❏ Can you (the homeowner) terminate the agreement without cause but with reasonable notice? (Best answer: Yes.)

_____

_____

_____

❏ Can you provide at least three names of clients who will serve as references? (Only acceptable answer: Yes.)

_____

_____

_____

Combine Do-It-Yourself Activities With Limited Use of a Management Company

When it comes to managing your property, you don't need to take an all-or-nothing approach. Depending on the company, you may be able to strike a middle ground and share responsibilities. By sharing the work, you can save money on fees, but not have the burden of handling everything on your own.

If a particular company doesn't advertise a collaborative option, there's nothing wrong with simply asking them. If the company is willing to work with you, be sure to clearly identify who does what and how the pricing structure works. For example, your arrangement may involve having you handle every step short of getting the renter in place, such as marketing the property, finding and screening tenants, finalizing the paperwork, and collecting the security deposit. Then, once the renter is in the place, the property management company takes over, dealing with general upkeep, repairs, and improvements, and handling complaints or requests from the tenants.

Protecting Your Home, Your Stuff, and Yourself

As with your primary residence, your mortgage lender will require you to carry insurance to protect your property from damage. Even if this isn't a requirement, it's still a good idea. But protection doesn't end with your home. As a landlord, you'll also want to make certain that you're covered personally, say, if someone slips on a wet walkway and decides to sue you.

Beyond your lender's requirements, the type and amount of insurance coverage you get is a personal choice based on your own comfort zone—that is, how much risk you can stomach. The more risk you're willing to take on—hopefully within the bounds of financial reasonableness—the lower your insurance premium, and vice versa. Below are the various options for insuring rental properties:

Protecting the Structure

Any property that you're going to rent out (long- or short-term) will probably need to have what is called a dwelling policy, rather than a normal homeowners' policy such as you have on your primary home. The difference is that a dwelling policy is tailored towards non-owner occupied homes (meaning you don't live there full time), and take into account the increased risk for damage due to vacancies and multiple renters.

Like a regular homeowners' policy, a dwelling policy covers the house against physical damage that occurs either outside or inside. This damage might come from perils such as fire and lightning, windstorm, hail, smoke, weight of snow, ice and sleet, theft, and vandalism, to name the major ones. Only the living structure is covered, both inside and out, minus any detached garage, shed, or other cottage. These can be added to the policy for an additional fee.

If you purchase a condo or townhouse, you may find that the homeowners' association already takes care of buying insurance for the exterior of the building and other jointly owned areas. This is usually called a blanket or master policy. However, you'll likely need to supplement this with your own insurance to cover the interior (such as the carpeting, built-in cabinets, countertops, drywall, wallpaper, paneling, fixtures, and flooring.) Not all master policies are the same, so be sure to review it to find out exactly what is covered.

Where your property is located can greatly impact the cost of your insurance premium. For one thing, different geographies are subject to different natural risks, such as floods, hurricanes, or earthquakes. A standard policy usually excludes damage from a natural disaster, so if you want protection, you'll need to supplement the policy. In some cases, this supplemental insurance is optional; in other cases it's required, such as when a property is located in a designated flood zone. Be sure to understand whether your new home is exposed to any natural disaster risks for which you should get additional insurance. These types of insurance can be expensive, so you'll need to make your own choice after analyzing the risks.

Protecting Personal Property

For a vacation rental, you'll need to provide furnishings, utensils, and other possessions inside the home for use by guests (and maybe yourself). If you will be using the place personally, you're also likely to leave some personal belongings tucked away in a locked closet. And regardless of what you need to provide, you may want to decorate your house with paintings, craft items, and more. If any of these various belongings were damaged during a storm or fire, or if they were stolen or vandalized, your basic dwelling policy would not cover the losses. (For a complete list of perils covered, it's best to contact your insurance carrier or agent.) But you can add personal property coverage to your dwelling policy, for a fee. (See the chart below for average coverage and premiums.)

If you're renting to long-term tenants, your tenants will have their own personal furnishings and belongings. They would be well advised to get renters' insurance, which they would pay for out of their own pocket. Your policy will not cover guests' property.

Protecting Yourself From Legal and Medical Liability

With tenants living in your property or vacation renters coming and going, you'll want to get liability and medical coverage, in order to protect yourself against paying for any personal injuries that occur on your property involving your tenants or guests, their family and friends, or anyone else, such as the mailman or delivery person. These injuries could be the result of your negligence (such as procrastinating in fixing a loose railing), the negligence of the injured person, or just a simple accident that wasn't anyone's fault. Such coverage pays, at a minimum, for the injured party's medical expenses up to a specified dollar amount, usually $1,000 per occurrence. If the matter goes to court, it would also pay not only for your lawsuit settlements and judgments, but the legal fees to defend against them, up to a specified dollar amount as defined in your policy (see chart below).

Unfortunately, in our society it has become very common to take legal action even for minor injuries. Many "victims" know that it's cheaper for you to settle than to go to court, so they play the odds, hoping for a few thousand dollars regardless of actual liability and responsibility. Most of the time, they win, since even if you fight back and a judge or jury end up deciding in your favor, your legal defense can be costly.

And real accidents can happen, too. Despite your intentions of keeping a safe and well-maintained home, you might overlook something and open yourself up to liability. Was the fence around the pool high enough? Was the latch on the gate to the busy road secure enough? Should you have installed nonslip floor tile in the bathroom? Maybe your actions or inactions will lead to an innocent person's injury, in which case your obligations will be clear— it's just a question of where the compensation money will come from.

Medical and liability coverage is usually added to your dwelling policy as a separate clause. To further reduce your risk, you can also purchase what's known as an "umbrella policy," which provides additional coverage up to a specific dollar amount (typically starting at $1 million) against medical and legal expenses. The premiums for this type of insurance are relatively low compared with the protection you receive.

Protecting Yourself from Loss of Rent

Suppose significant damage occurs to your home from a fire and you discover that you won't be able to rent out the property for six months until the rebuilding is complete. To complicate matters, you need some of the rental income to help pay the mortgage on your place. As long as you add "loss of rent" coverage to your policy, you're protected. This added coverage means that your insurance company will pay you the monthly rent you would have received if your place had been rentable. The amount is capped, say at $25,000, and is determined based on your estimated monthly rent.

Your coverage and premiums will vary greatly based on the type of home you have, where it's located, and the extent of coverage.

Average Insurance Coverage and Premiums		
(Based on a $400,000 single-family house)		
	Average Coverage	Average Premium
Dwelling	$300,000	$375
Personal Property	$50,000	$275
Liability and Medical	$500,000	$200
Loss of Rent	$25,000	$75

POINTS TO REMEMBER
Renting out your property can be a great way to turn a profit or help offset your mortgage and other house-related expenses. However, there's more to it than most people think. In addition to having the time and inclination to be a landlord, you'll need to familiarize yourself with landlord law, decide on your rental policies, and take steps to protect your property and your tenants. How much you do on your own depends on whether using a property management company is worth the cost.

14

Tax-Saving Strategies

L ord Bramwell, a 19th Century English judge, once said, "Like mothers, taxes are often misunderstood, but seldom forgotten." For many second-home owners, this statement rings especially true.

The tax implications of owning a second home can be straightforward or complex, depending on whether you plan to use your home exclusively for personal use, strictly as a rental, or for a combination of the two. Plus, if you switch gears down the road—say, you start off renting out your house year-round, but decide a few years into it that you'd like to use it as a family getaway sometimes—the tax impact may shift. Whether that shift is positive, negative, or has no effect at all depends on your balance between personal and rental usage.

Smart second-home owners give at least some thought to tax implications before purchasing the home. Doing so helps you make educated decisions about the best way to use the home, and even where to buy it. Choosing a location based on tax consequences is particularly smart for vacationers looking to use the home just for themselves, and future retirees who will one day live in their second home year-round.

EXPERT

This chapter will give you enough information to do some constructive advance planning. However, we can't possibly cover all the tax intricacies involved in your ongoing ownership of a second home—we advise consulting with an accountant for that.

Let's begin by shedding some light on the different types of taxes that second-home owners face, then explore ways to lower them. You'll be happy to learn that several tax deductions are available to reduce the burden of second-home ownership. And, though you haven't even bought a home yet, we'll talk about how selling it can affect your taxes.

Types of Taxes Second-Home Owners Pay

For a country that revolted against Britain because we were fed up with taxation, we sure have our share of taxes today. For the potential second-home owner, there are five types of taxes to plan for:

- property tax
- personal income tax (on rental income)
- capital gains tax
- estate tax, and
- sales tax (on vacation rentals).

Some of these taxes will take a bite out of your wallet each year, while others will surface only after you either sell your home or you die.

Property Tax

As a current homeowner, you should be all too familiar with property taxes. But in case you've forgotten, or more likely, have gone into denial, these are taxes charged annually to all homeowners by state and local governments (the city or town in which your property is located). The money derived from these taxes is used to fund schools, libraries, police and fire departments, and other government services.

Property taxes are usually calculated as a percentage of your home's assessed value, as determined by your area's tax assessor. Given all the variables—local bonds and elections and changing property values—it's easy to see why the amount charged for an average house may vary greatly between cities or locales. The fact that your house will be a second home rather than a primary residence will, however, make no difference to your property tax bill.

Sometimes buying a property just over a town's or a state's border can make a difference of thousands of dollars a year, so be sure to compare the property tax rates in neighboring towns. Even if home prices are equivalent, the tax rates may not be. Once you're seriously considering a home, pay a visit to the town hall and pull a history of its tax records.

Also make sure you understand the town's policy about raising property taxes (for example, is there an annual cap?) and whether any changes are pending, such as overrides (allowing the town to increase property taxes beyond the annual cap, usually after approval by voters). The best way to research this is to actually sit down with the town's tax collector and ask for an explanation of how property taxes are calculated and the policy for increases. Another good idea is to check the local newspaper for past articles and letters to the editor related to property taxes (either using an online search or a call directly to the paper). Many towns throughout the United States are struggling with how to pay for community services at increased costs, and property taxes have become an increasingly common source of funding. If property taxes are of concern to the town's residents, it's sure to come out in the local news.

FUTURE RETIREE

If you'll be on a fixed income after retirement, property taxes can severely impact your cost of living. First, make sure you understand and compare the property taxes of any towns or areas in which you're interested. Then, since you'll become a permanent resident at some point in the future, fully analyze every other type of tax you're likely to owe. This should include not just your property taxes, but also your likely state income tax and sales taxes. Finding a U.S. state that charges low taxes across the board, however, is nigh on impossible. If the state doesn't tax your property at high rates, it will probably charge high taxes in another area, such as sales or income.

Personal Income Tax

Anyone who makes money is all too familiar with paying income taxes. As you probably know, your tax rate is based on the amount of money you make each year minus any deductions, as well as your marital and filing status (see the "2006 Federal Tax Rates" chart, below). And income doesn't just mean the salary from your job. If your second home generates income, you may need to pay tax on that income.

Specifically, the money you receive from rent and any other sources associated with renting out your place, such as coin-operated laundry machines, parking spaces, late fees on paying rent, or vending machines, is considered income. You'll need to add it to the personal income that you report at tax time, usually using Form 1040.

There are some exceptions. For example, if you rent out your property for fewer than 15 days each year, you don't have to pay income tax on rental and other income. (See the discussion in "Tax-Free Vacation Homes," below.)

Capital Gains Tax

If, someday, you sell your second home, any profits realized from that sale are considered capital gains, and you'll have to pay the appropriate tax. For example, if you buy a house for $200,000 and you sell it for $300,000, you'll be taxed on your $100,000 profit. Of course, no tax matter is ever quite that simple. Certain home-related expenses, such as home renovations, can be subtracted from your profit and result in your paying a lower capital gains tax.

The rate at which your capital gains will be taxed depends upon whether you earned:

- *short-term capital gains,* meaning you owned your home for 365 days or less. Short-term capital gains are taxed at the same rate as your personal income tax bracket, or
- *long-term capital gains,* meaning you owned your home for more than 365 days. Long-term capital gains are taxed at a rate of 5%, 10%, 15%, 25%, or 28%, depending on which personal income tax bracket you fall under.

Come tax time, capital gains are added to the income section listed on your Form 1040. For information on how you can reduce your taxable profits, see "How Deductions Can Lower Your Taxes," below.

Estate Tax

If you still own your second home when you die, an estate tax of up to 46% (as of 2006) can be levied on the transfer of this property to your beneficiaries. However, whether the estate tax applies to your assets at all depends on your overall worth. The good news is that in its current form, the estate tax affects only the top 2% of Americans—the very wealthiest. Estates valued at up to $2 million per individual are exempt from paying estate tax. This exemption is set to remain at $2 million through 2008 and increase to $3.5 million in 2009. In 2010 the federal estate tax will be completely repealed (disappear). But in 2011, the estate tax will return to the old rates that were in place prior to the repeal, unless Congress takes action to the contrary such as extending the repeal.

Because the estate tax, not to mention the underlying issue of how asset ownerships are structured within estates, is a complex subject that impacts very few people, we won't address it further in this book. Keep in mind, however, that real estate often constitutes the majority of a person's worth. Keep an eye on the appreciation of both your primary and second homes. If the values begin to approach the estate tax exemption limits, consult with an estate planning professional.

Sales Tax

If you plan on using your property as a short-term vacation rental, most states expect you to pay sales taxes on the income—often monthly or quarterly, rather than yearly. Even some cities and counties impose such taxes. These may go by other names, such as lodging, accommodations, hotel, bed, tourist, or transient occupancy taxes. You'll need to check and possibly register with your state's department of revenue and your local government for details.

Look carefully for any exemptions allowing you to wiggle out of this obligation. In many states, for instance, if you're renting the property only once or twice a year, you can avoid paying sales tax.

EXAMPLE: Thor owns a cottage near an apple grove in Spokane, Washington. In that state, anyone who rents out a second home three or more times annually for periods of less than 30 days each time must pay retail sales tax, as well as a lodging tax. Suppose Thor rents out the cottage four times in a given year. The renters stay 14, 10, 30, and 32 days respectively. Under Washington tax law, Thor would not owe sales tax, because only two of those stays were for less than 30 days, so Thor fell below the three-or-more rule. However, if Thor's renters stayed 14, 10, 10, and 32 days respectively, he would owe sales tax.

Free Private Loan Information

"CircleLending handles every aspect of the [private loan] experience from drawing up formal promissory notes to collecting payments each month."

~ Time Magazine

☑ **YES!** I'm considering lending to or borrowing from someone I know for:

☐ Real estate   ☐ Business   ☐ Personal use

Please have a private loan specialist:

☐ Call me for a free phone consultation at (____) ____ - ____

☐ Email me a brochure at _____

☐ Send me a brochure at _____

_____
name

_____
address

_____ _____ _____
city   state   zip

Use CircleLending when you want to lend to or borrow from someone you know for:

- **Mortgage loans**
- **Personal loans**
- **Business loans**

Free Private Loan Guides available at www.circlelending.com

Circle Lending℠

Mark our words…

CircleLending

is the Smart Way to

Manage Loans Between

Relatives and Friends

Call: **1.800.805.2472**

Email: **info@circlelending.com**

Visit: **www.circlelending.com**

There's good news, even if you're stuck paying the tax: You can pass it along to your renters, on top of the regular rent you charge them (you'd be wise to warn them in advance). But the bad news is that the tax is usually just a straight percentage (often 6% to 12% of revenues), and you won't be able to claim any deductions.

How Deductions Can Lower Your Taxes

If, during a given year or over time, you pay expenses that reduce your total, or gross income, these can be claimed as tax deductions. Figuring out gross income is one of the final steps toward calculating how much of your income can be taxed (called your adjusted gross income). A number of home-related expenses qualify as tax deductions. The more tax deductions you have, the less you end up paying in taxes. It's that simple.

Now, that doesn't mean that after buying your home, you should rack up needless expenses in the hopes of getting more tax deductions. What it does mean, however, is that you should leave no stone unturned in identifying and recording your deductions. Missing out on a tax deduction is no different than leaving money on the table.

Before we start examining the various deductions available to you, let's clear up one common misconception: While tax deductions lower your taxable income, they don't save you money dollar for dollar. (If you already consider yourself tax savvy, you can now skip to the next section.) For example, if you've accumulated a total of $5,000 in tax deductions, you won't save $5,000 in taxes. Rather, a tax deduction will lower your gross income, thus shrinking the pie that Uncle Sam can take a bite from. To give you an idea as to how much less you might pay, we need to look at how your tax rate is calculated.

Individuals are taxed, both at the federal and state level, at varying rates referred to as tax brackets. These brackets are based on the size of people's income. There are six federal tax brackets, ranging from a low of 10% to a high of 35%. Your marital status (single, married, or widowed) and how you file (jointly with your spouse or separately, or as the head of your household) also figure in, by impacting the income range that qualifies you for any given tax bracket. (See the "2006 Federal Tax Rates" chart below, or go to www.irs.gov.)

How Your Manner of Holding Title Impacts Your Taxes

Title (legal ownership) of your second home can be held in several ways, each of which can impact the amount of your potential tax deductions and the manner in which you pay taxes.

- **Individual ownership.** The simplest and most common form of holding title is individual ownership by a sole owner (or a married couple filing jointly). In this case, you realize all allowable deductions by including them on your personal tax return. If you've received rental income, you pay taxes on this by adding it to any personal income derived from wages, salary, and other income reported on your tax return.

- **Tenancy in common.** If you split ownership with someone other than your spouse or significant other, you will probably hold title as tenants in common. In this case, you and your co-owner will each realize only a portion of the total allowable deductions, based on your percent of ownership, which can be an equal or unequal interest. Both you and your co-owner would claim your share of allowable deductions on your personal tax returns. If you receive rental income, each of you will pay taxes only on your proportional share, which is added to any personal income derived from wages, salary, and other income reported on your tax return.

- **Ownership through a business entity.** You can also hold title through any of various legal entities, including a partnership, limited partnership, corporation, or limited liability company (LLC). With the exception of C corporations, which pay corporate taxes, these are "pass-through entities", which means the businesses themselves don't pay the taxes. Instead, tax responsibilities are passed through to the partners or shareholders, who factor their shares of allowable deductions into their personal tax returns. Each partner or shareholder claims his or her share of income and expenses on the personal return. If the house produces rental income, a proportional share is added to any personal income you derived from wages, salary, and other income as reported on your tax return.

Each year, the U.S. government accounts for any inflation by raising the income ranges across each tax bracket. The higher your income, the higher your tax bracket. However, you don't pay the percentage associated with your bracket on your entire income—only on the portion of your income that exceeds the previous bracket.

For example, suppose you are single and your adjusted gross income (after deductions) is $73,000 for the year. That puts you in the 25% federal tax bracket. But you don't pay 25% in taxes on the full $73,000. Instead, you pay 10% on the first $7,550 you made, 15% on the next $30,650, and 25% on the final $34,800.

But here's the crucial thing to understand when keeping track of your tax deductions: They're based entirely on your tax bracket (25% in the example above). That means if you had a total of $5,000 in deductions, you'd save $1,250 in taxes (0.25 multiplied against $5,000)—no need to divide it up between the separate brackets, as you do with your income.

2006 Federal Tax Rates				
Tax Bracket	Income for Single Filers	Income for Married Filing Jointly or Qualifying Widow/ Widower	Income for Married Filing Separately	Income for Head of Household
10%	Up to $7,550	Up to $15,100	Up to $7,550	Up to $10,750
15%	$7,551 - $30,650	$15,101 - $61,300	$7,551 - $30,650	$10,751 - $41,050
25%	$30,651 - $74,200	$61,301 - $123,700	$30,651 - $61,850	$41,051 - $106,000
28%	$74,201 - $154,800	$123,701 - $188,450	$61,851 - $94,225	$106,001 - $171,650
33%	$154,801- $336,550	$188,451 - $336,550	$94,226 - $168,275	$171,651 - $336,550
35%	$336,551 or more	$336,551 or more	$168,276 or more	$336,551 or more

On a state level, taxes on personal income can range from 0 to 9% (based on 2006 tax rates across the United States). There are seven states that don't have a personal income tax at all. But before you hightail it to one of these states, check whether it's filling its coffers by charging higher sales and property taxes.

RESOURCES
To find out more about income taxes in individual states: Visit www .taxsites.com/state.html, which contains links to state tax information.

U.S. States With No Personal Income Tax
Seven of the fifty U.S. states don't have a personal income tax, including:

Alaska	Nevada	Texas	Wyoming.
Florida	South Dakota	Washington	

Basic Home-Related Deductions: Mortgage Interest, Points, and Property Taxes

All second-home owners are entitled to the three deductions described below.

- *Mortgage interest.* The interest on your second-home mortgage will probably be one of the largest tax deductions available to you (assuming you don't use the loan money for anything other than to buy, build, or improve your home). All those dollars of interest that you pay to your lender can, as with your current home, be turned into deductions each year. It doesn't matter whether you borrowed from a bank, credit union, other institutional lender, or a friend or family member. The exact amount of interest can be found on the year-end statement from your lender. How exactly you claim the deduction (as a personal deduction, a rental expense, or split between the two) depends on whether or not you rent out the property and to what degree you use it yourself. It's a valuable deduction either way, especially in the early years of owning the home, since most mortgages are frontloaded with interest. For example, in the early years of a mortgage with an amortized schedule (in which you pay the same total amount each month), upwards of 85% of each payment is allocated towards interest. As you pay down your mortgage, the balance will shift to paying more principal, and your potential deduction will become less and less. But on a 30-year amortized mortgage, it takes at least ten years before you begin to see the difference. You can also deduct any late-payment or prepayment penalties that you incur.

> ⚠ **WARNING**
> **In certain situations, your mortgage interest deduction may not be fully deductible.** According to the IRS, if all of the mortgages on your home exceed the fair market value of your home or $1 million ($500,000 if you're married and filing separately from your spouse) or if the equity in your second home is more than $100,000 ($50,000 if you're married and filing separately from your spouse), you may not be able to fully deduct mortgage interest. For details, see page 3 of IRS Publication 936 (*Home Mortgage Interest Deduction*), available at www.irs.gov.

- *Points.* These one-time fees charged by lenders in order to process your loan are considered prepaid interest and are, therefore, tax deductible. (Your interest rate is usually lowered in return for choosing a loan with points.) According to the IRS, "you generally cannot deduct the full amount of points in the year paid." Instead, they are usually deducted over the life of the loan. Of course, as you'd expect with the IRS, certain exceptions exist, allowing you to deduct the full amount in the year paid. For details on these exceptions, see page 5 of IRS Publication 936, *Home Mortgage Interest Deduction*, available at www.irs.gov.

- *Property taxes.* Your state and local tax payments are deductible each year regardless of how you use your home. In the year that you buy your home, the property taxes will most likely be divided between you and the sellers based on the number of days that each of you held ownership. Expect to deduct only your proportional share of property taxes for that particular year.

While every second-home owner can take advantage of the basic tax deductions described above, those who rent out their property may qualify for additional deductions based on the house's depreciation, expenses for repairs, and more. It all depends on whether or not you use your place personally and, if so, to what extent.

Additional Deductions If Your Rent Out Your Property

Broadly speaking, the more you rent out your property and the less you use it personally, the more deductions you can take beyond mortgage interest, points, and property taxes. For some potential landlords, the list of additional deductions can be extensive, while others may find they can't claim anything more than the basic deductions already discussed. In order to figure out which deductions you can take when renting out your property, you must first determine the amount you will use your place personally, if at all.

EXPERT
This is meant to be an overview of tax issues relevant to second-home owners. Your own tax situation may vary from our examples, and could be quite complex depending on how you mix personal usage with renting. Seek the advice of a tax professional before making any tax-related decisions about buying a second home.

How Your Personal Usage Determines Your Tax Category

The chart below shows your four potential tax categories, based on your mix of personal usage and renting. These categories cover a spectrum, ranging from people who never personally use their property to people who never— or almost never—open it up to renters. Each category, and the deductions typically associated with it, is discussed in further detail below the chart.

Tax Categories for Personal and Rental Use		
Tax Category	**Personal Use**	**Rental Use**
Regular rental property	0 days	Any number of days
Vacation home used as rental property	Fewer than 15 days or no more than 10% of the total days rented to others at fair rental value	15 days or more
Tax-free vacation home	15 days or more	Fewer than 15 days
Vacation home used as residence	More than 14 days OR more than 10% of the total days rented to others at fair rental value	15 days or more

Regular Rental Property

A property that you never use yourself, but rent out exclusively to others, is the most advantageous from a tax perspective. If you're an investor looking to generate steady cash flow with no intent of using the home personally, or a future retiree who doesn't plan on using the home until retirement, this is probably the tax category you'll start out in.

In addition to taking deductions for mortgage interest, points (if applicable), and property taxes, "regular rental property" owners can usually write off depreciation, repairs, and other expenses, such as local travel, utilities, and insurance, that result in a gain or loss. These deductions are covered in more detail in "Depreciation, Rental Losses, Repairs, Improvements, and More," below.

Vacation Home Used as a Rental Property

A property that is used largely as a rental, with minimal personal use, is the next most advantageous tax category. If you're an investor or future retiree looking to generate cash flow, but you also intend to use the property personally on a limited basis, this will probably be the category you'll fall into. This category may also apply to you if you're a vacationer who will use your second home only for a limited amount each year (say, because it's on the other side of the country), and you want to rent it out the rest of the time.

If the property is rented out at least 15 days a year and is used by its owner or owner's family for either fewer than 15 days or less than 10% of the number of rental days, then it's considered a "vacation home used as a rental property."

EXAMPLE: John owns a beach house in Sanibel Island, Florida, and spends a two-week vacation there each year. The rest of the year he rents it out (for at least 15 days). John's second home is considered a "vacation home used as a rental property." However, one year, John takes a three-week (21 day) vacation at the beach house. As long as he rents it out for at least 210 days that same year, he still qualifies under this category (21 days being 10% of the 210 rental days). But if he doesn't make the 210-day threshold that year, his tax status changes to either "tax-free vacation home" or "vacation home used as residence," depending on how many days he rents out his place that year.

When figuring out what expenses you can deduct under this tax category, the IRS insists that you report those expenses that are directly related to your rental business separately from all your other expenses of keeping and maintaining the home. These "direct rental expenses," as they are known, can be deducted from your rental income at 100% of their value and are covered in more detail in "Depreciation, Rental Losses, Repairs, Improvements, and More," below.

For all other expenses, such as mortgage interest, property taxes, insurance, repairs and utilities, and depreciation, you'll need to figure the percentage of the total time the house was devoted to rental, as opposed to personal, use.

For example, suppose that one year you rent out your house for 215 days and stay in it personally for 21 days. That meets the standard for "vacation home used as a rental property." To figure how much of its expenses you can deduct, take the total number of days it was used (21 personal days + 215 rental days = 236 days) and divide by the days of rental use. That's 215/236, or 91%. That means you can deduct 91% of those expenses. The other 9% of your mortgage interest and property taxes can be taken as a personal (as opposed to rental) deduction, since they're considered costs associated with your personal residence.

Tax-Free Vacation Home

If just you and your family plan on using your second home most of the time, the IRS will most likely consider it a "tax-free vacation home." Despite the name, this doesn't mean you're exempt from paying any taxes on your home. It simply means the IRS views the property as a true second home (meaning it will be used primarily for personal reasons) as opposed to an investment property in which you're trying to turn a profit. If you're a vacationer or future retiree who plans on using the home primarily for personal use, you'll most likely fall into this tax category.

As the owner of a "tax-free vacation home" you can still rent out your property, but only for up to 14 days a year. The great part is that you don't have to pay any tax on that rental income. It doesn't matter if you earn big bucks from these 14 days' worth of rent—none of it is taxable, period.

Basically, tax-free homes are treated similarly to your current home. You can deduct property taxes and mortgage interest (for mortgages up to $1 million), but you can't take any of the deductions available to landlords, such as for depreciation, repairs, and other expenses like utilities, mileage, insurance, and more.

Vacation Home Used as Residence

This is the least tax-friendly category, and one you might want to change your personal use patterns to avoid. The idea is that you're mostly a personal user, but have your toes pretty deeply into landlord waters, too. If you're a vacationer or future retiree who plans on using your home a lot personally but you're also looking to generate significant rental income to offset expenses, you may fall into this tax category.

The IRS defines "vacation home used as residence" as a property that is rented out for at least 15 days and is used personally for more than 14 days, or more than 10% of the total rental days, a year. The rules for tax deductions here are particularly complicated, and designed to make sure you don't try deducting more rental expenses than is fair given your heavy personal use of the property.

For starters, you'll be able to deduct your home's expenses only to the extent of your rental income. Your "direct rental expenses" (see "Depreciation, Rental Losses, Repairs, Improvements, and More", below) can be deducted at 100%. For all other expenses, you'll need to figure out the percentage of use that was for renting, and then deduct only that percentage of those expenses. While any unused deductions can be carried over to future years, many people in this category find they're rarely able to realize those deductions, because each year they continue to hit their rental limits. That means the carryover portion just builds up.

The strictest limitation is that the IRS requires you to take the deductions in specific order, with mortgage interest and taxes coming off the income total first, followed by direct rental expenses, then other expenses such as repairs and utilities, and finally (if there is any income left to offset), depreciation. In theory, mortgage interest, property taxes, and any direct rental expenses are fully deductible regardless of income. However, this is hardly helpful in situations where there's not much income to offset, given the fact that these deductions must be taken before any of the operating expenses.

EXAMPLE: Lisa has a second home on Lake Champlain, in Vermont. She uses the home for 21 days during the year and rents it out for 60 days, for which she receives $6,000. Since the house was used a total of 81 days (21 personal days + 60 rental days), Lisa can deduct 100% of her direct expenses and 74% (60 rental days divided by 81 total days) of her remaining expenses. However, she must deduct them in the order indicated above, and only up to the amount of her rental income, then carry over any unused deduction to future years. The remaining 26% of her mortgage interest, points (if any), and property taxes can be used as personal itemized deductions.

Depreciation, Rental Losses, Repairs, Improvements, and More

FAST TRACK
If you fall into the category of "tax-free vacation home" you can skip this entire section. The deductions described below won't apply to you.

To help you understand the key deductions available to you when renting out your property, we've divided them into:

- depreciation
- rental losses
- repairs and improvements, and
- other expenses.

RESOURCES
Looking for in-depth information on tax deductions for landlords? See Nolo's *Every Landlord's Tax Deduction Guide*, by Stephen Fishman, which contains comprehensive, plain-English information on tax-saving strategies.

Depreciation

The idea behind depreciation is that assets, such as a car, equipment, or a house (the structure only, not the land) will lose value over time. At some point, these assets will, in theory, be reduced to dust. That means the cost of purchasing a property is part of the expense of the business, and should be deductible. The government has determined, quite arbitrarily, that the life span of a house is 27.5 years. Each year, you can take a depreciation deduction that's a portion of the purchase price of the home, plus transaction fees and minus the cost of the land.

By depreciating the structure and any improvements you make to it each year, you can lower your taxes. The catch is that when you eventually sell the property, you'll have to pay all that depreciation back (since it's obvious that the house didn't turn to dust after all). Currently, the federal government assesses a 25% tax rate against your excess depreciation, regardless of the tax bracket(s) you were in during the years the property was being depreciated. So if you're in a lower tax bracket when you sell, the depreciation may have saved you only 15 cents on the dollar in taxes, but you'll have to pay 25 cents on every dollar back to the government. (Of course, if you're in the 28% tax bracket, you'll come out ahead.)

EXAMPLE: Liam bought an investment property five years ago for $195,000. During that time, he depreciated a total of $43,000. He sells the place for $300,000 and his accountant determines that Liam has made of profit of $75,000. Liam would be taxed at the 25% rate on $43,000 of the $75,000, which accounts for the depreciation, while he would be taxed at the long-term capital gains rate (we'll say 28%, for the sake of argument) on the remaining $32,000.

If you're tempted to just avoid all this trouble, realize that depreciation is not an optional deduction, but is required by the IRS. If you don't take it, the IRS will impute the depreciation you should have taken when you sell. In other words, they'll pretend you took it and make you pay it back regardless, thus increasing your tax burden.

Depreciation is often one of the largest deductions for a landlord. It can mean the difference between showing a profit or a loss on a property, even when that property is increasing in value. From a tax perspective, showing a loss (at least on paper) is a good thing, since it lowers the amount of taxes you must pay. However, not everyone who rents out their property can deduct that loss.

FAST TRACK
If you fall under the "vacation used a residence" tax category, skip this section. You can't claim this deduction.

A rental loss occurs when your expenses exceed the amount of rent received. Up until about 20 years ago, you could simply deduct a rental loss from your other income such as your salary or non-real estate investment income. But the wealthy abused this deduction and, in 1986, Congress enacted the so-called passive activity loss rule. This rule severely limits people's ability to use real estate losses to offset other income, by characterizing rental losses as "passive losses," which can only be deducted against "passive income."

What's passive income? It includes income from this or other rental properties or businesses in which you don't materially participate. Your salary or other wages are considered to be "active income," and you can't deduct your rental losses against it. Your non-real estate investment income received from dividends, interest, gains on the sale of stock, and the like, falls into another category referred to as "portfolio" income, and you can't deduct your rental losses against it, either.

Fortunately for beginning investors like you, there's an exception available: the so-called $25,000 offset. If your deductions total more than your total rental income—which is likely to be the case—you may deduct up to $25,000 against your other sources of income, such as wages or a salary from your employer. To take advantage of this offset, you must meet the following criteria:

- *Your modified adjusted gross income (MAGI) must be under $150,000 a year.* Currently, you get the full amount of the $25,000 exception if your MAGI (all of your income for the year minus certain expenses) is less than $100,000. You get an increasingly smaller proportion of the deduction as your MAGI incomes moves up toward $150,000, at which point the deduction phases out altogether.

- *You must be actively involved in your real estate business.* Landlords who are driven to earn rental profits while being actively and regularly involved in running the business—either directly or by managing others—are considered business owners and can therefore deduct rental losses. Examples of actively and regularly running a business may include advertising and marketing your rental property, finding and screening tenants, dealing with tenant complaints, and handling or overseeing repairs and upkeep. It's not necessary for you to do everything yourself. If you're managing others, such as real estate agents or property managers, who help you rent out and maintain your property, the IRS may still consider you to be a business owner. A good rule of thumb is that the more tasks you do (or manage), and the more time you spend on those tasks, the more likely the IRS is to consider you a business owner. Be sure to keep accurate records of what you do and when, just in case the IRS audits you.

- *You must own at least a 10% interest in the property.* Your percentage interest is determined by the value of your property. For example, if the property is valued at $200,000, you must own at least $20,000 worth. If you're married, your spouse's ownership interest can be added to yours with the total being at least 10%.

TIP

Spending 750 hours a year or more handling your real estate business? You may fit the IRS definition of a real estate professional. In that case, you aren't limited by the $25,000 offset, but can deduct all of your rental losses against your other income. Due to the complexity of this exemption, however, it will not be addressed in this book. It probably doesn't apply to most readers: Again, you'd have to work at least 750 hours a year at being a landlord or in any other real-estate-oriented business or profession such as real estate agent, mortgage broker, or property manager.

Repairs and Improvements

You say *tomato* and I say *tomahto*. You say *repair* and I say *improvement*. Why should your word choice matter when, in the end, it's all about fixing up your house? Because the IRS says it matters, and makes repairs a lot easier to deduct than improvements.

The IRS views the distinction between repairs and improvements, and their tax implications, as follows:

- *Repairs.* This is work that keeps your property in good condition but doesn't add value or substantially extend its life. Repairs might include painting the interior or exterior, fixing a leaky faucet, or replacing a broken window. Such work returns the property to more or less its original condition. As a landlord, you can fully deduct the cost of repairs each year as a rental expense (unless they were done as part of a larger improvement project, as described below). However, if you are using the property partly for personal use, you can deduct only those expenses related to rental use of the property. Also, if you're doing the repair work yourself, you can deduct only your out-of-pocket expenses, not your time spent on labor.

- *Improvements.* This is work that adds to the value of your property, prolongs its useful life, or adapts it to new uses. It includes such work as adding a new deck, replacing the heating system, or putting on a new roof. As a landlord, you can deduct this type of work, but only in yearly increments over a long period of time (currently 27.5 years) instead of all at once within the same year. Sound familiar? Yes, the concept of depreciation must be factored in when deducting the cost of improvements. As with repairs, if you're doing the work yourself, you can deduct only your out-of-pocket expenses, and not your time spent on labor. By the way, land improvements such as fences and driveways are depreciated over 15 years.

As you can see, there's a fine line between what's considered a repair and what's considered an improvement. To help you determine which is which, try to answer the following question: "Will this particular work bring the property back to the state it was in prior to the work being done?" If you can answer "Yes," then the work is most likely a repair. But as an added check, answer the following question: "Did the work make the property better than it was before and/or did it add to the property's value?" If you answer "No," then the work is still most likely a repair. But if you answer "Yes," that work may in fact be an improvement.

EXAMPLE: Sean has a rental house that has a leaky roof. He pays a contractor $1,200 to fix it. That's considered a repair, because the work brings the property back to its original state without adding value. Sean can fully deduct the $1,200 during the year in which he paid it out. But what if Sean decides his property will be better off in the long run if he pays the contractor $8,500 to tear off the old roof and put on a new one? This would be considered an improvement, because the work makes the property better than it was before and adds to its value. The IRS will allow Sean to depreciate the $8,500, by deducting roughly $309 each year for the next 27.5 years.

Use the list below to help you distinguish between a repair and an improvement. The more work you do that's classifiable as a repair rather than an improvement, the more you'll be able to deduct in a given year.

Repairs Versus Improvements	
Repairs	**Improvements**
Interior painting	Adding new rooms (bedroom, bathroom, etc.)
Exterior painting	Adding a garage
Fixing gutters	Adding a porch, deck, patio, or fence
Fixing damaged floors	Landscaping
Fixing leaks	Installing a fence or retaining wall
Patching plaster/drywall	Installing a swimming pool
Replacing broken windows	New roof
Replacing cedar shingles/clapboard	Wall-to-wall carpeting
Patching stucco exteriors	New flooring
Patching damaged roof	Wiring upgrades
	Adding built-in appliances
	Installing a new furnace
	Adding insulation
	Installing security system
	Central air conditioning

TIP

Keep accurate records of all the work done on your house, making sure to distinguish between repair and improvement costs. This includes keeping a list of when and how much you've spent in a given year. Be sure to keep copies of all receipts in case the IRS asks you for proof of your expenditures.

Other Expenses

Now we get to the day-to-day, miscellaneous expenses associated with maintaining your rental and running your landlord business. Many, but not necessarily all, of them are deductible. The IRS says you can deduct expenses that are:

- "ordinary and necessary" (usually interpreted to mean common and appropriate for your business)
- current
- directly related to the rental activity, and
- reasonable.

As you can see, these definitions leave some room for interpretation. Refer to "Commonly Recognized Expenses for Landlords," below, for a practical list. While by no means exhaustive, this list gives you an idea of the breadth of deductions available.

If you plan on doing work around the property yourself, you cannot deduct the cost of your own labor, although you can deduct the cost of the supplies as indicated in the table above. Also, you can deduct labor if you pay for it—either to an independent contractor or an employee. You can also have family members do some of the work, and deduct what you pay them, as long as it is a reasonable amount.

Commonly Recognized Expenses for Landlords

The IRS has, in the past, allowed landlords to take deductions for:

- advertising
- car mileage
- casualty losses (from thefts, fires, and other such damage)
- cleaning
- commissions paid to rental brokers
- educational expenses related to running rental property
- insurance
- interest (paid on credit cards for property-related expenses)
- landscaping
- legal and professional fees, including accounting
- licenses and fees required by local governments
- management company fees
- meals and entertainment (subject to strict IRS guidelines)
- membership fees in landlord associations
- office expenses, including rent, software, postage, and other supplies
- subscriptions and publications (including this book!) related to owning and renting property
- supplies for cleaning and refurbishing the property, and
- utilities.

Summary of Deductions for Different Tax Categories	
If you own a:	**You can usually deduct:**
Regular rental property	• mortgage interest • points • property taxes • depreciation • real estate losses (provided you meet certain criteria) • repairs, and • other expenses (such as local travel, utilities, and insurance).
Tax-free vacation home	• mortgage interest • points, and • property taxes.
Vacation home used as residence	• mortgage interest • points • property taxes • direct rental expenses (against rental income only) • repairs (against rental income only) • other expenses (against rental income only), and • depreciation (against rental income only).
Vacation home used as rental property	• mortgage interest • points • property taxes • depreciation (for the rental portion only) • rental losses (with limitations) • repairs (for the rental portion only) • other expenses (for the rental portion only), and • direct expenses (related to your rental business and usually a subset of other expenses).

How to Minimize Capital Gains Taxes If You Sell

Even if you think you'll never sell, it's worth knowing how to position yourself to avoid capital gains taxes upon sale. By strategizing appropriately, you can defer paying, or save, tens of thousands of tax dollars. The most valuable IRS rules to know about are the:

• $250,000/$500,000 capital gains tax exclusion for primary residences

• like-kind exchange for investment properties, and

• reduction in gains for the costs of capital improvements to your property.

Primary Residence Tax Exclusion

Thanks to the 1997 Taxpayer Relief Act, you can, if you've converted your second home to your primary residence before selling it, exclude up to $250,000 of profit—meaning you get that money tax-free. The exclusion turns to $500,000 if you're married and filing jointly. And if you co-own the house with someone other than a spouse, each of you can, if you separately meet the other criteria described below, take the $250,000 exclusion.

To qualify for the exclusion, you must live in the property for at least two years out of the five years prior to the sale. Those two years don't need to be consecutive—you could live in the house as your main home for a year, then move out for up to three years, and move back for another year, and still take advantage of the exclusion. Also, the required years are reduced to one out of five if you enter a nursing home.

The IRS will look at various pieces of evidence, such as the address shown on your driver's license, utility bills, voter registration, and the like to verify your usage. So if you're expecting to use this exclusion, make sure you understand the rules and can document your periods of living in the house.

Also, if you took depreciation on your house as a landlord, you may end up owing taxes on the recaptured depreciation losses. Since you are now treating the home as a primary residence, depreciation does not apply. Be sure to review your options with your tax advisor.

RESOURCES

Ready to learn more about capital gains taxes upon selling your home? See IRS Publication 523, *Selling Your Home*, available at www.irs.gov.

Reduction in Gains for Capital Improvement Costs

If you're not renting out your property, you can't depreciate any improvements you make to it. You can, however, use these improvements to lower your capital gains tax on the sale of your house. The amount you spend on improvements gets subtracted directly from your profits.

EXAMPLE: Xavier sells his vacation home in Savannah, Georgia, for $225,000. During the time he owned the home, he spent $12,000 to renovate the bathroom and upgrade the kitchen. After paying off the mortgage and covering real estate commissions and other selling expenses, Xavier ends up with $60,000 in profit. Fortunately, he saved proof of his improvement expenses. At tax time, Xavier can subtract the $12,000 he spent from the $60,000 profit, leaving $48,000 upon which he owes capital gains. This saves him a few thousand dollars in taxes.

Make sure you keep accurate records and have all receipts for any improvements made to your home. If you do the improvements yourself, you won't be able to include your labor, but you can still factor in materials used.

Like-Kind Exchanges

If you rent out your second home and it doesn't become your main residence, you can take advantage of another IRS rule that allows investment property owners to put off paying capital gains taxes (and recaptured depreciation) by "exchanging" it for another property of the same or higher value. Known variously as a "like-kind," "Starker," or "1031" exchange, this has become wildly popular with real estate investors. It allows them to acquire increasingly valuable assets with pretax money.

The word "exchange" is a bit misleading, since you aren't really swapping your property for the new one you acquire. Instead, you are rolling over the equity in your property into the new purchase.

The words "like kind" need some defining, too. As long as you're buying for investment purposes, you'll probably be on safe ground. For example, you could sell a duplex, multifamily home, or commercial building, and reinvest into raw land or a resort home. However, you can't make the exchange with a property owned by a relative. Consult a professional if you're considering this.

REAL-LIFE EXAMPLE: Ellie Herrmann sold her share of the family home in Cohasset, Massachusetts, where she grew up. Her family had been renting it out for over 20 years. Ellie wanted to continue investing the money, and explored many different options. Deciding that land in the Northwest had potential for appreciation, she purchased five acres of partially developed land (with an infrastructure of septic system, water pipes, and electricity) in a budding residential area near Portland, Oregon. She hopes to sell it for a profit in several years This exchange meets the rules of a like-kind exchange. Eventually, she'll sell the land to someone who wants to have a house custom built.

There are strict time limits on such exchanges: You must identify the new property within 45 days of selling your current property, and you must complete the new purchase within 180 days. You also need to use the services of a "qualified intermediary" (usually an escrow or title company) to complete the transaction.

The process of selling and buying "exchange" properties is, in most ways, similar to the regular real estate process. You look for properties the same way, use a real estate agent, pay commissions upon sale, and pay closing costs upon purchase. The involved parties may not even realize you're doing an exchange. It's really only important to you, your tax advisors, and the IRS.

The steps for an exchange are as follows:

1. Upon sale of your current investment property, you have 45 days to identify the replacement property. The IRS allows you to identify up to three potential properties. The replacement property does not have to be a single property of equal value. You could decide to buy two properties of lesser value that add up to your reinvestment amount.

2. You must reinvest the full amount (equity) received from your sale. Closing costs and expenses can be included in calculating the investment amounts. If you don't reinvest the full amount, you'll be taxed on the prorated amount not included in the exchange. (Your tax advisor can tell you more.)

3. You have 180 days within which to close on the new property.

The like-kind exchange can be a wonderful tool not just for avid investors, but also for people exploring different communities in which to spend time. You can spend a couple of weeks in your rental property without affecting its investment status. Perhaps you and your spouse are debating which leisure activities are most important to you. You might start by buying a second home on a lake in South Carolina, but decide that snow sports are more fun than water sports. You can sell the property that you'd been renting out in South Carolina and purchase a second home in a ski town in Utah, all without paying capital gains. Be sure to begin renting the new property right away so that it meets the rules of investment properties. And if you eventually find the perfect place, you can use it for more personal time than rental, or even retire there.

Combining the Primary-Residence Exemption With a Like-Kind Exchange

Some investors have sold their rental properties and exchanged them for a property they'd eventually like to live in themselves. After obtaining the property, they rent it out for a period of time and then move in. (They're careful to gather and save documentation proving their rental-versus-residence time periods.) As long as they continue to hold the property for five years, and live in it for at least two, they can claim the $250,000/$500,000 homeowners' capital gain exclusion. They'll still have to repay the depreciation deductions taken over the years on both properties, but a savvy investor can nevertheless reap significant tax-free profits this way.

When considering this option, check the rules carefully. The IRS prohibits 1031 exchanges on personal use property. And the conversion of 1031 exchange properties into primary residences is a gray area. Some experts suggest renting the property for three years before turning it into a primary residence. It's best to consult with legal and tax professionals regarding your plans.

POINTS TO REMEMBER

A certain amount of property-related taxes can't be avoided, though they can be planned and budgeted for. If you're a prospective landlord, realize that the taxes you pay on your second home are ultimately decided by the degree to which you rent it out, balanced against how much you use it personally. And don't forget to keep your eye on the possibility of some day selling your home, so that you can strategize ways to avoid paying capital gains taxes.

Appendix A – How to Use the CD-ROM

The tear-out forms in Appendix B are included on a CD-ROM in the back of the book. This CD-ROM, which can be used with Windows computers, installs files that you use with software programs that are already installed on your computer. It is not a stand-alone software program. Please read this Appendix and the README.TXT file included on the CD-ROM for instructions on using the Forms CD.

Note to Mac users: This CD-ROM and its files should also work on Macintosh computers. Please note, however, that Nolo cannot provide technical support for non-Windows users.

How to View the README File

If you do not know how to view the file README.TXT, insert the Forms CD-ROM into your computer's CD-ROM drive and follow these instructions:

- **Windows 98, 2000, Me, and XP:** (1) On your PC's desktop, double click the My Computer icon; (2) double click the icon for the CD-ROM drive into which the Forms CD-ROM was inserted; (3) double click the file README.TXT.

- **Macintosh:** (1) On your Mac desktop, double click the icon for the CD-ROM that you inserted; (2) double click on the file README.TXT.

While the README file is open, print it out by using the Print command in the File menu.

Two different kinds of forms are contained on the CD-ROM:

- Word processing (RTF) forms that you can open, complete, print, and save with your word processing program (see "Using the Word Processing Files to Create Documents", below), and

- PDF forms that can be viewed only with Adobe Acrobat Reader 4.0 or higher (see "Using PDF Forms," below). One of these forms has "fill-in" text fields and can be completed using your computer. You will not, however, be able to save the completed forms with the filled-in data. PDF forms without fill-in text fields must be printed out and filled in by hand or with a typewriter.

A list of forms, their file names, and file formats is included at the end of this appendix.

Installing the Form Files Onto Your Computer

Before you can do anything with the files on the CD-ROM, you need to install them onto your hard disk. In accordance with U.S. copyright laws, remember that copies of the CD-ROM and its files are for your personal use only.

Insert the Forms CD and do the following:

Windows 98, 2000, Me, and XP Users

Follow the instructions that appear on the screen. (If nothing happens when you insert the Forms CD-ROM, then (1) double click the My Computer icon; (2) double click the icon for the CD-ROM drive into which the Forms CD-ROM was inserted; and (3) double click the file WELCOME.EXE.)

By default, all the files are installed to the \Second Home Forms folder in the \Program Files folder of your computer. A folder called "Second Home Forms" is added to the "Programs" folder of the Start menu.

Macintosh Users

Step 1: If the "Second Home CD" window is not open, open it by double clicking the "Second Home CD" icon.

Step 2: Select the "Second Home Forms" folder icon.

Step 3: Drag and drop the folder icon onto the icon of your hard disk.

Using the Word Processing Files to Create Documents

This section concerns the files for forms that can be opened and edited with your word processing program.

All word processing forms come in rich text format. These files have the extension ".RTF." For example, the form for the Fixer-Upper Cost-Tracking Form discussed in Chapter 7 is on the file FixUpForm.rtf. All forms, their file names, and file formats are listed at the end of this appendix.

RTF files can be read by most recent word processing programs including all versions of MS Word for Windows and Macintosh, WordPad for Windows, and recent versions of WordPerfect for Windows and Macintosh.

To use a form from the CD to create your documents you must: (1) open a file in your word processor or text editor; (2) edit the form by filling in the required information; (3) print it out; and (4) rename and save your revised file.

The following are general instructions. However, each word processor uses different commands to open, format, save, and print documents. Please read your word processor's manual for specific instructions on performing these tasks.

Do not call Nolo's technical support if you have questions on how to use your word processor.

Step 1: Opening a File

There are three ways to open the word processing files included on the CD-ROM after you have installed them onto your computer.

- Windows users can open a file by selecting its shortcut as follows: (1) Click the Windows Start button; (2) open the Programs folder; (3) open the Second Home Forms folder; (4) open the RTF subfolder; and (5) click on the shortcut to the form you want to work with.

- Both Windows and Macintosh users can open a file directly by double clicking on it. Use My Computer or Windows Explorer (Windows 98, 2000, Me, or XP) or the Finder (Macintosh) to go to the folder you installed or copied the CD-ROM's files to. Then, double click on the specific file you want to open.

- You can also open a file from within your word processor. To do this, you must first start your word processor. Then, go to the File menu and choose the Open command. This opens a dialog box where you will tell the program the type of file you want to open (*.RTF), and the location and name of the file. (You will need to navigate through the directory tree to get to the folder on your hard disk where the CD's files have been installed.) If these directions are unclear you will need to look through the manual for your word processing program—Nolo's technical support department will not be able to help you with the use of your word processing program.

Where Are the Files Installed?

Windows Users
- RTF files are installed by default to a folder named \Second Home Forms\RTF in the \Program Files folder of your computer.

Macintosh Users
- RTF files are located in the "RTF" folder within the "Second Home Forms" folder.

Step 2: Editing Your Document

Fill in the appropriate information according to the instructions and samples in the book. Underlines are used to indicate where you need to enter your information, frequently followed by instructions in brackets. Be sure to delete the underlines and instructions from your edited document. You will also want to make sure that any signature lines in your completed documents appear on a page with at least some text from the document itself. If you do not know how to use your word processor to edit a document, you will need to look through the manual for your word processing program—Nolo's technical support department will *not* be able to help you with the use of your word processing program.

Editing Forms That Have Optional or Alternative Text

Some of the forms have optional or alternate text:

- With optional text, you choose whether to include or exclude the given text.
- With alternative text, you select one alternative to include and exclude the other alternatives.

When editing these forms, we suggest you do the following:

Optional text

If you **don't want** to include optional text, just delete it from your document.

If you **do want** to include optional text, just leave it in your document.

In either case, delete the italicized instructions.

Alternative text

First delete all the alternatives that you do not want to include, then delete the italicized instructions.

Step 3: Printing Out the Document

Use your word processor's or text editor's Print command to print out your document. If you do not know how to use your word processor to print a document, you will need to look through the manual for your word processing program—Nolo's technical support department will *not* be able to help you with the use of your word processing program.

Step 4: Saving Your Document

After filling in the form, use the Save As command to save and rename the file. Because all the files are "read-only," you will not be able to use the Save command. This is for your protection. *If you save the file without renaming it, the underlines that indicate where you need to enter your information will be lost, and you will not be able to create a new document with this file without recopying the original file from the CD-ROM.*

If you do not know how to use your word processor to save a document, you will need to look through the manual for your word processing program—Nolo's technical support department will *not* be able to help you with the use of your word processing program.

Using PDF Forms

Electronic copies of useful forms are included on the CD-ROM in Adobe Acrobat PDF format. You must have the Adobe Reader installed on your computer to use these forms. Adobe Reader is available for all types of Windows and Macintosh systems. If you don't already have this software, you can download it for free at www.adobe.com.

All forms, their file names, and file formats are listed at the end of this appendix.

The HUD-1 Settlement Statement has fill-in text fields. To create your document using this file, you must: (1) open a file; (2) fill in the text fields using either your mouse or the tab key on your keyboard to navigate from field to field; and (3) print it out.

Note: You will *not* be able to save the HUD-1 Settlement Statement form, but you can still print out completed versions of this form. This form file was created by the U.S. Department of Housing and Urban Development, not by Nolo.

Forms without fill-in text fields cannot be filled out using your computer. To create your document using these files, you must: (1) open the file; (2) print it out; and (3) complete it by hand or typewriter.

Step 1: Opening a Form

PDF files, like the word processing files, can be opened one of three ways.

• Windows users can open a file by selecting its shortcut as follows: (1) Click the Windows Start button; (2) open the Programs folder; (3) open the Second Home Forms folder; (4) open the PDF folder; and (5) click on the shortcut to the form you want to work with.

- Both Windows and Macintosh users can open a file directly by double clicking on it. Use My Computer or Windows Explorer (Windows 98, 2000, Me, or XP) or the Finder (Macintosh) to go to the folder you created and copied the CD-ROM's files to. Then, double click on the specific file you want to open.

- You can also open a PDF file from within Adobe Reader. To do this, you must first start Reader. Then, go to the File menu and choose the Open command. This opens a dialog box where you will tell the program the location and name of the file. (You will need to navigate through the directory tree to get to the folder on your hard disk where the CD's files have been installed.) If these directions are unclear you will need to look through Adobe Reader's help—Nolo's technical support department will not be able to help you with the use of Adobe Reader.

Where Are the PDF Files Installed?

- Windows Users: PDF files are installed by default to a folder named \ Second Home Forms\PDF in the \Program Files folder of your computer.

- Macintosh Users: PDF files are located in the "PDF" folder within the "Second Home Forms" folder.

Step 2: Filling in a Form

Use your mouse or the Tab key on your keyboard to navigate from field to field within these forms. Be sure to have all the information you will need to complete a form on hand, because you will not be able to save a copy of the filled-in form to disk. You can, however, print out a completed version.

Note: This step is only applicable to forms that have been created with fill-in text fields. Forms without fill-in fields must be completed by hand or typewriter after you have printed them out.

Step 3: Printing a Form

Choose Print from the Acrobat Reader File menu. This will open the Print dialog box. In the Print Range section of the Print dialog box, select the appropriate print range, then click OK.

List of Forms Included on the Forms CD-ROM

The following files are in rich text format (RTF):

Form	File name
Affordable Monthly Expenditures Worksheet	Affordable.rtf
Annual Nonessential Expenditures Adjustment Worksheet	Nonessential.rtf
Borrowing Against Home Equity: Comparison Worksheet	Borrowing.rtf
Estimated Maximum Loan Amount Worksheet	Loan.rtf
Fixer-Upper Cost-Tracking Form	FixUpForm.rtf
Maximum Purchase Price Worksheet	Purchase.rtf
Promissory Note	Promissory.rtf
Rental Property Annual Pretax Cash Flow Worksheet	Rental.rtf
Return on Investment (ROI) Worksheet	ROI.rtf

The following files are in Adobe Reader PDF format (asterisk indicates a form with fill-in text fields):

Form	File name
Attorney Interview Questionnaire	Attorney.pdf
Fixer-Upper State-of-Mind Quiz	FixUpQuiz.pdf
Fixer-Upper Walk-Through Checklist	FixUpList.pdf
Home Inspector Interview Questionnaire	Inspector.pdf
HUD-1 Settlement Statement*	1.pdf
Initial Walk-Through Checklist	Initial.pdf
Mortgage Broker Interview Questionnaire	Broker.pdf
Property Management Company Interview Questionnaire	Company.pdf
Real Estate Agent Interview Questionnaire	Agent.pdf
Mortgage (Massachusetts)	MortgageMA.pdf
Deed of Trust (California)	DeedofTrustCA.pdf

Appendix B – Forms and Checklists

HUD-1 Settlement Statement

A. Settlement Statement	U.S. Department of Housing and Urban Development	OMB Approval No. 2502-0265 (expires 11/30/2009)

B. Type of Loan

1. ☐ FHA 2. ☐ FmHA 3. ☐ Conv. Unins.	6. File Number:	7. Loan Number:	8. Mortgage Insurance Case Number:
4. ☐ VA 5. ☐ Conv. Ins.			

C. Note: This form is furnished to give you a statement of actual settlement costs. Amounts paid to and by the settlement agent are shown. Items marked "(p.o.c.)" were paid outside the closing; they are shown here for informational purposes and are not included in the totals.

D. Name & Address of Borrower:	E. Name & Address of Seller:	F. Name & Address of Lender:

G. Property Location:	H. Settlement Agent:	
	Place of Settlement:	I. Settlement Date:

J. Summary of Borrower's Transaction		**K. Summary of Seller's Transaction**	
100. Gross Amount Due From Borrower		**400. Gross Amount Due To Seller**	
101. Contract sales price		401. Contract sales price	
102. Personal property		402. Personal property	
103. Settlement charges to borrower (line 1400)		403.	
104.		404.	
105.		405.	
Adjustments for items paid by seller in advance		**Adjustments for items paid by seller in advance**	
106. City/town taxes to		406. City/town taxes to	
107. County taxes to		407. County taxes to	
108. Assessments to		408. Assessments to	
109.		409.	
110.		410.	
111.		411.	
112.		412.	
120. Gross Amount Due From Borrower		**420. Gross Amount Due To Seller**	
200. Amounts Paid By Or In Behalf Of Borrower		**500. Reductions In Amount Due To Seller**	
201. Deposit or earnest money		501. Excess deposit (see instructions)	
202. Principal amount of new loan(s)		502. Settlement charges to seller (line 1400)	
203. Existing loan(s) taken subject to		503. Existing loan(s) taken subject to	
204.		504. Payoff of first mortgage loan	
205.		505. Payoff of second mortgage loan	
206.		506.	
207.		507.	
208.		508.	
209.		509.	
Adjustments for items unpaid by seller		**Adjustments for items unpaid by seller**	
210. City/town taxes to		510. City/town taxes to	
211. County taxes to		511. County taxes to	
212. Assessments to		512. Assessments to	
213.		513.	
214.		514.	
215.		515.	
216.		516.	
217.		517.	
218.		518.	
219.		519.	
220. Total Paid By/For Borrower		**520. Total Reduction Amount Due Seller**	
300. Cash At Settlement From/To Borrower		**600. Cash At Settlement To/From Seller**	
301. Gross Amount due from borrower (line 120)		601. Gross amount due to seller (line 420)	
302. Less amounts paid by/for borrower (line 220)	( )	602. Less reductions in amt. due seller (line 520)	( )
303. Cash ☐ From ☐ To Borrower		**603. Cash** ☐ To ☐ From Seller	

Section 5 of the Real Estate Settlement Procedures Act (RESPA) requires the following: • HUD must develop a Special Information Booklet to help persons borrowing money to finance the purchase of residential real estate to better understand the nature and costs of real estate settlement services; • Each lender must provide the booklet to all applicants from whom it receives or for whom it prepares a written application to borrow money to finance the purchase of residential real estate; • Lenders must prepare and distribute with the Booklet a Good Faith Estimate of the settlement costs that the borrower is likely to incur in connection with the settlement. These disclosures are manadatory.

Section 4(a) of RESPA mandates that HUD develop and prescribe this standard form to be used at the time of loan settlement to provide full disclosure of all charges imposed upon the borrower and seller. These are third party disclosures that are designed to provide the borrower with pertinent information during the settlement process in order to be a better shopper.

The Public Reporting Burden for this collection of information is estimated to average one hour per response, including the time for reviewing instructions, searching existing data sources, gathering and maintaining the data needed, and completing and reviewing the collection of information.

This agency may not collect this information, and you are not required to complete this form, unless it displays a currently valid OMB control number.

The information requested does not lend itself to confidentiality.

Source: U.S. Department of Housing and Urban Development

HUD-1 Settlement Statement (cont'd)

L. Settlement Charges		Paid From Borrowers Funds at Settlement	Paid From Seller's Funds at Settlement
700. Total Sales/Broker's Commission based on price $ @ % =			
Division of Commission (line 700) as follows:			
701. $ to			
702. $ to			
703. Commission paid at Settlement			
704.			
800. Items Payable In Connection With Loan			
801. Loan Origination Fee %			
802. Loan Discount %			
803. Appraisal Fee to			
804. Credit Report to			
805. Lender's Inspection Fee			
806. Mortgage Insurance Application Fee to			
807. Assumption Fee			
808.			
809.			
810.			
811.			
900. Items Required By Lender To Be Paid In Advance			
901. Interest from to @ $ /day			
902. Mortgage Insurance Premium for months to			
903. Hazard Insurance Premium for years to			
904. years to			
905.			
1000. Reserves Deposited With Lender			
1001. Hazard insurance months @ $ per month			
1002. Mortgage insurance months @ $ per month			
1003. City property taxes months @ $ per month			
1004. County property taxes months @ $ per month			
1005. Annual assessments months @ $ per month			
1006. months @ $ per month			
1007. months @ $ per month			
1008. months @ $ per month			
1100. Title Charges			
1101. Settlement or closing fee to			
1102. Abstract or title search to			
1103. Title examination to			
1104. Title insurance binder to			
1105. Document preparation to			
1106. Notary fees to			
1107. Attorney's fees to			
(includes above items numbers:)			
1108. Title insurance to			
(includes above items numbers:)			
1109. Lender's coverage $			
1110. Owner's coverage $			
1111.			
1112.			
1113.			
1200. Government Recording and Transfer Charges			
1201. Recording fees: Deed $; Mortgage $; Releases $			
1202. City/county tax/stamps: Deed $; Mortgage $			
1203. State tax/stamps: Deed $; Mortgage $			
1204.			
1205.			
1300. Additional Settlement Charges			
1301. Survey to			
1302. Pest inspection to			
1303.			
1304.			
1305.			
1400. Total Settlement Charges (enter on lines 103, Section J and 502, Section K)			

Source: U.S. Department of Housing and Urban Development

Affordable Monthly Expenditures Worksheet

Section A - Monthly income:

Net salary/wages (after taxes and other deductions) $_____

Interest income/dividends   + $_____

Other income:

Profits on investments	$_____
Part-time work or home-based business	$_____
Other	$_____
Total	$_____

                (Insert total other income)   + $_____

Rental income (if you plan on renting out your second home)   + $_____

Line 1: Total monthly income   = $_____

Section B - Monthly expenses for your existing home:

Mortgage/loan payment $_____

Property taxes (annual cost/12)   + $_____

Property insurance (annual cost/12)   + $_____

Household bills:

Electric	$_____
Heating	$_____
Water and sewer	$_____
Internet	$_____
Phone (landline and cell)	$_____
Cable	$_____
Other	$_____
Total	$_____

              (Insert total household bills)   + $_____

Maintenance and repairs (average annual cost/12)   + $_____

Line 2: Total monthly expenses for your existing home   = $_____

Affordable Monthly Expenditures Worksheet (cont'd.)

Section C - Other monthly expenses:

Auto loans $_____

Credit card payment (bank cards and store cards)   + $_____

Other loans or debt   + $_____
(student loan, consumer loan, child support, etc.)

Line 3: Total other monthly expenses   = $_____

Section D - Monthly savings not related to second home:

IRA contributions (Note: 401(k) contributions are already factored $_____
into the "Net salary/wages" line under "Monthly income.")

Self-imposed savings, such as for school tuition or wedding   + $_____

Line 4: Total monthly savings not related to second home   = $_____

Section E - What's left? Calculate what you can spend each month for a second home

Line 1: Total monthly income $_____

Line 2: Total monthly expenses for existing home   – $_____

Line 3: Total other monthly expenses   – $_____

Line 4: Total monthly savings not related to second home   – $_____

Amount left for your second home each month   = $_____

Estimated Maximum Loan Amount Worksheet

Amount left for your second home each month (from final line of the Affordable Monthly Expenditures Worksheet)	$_____
Percent allocation towards your loan payments (see table above)	x _____ %
Affordable monthly loan payment	= $_____
Number of months for loan term (most likely 360 months)	x _____
Total payback amount (loan principal plus interest)	= $_____
Percentage of payback amount allocated towards loan principal only*	x $_____ %
Estimated maximum loan amount	= $_____

* The easiest way to figure out this loan principal allocation is to use an online mortgage calculator. Simply plug in your anticipated loan terms (such as loan amount, interest rate, and number of years) to determine the total amount paid (principal and interest) at the end of your loan period. To calculate the percentage of principal only, divide the total principal paid by the total amount paid on your loan. For example, a $200,000 loan at 6% interest over 30 years means you'll pay back a total of $431,677 ($200,000 in principal plus $231,677 in total interest). That means your principal-only percentage is 46% ($200,000 divided by $431,677).

Maximum Purchase Price Worksheet

Your estimated maximum loan amount
(from Estimated Maximum Loan Amount Worksheet, above)

$ _____

Down payment amount
(how much you have currently saved)

+ $ _____

Estimated closing costs

– $ _____

Total amount you can pay for a second home

= $ _____

Initial Walk-Through Checklist

❏ **General appearance.** _____
_____
_____

[Needs new paint? Are the shingles on the roof or side of the house buckled or broken?
Are there no broken or cracked windows? Inside, is the home is dirty and cluttered?
Are the walls chipped and crying for a fresh coat of paint?]

❏ **Water leaks.** _____
_____
_____

[Telltale signs include yellowish-brown stains, bulges, or soft spots on ceilings and walls.]

❏ **Appliances and fixtures.** _____
_____
_____

[Test all light switches, faucets, toilets, thermostats, and all major appliances.]

❏ **Floors.** _____
_____
_____

[Should be smooth, even, and solid. Watch out for soft, springy sections or excessive
squeaking.]

❏ **Doors and windows.** _____
_____
_____

[Do doors and windows fit snugly and operate smoothly? Any flaking paint, loose caulking,
or gaps that can create drafts?]

❏ **Grout and caulking.** _____
_____
_____

[Is the grout and caulking around bathroom and kitchen tiles loose and crumbling?]

❏ **Furnishings.** _____
_____
_____

[Will yours or a potential renter's fit into the rooms?]

❏ **Storage space.** _____
_____
_____

[Is there enough for your belongings or those of potential renters?]

Rental Property Annual Pretax Cash Flow Worksheet

Annual rental income	$_____
Annual mortgage payments (include principal and interest plus property taxes and insurance)	– $_____

Annual operating expenses

Liability insurance	$_____
Utilities (if not covered by tenant)	$_____
Upkeep and maintenance fees (if not covered by property management fees if you're using an outside company)	$_____
Advertising and tenant-screening costs (if not covered by property management fees if you're using an outside company)	$_____
Property management fees (if you're using a management company)	$_____
Professional services fees (legal, accounting, etc.)	$_____
Prorated repair and improvement costs	$_____
Total	$_____

(Insert total annual operating expenses)	– $_____
Cash flow (+ or –)	= $_____

Return-On-Investment Worksheet

Year	Pretax Cash Flow*		Unrealized Home Appreciation**		Unrealized Gain/(Loss)		Total Investment in Property***		Return on Investment After Sale****
0	n/a		n/a		n/a	$			n/a
1	$	+	$	=	$	/	$	=	%
2	$	+	$	=	$	/	$	=	%
3	$	+	$	=	$	/	$	=	%
4	$	+	$	=	$	/	$	=	%
5	$	+	$	=	$	/	$	=	%
6	$	+	$	=	$	/	$	=	%
Total	$	+	$	=	$	/	$	=	%

*Cash flow will change over the years based on changes in rents and expenses. For purposes of this example, Ralph has assumed that rents will not rise. Property taxes, which have been calculated at $12 per $1,000 in house value, will also rise based on the current value of the house. Note that "( )" indicates negative cash flow.

**Based on local average of 5% per year

***Down payment of $40,000 + subsequent principal payments made on mortgage

****Not including real estate commissions

Real Estate Agent Interview Questionnaire

Ask potential agents the following questions.

❏ Do you work full time as a real estate agent? (Best answer: Yes.)

_____

_____

❏ How long have you been in the real estate business? (The longer the better, but preferably at least three years.)

_____

_____

❏ Do you have additional certification beyond your general real estate license? (More certifications show a commitment by the agent. A REALTOR®'s RSPS certification is particularly appropriate for second-home buyers. However, since this is a relatively new certification, few REALTOR®s may have it.)

_____

_____

_____

❏ How many real estate transactions have you been a part of in the past year? (Should be a minimum of ten.)

_____

_____

❏ In how many of those transactions have you represented the buyer? (Should be at least half; however, an even better answer is "all of them.")

_____

_____

❏ In how many of the transactions where you represented the buyer was it specifically for buying a second home? (Should be at least half; however, an even better answer is "all of them.")

_____

_____

_____

❏ Can you provide at least three names of previous clients who will serve as references, preferably at least one of whom used you to buy a second home? (Only acceptable answer: Yes.)

_____

_____

Mortgage Broker Interview Questionnaire

To make sure you have the best mortgage broker on your team, ask potential brokers the following questions:

❏ Do you work full time as a residential mortgage broker? (Best answer: Yes.)

_____

_____

_____

❏ How long have you been in the residential mortgage business? (The longer the better, but should be at least two years.)

_____

_____

_____

❏ Are you certified by the National Association of Mortgage Brokers? (Best answer: Yes.)

_____

_____

_____

❏ How many residential mortgages have you brokered in the past year? (Should be a minimum of ten.)

_____

_____

_____

❏ How many of those transactions were for second homes? (Should be at least half; however, an even better answer is "all of them.")

_____

_____

_____

❏ Can you provide at least three names of previous clients who will serve as references, at least one of whom used you to help finance a second home? (Only acceptable answer: Yes.)

_____

_____

_____

Real Estate Attorney Interview Questionnaire

To make sure you have the best attorney on your team, ask potential attorneys the following questions:

❏ Do you spend most of your time dealing with real estate legal matters? (Best answer: Yes.)

_____

_____

❏ How many years have you been handling real estate legal matters? (The longer the better, but should be at least two years.)

_____

_____

❏ Do you charge hourly rates (if so, at what rate) or flat fees for services? (You'll want to compare fees between attorneys—but try not to base your decision solely on how high or low the fees are.)

_____

_____

❏ Are you a member of the state bar association? (Only acceptable answer: Yes.)

_____

_____

_____

❏ Have you ever been subject to any bar association disciplinary proceedings? (Only acceptable answer: No.)

_____

_____

_____

❏ How many individual home-buying clients have you represented in the past year? (Should be a minimum of ten.)

_____

_____

_____

❏ Can you provide at least three names of previous clients who will serve as references? (Only acceptable answer: Yes.)

_____

_____

_____

Home Inspector Interview Questionnaire

Ask potential inspectors the following questions:

❏ Do you work full time as a home inspector? (Best answer: Yes.)

_____

_____

❏ How long have you been in the home inspection business? (The longer the better, but should be at least two years.)

_____

_____

❏ Are you affiliated with any home inspection trade organizations such as the American Society of Home Inspectors, the National Association of Certified Home Inspectors, or the National Association of Home Inspectors? (Best answer: Yes.)

_____

_____

❏ How many home inspections have you done in the past year?
(Should be a minimum of fifteen.)

_____

_____

_____

❏ Do you have insurance that is currently active? (Only acceptable answer: Yes. And be sure to ask for a certificate of insurance.)

_____

_____

_____

❏ What did you do before you were a home inspector? (Ideally, should have been a contractor, building inspector, or even on a town planning board involved in issuing building permits and ensuring compliance on home renovations.)

_____

_____

_____

❏ Can you provide at least three names of previous clients who will serve as references? (Only acceptable answer: Yes.)

_____

_____

Fixer-Upper State-of-Mind Quiz

Rate yourself against the statements below. Total your ratings and see the scorecard at the bottom of this worksheet.

I'm comfortable managing and directing other people.

    (poor condition) 1 2 3 4 5 (good condition)

When things don't go as initially planned, I'm flexible in finding alternative solutions.

    (poor condition) 1 2 3 4 5 (good condition)

I'm a patient person.

    (poor condition) 1 2 3 4 5 (good condition)

When I commit to something, I stick with it until it's complete.
    (poor condition) 1 2 3 4 5 (good condition)

I'm good at tracking how I spend money.

    (poor condition) 1 2 3 4 5 (good condition)

How did you score?

Overall score of 20 or higher: Your head is in the right place.

Overall score of between 15 and 19: You have more or less the right state of mind, but should be aware of areas where you scored low, and plan around them.

Overall score of 14 or less: Think twice about what you're getting yourself into.

Fixer-Upper Walk-Through Checklist

Rate the condition of the house based on your own visual inspection during the walk-through. Write down any notes about particular items. Also try to take photos or video of the property.

Exterior

Roof: Reduce the rating for any cracked, missing, or worn down shingles or tiles.

(poor condition) 1 2 3 4 5 (good condition)

Notes:_____

_____

_____

Paint/Stain/Siding: Reduce the rating for any chips or cracks on paint, faded stain, or siding that is buckled and pulling away from the house.

(poor condition) 1 2 3 4 5 (good condition)

Notes:_____

_____

_____

Windows: Reduce the rating for any broken panes and rot around the frames.

(poor condition) 1 2 3 4 5 (good condition)

Notes:_____

_____

_____

Fence: Reduce the rating for any missing slats or sections, unevenness, and loose posts.

(poor condition) 1 2 3 4 5 (good condition)

Notes:_____

_____

_____

Driveway: Reduce the rating for any sagging spots, holes, or cracks.

(poor condition) 1 2 3 4 5 (good condition)

Notes:_____

_____

Walkways: Reduce the rating for any sagging spots, holes, or cracks in slates or bricks.

(poor condition) 1 2 3 4 5 (good condition)

Notes:_____

_____

Landscaping: Reduce the rating for any overgrown or dying shrubs, trees, and grass.

(poor condition) 1 2 3 4 5 (good condition)

Notes:_____

_____

Fixer-Upper Walk-Through Checklist (cont'd.)

Interior

Kitchen: Reduce the rating for any cracked or chipped countertops, poorly working fixtures, or old or worn-down appliances or cabinets.

(poor condition) 1 2 3 4 5 (good condition)

Notes:_____

_____

_____

Living room: Reduce the rating for any cracked or broken windows; chips, cracks, or holes in the walls or ceiling; sagging or squeaky floors; or worn carpets.

(poor condition) 1 2 3 4 5 (good condition)

Notes:_____

_____

_____

Dining room: Reduce the rating for any cracked or broken windows; chips, cracks, or holes in the walls or ceiling; sagging or squeaky floors; or worn carpets.

(poor condition) 1 2 3 4 5 (good condition)

Notes:_____

_____

_____

Bathroom #1: Reduce the rating for any cracked or chipped countertops, or poorly working fixtures, toilet, or tub/shower.

(poor condition) 1 2 3 4 5 (good condition)

Notes:_____

_____

_____

Hallways and stairs: Reduce the rating for any chips, cracks, or holes in the walls or ceiling; sagging or squeaky floors, or worn carpets.

(poor condition) 1 2 3 4 5 (good condition)

Notes:_____

_____

_____

Master bedroom: Reduce the rating for any cracked or broken windows; chips, cracks, or holes in the walls or ceiling; sagging or squeaky floors; or worn carpets.

(poor condition) 1 2 3 4 5 (good condition)

Notes:_____

_____

_____

Fixer-Upper Walk-Through Checklist (cont'd.)

Bedroom #2: Reduce the rating for any cracked or broken windows; chips, cracks, or holes in the walls or ceiling; sagging or squeaky floors; or worn carpets.

(poor condition) 1 2 3 4 5 (good condition)

Notes:_____

_____

_____

Bedroom #3: Reduce the rating for any cracked or broken windows; chips, cracks, or holes in the walls or ceiling; sagging or squeaky floors; or worn carpets.

(poor condition) 1 2 3 4 5 (good condition)

Notes:_____

_____

_____

Bathroom #2: Reduce the rating for any cracked or chipped countertops, or poorly working fixtures, toilet, or tub/shower.

(poor condition) 1 2 3 4 5 (good condition)

Notes:_____

_____

_____

Furnace and Air Conditioning: Reduce the rating for an old, decrepit furnace (listen for rattling or clunky noises) or for an altogether insufficient heating or air conditioning system.

(poor condition) 1 2 3 4 5 (good condition)

Notes:_____

_____

_____

Electrical: Reduce the rating for any old and frayed wires. Also find out how many amps are coming into the house, and reduce the rating for anything less than 100 (depending on the size of the house).

(poor condition) 1 2 3 4 5 (good condition)

Notes:_____

_____

_____

Fixer-Upper Cost-Tracking Form

Project Description	Expense Description	Labor, Materials, or Both?	Date (Month/Year)	Budgeted Amount ($)	Actual Amount ($)	Budget Reconciliation (+/_)
				$	$	$
				$	$	$
				Budget Totals		
				$	$	$

Annual Nonessential Expenditures Adjustment Worksheet

Instructions:

1. In Column A, list all items and activities you can do without in the short term.

2. In Column B, estimate how much you currently spend annually on each of these nonessentials.

3. In Column C, enter the new, lower amount you plan to spend for each item and activity.

4. Finally, subtract the amount in Column C from the amount in Column B and write that number in Column D. The TOTAL of all your entries in Column D is the annual amount you will be able to put towards your down payment.

(A) Description of expense	(B) Current expense		(C) Reduced expense		(D) Amount allocated toward down payment
	$	–	$	=	$
	$	–	$	=	$
	$	–	$	=	$
	$	–	$	=	$
	$	–	$	=	$
	$	–	$	=	$
	$	–	$	=	$
	$	–	$	=	$
	$	–	$	=	$
	$	–	$	=	$
	$	–	$	=	$
	$	–	$	=	$
	$	–	$	=	$
	$	–	$	=	$
Total	$	–	$	=	$

Borrowing Against Home Equity: Comparison Worksheet

Type of Loan	Name of Lender	Loan Amount[1]	Points and Loan Fees[2] ($)	Interest Rate[3] (%)	Monthly Payment ($)
Home Equity Loans					
Loan #1		$	$	%	$
Loan #2		$	$	%	$
Loan #3		$	$	%	$
Home Equity Lines of Credit					
Loan #1		$	$	%	$
Loan #2		$	$	%	$
Loan #3		$	$	%	$
Cash-Out Refinances					
Loan #1		$	$	%	$
Loan #2		$	$	%	$
Loan #3		$	$	%	$

[1] For a cash-out refinance, enter only the portion of the loan that applies to the equity being pulled out of your primary home.

[2] Include all costs, such as points, application fee, and credit report fee, that you'll need to pay in connection with the loan.

[3] If the loan will have an adjustable interest rate, don't base your comparison on the lower introductory rate.

Promissory Note (amortized loan)

1. Identity of Borrower and Lender

Borrower's name: Joe Borrowguy

Lender's name: John Lenderman

The term "Borrower" may refer to more than one person, in which case they agree to be jointly and severally liable under this note. The term "Lender" may refer to any person who legally holds this note, including a buyer in due course.

2. Promise to Pay

For value received, Borrower promises to pay Lender $100,000 plus interest at the yearly rate of 6% on the unpaid balance as specified below. Payments will be made to Lender at 123 Main Street, San Mateo, CA 12345, or such other place as Lender may designate.

3. Payment Schedule

Borrower agrees that this note will be paid in monthly installments of principal and interest. Accordingly, Borrower will pay 360 installments of $599.55 each.

4. Payment Due Dates

Borrower will make installment payments on the 1st day of each month beginning May 2006, until the principal and interest have been paid in full, which will be no later than May 2036. If Borrower fails to make a payment until the 10th day of the month or later, Borrower will owe a late fee of $15.

5. Prepayment

Borrower may prepay all or any part of the principal without penalty.

6. Loan Acceleration

If Borrower is more than 15 days late in making any payment, Lender may declare that the entire balance of unpaid principal is due immediately, together with any interest that has accrued.

7. Security

Borrower agrees that until the principal and interest owed under this promissory are paid in full, this note will be secured by a mortgage covering the real estate commonly known as 456 Main Street, City of Swampscott, County of Essex, State of Massachusetts.

8. Attorney's Fees

If Lender prevails in a lawsuit to collect on this note, Borrower will pay Lender's costs and attorney's fees in an amount the court finds to be reasonable.

9. Governing Law

This note will be governed by and construed in accordance with the laws of the state of Massachusetts.

BORROWER:

Signature: *Joe Borrowguy*

Printed name: Joe Borrowguy

Address: 789 Main Street, Marblehead, MA 12345

Dated: April 3, 2007

Property Management Company Interview Questionnaire

Ask potential property management companies the following questions:

❏ How long has your company been around? (Best answer: Ten or more years.)

_____

_____

_____

❏ What is the percentage breakdown of the types of properties (single-family, condo, etc.)
your company handles? (At least half should be the same type of property as yours.)

_____

_____

_____

❏ What is the average vacancy rate of all the properties you handle?
(Should be less than 20%; ideally, under 10%.)

_____

_____

_____

❏ Are you licensed or affiliated with any trade organizations?
(Best answer: Yes, such as with the National Association of Residential Property
Managers or the Property Management Association.)

_____

_____

_____

❏ Can you provide me with a list and explanation of all the services you offer?
(Best answer: Yes.)

_____

_____

_____

❏ How do you typically communicate (both with the landlord and the renter)?
(Should be by phone, as well as email to allow for more personal communication.)

_____

_____

_____

❏ How and where will you advertise my property? (Best answer: At the very least,
it should be listed in the local newspapers, appear online in rental and other relevant
websites, and have a "for rent" sign in the window.)

_____

_____

_____

Property Management Company Interview Questionnaire (cont'd.)

❏ Do you provide documentation of any charges, bids, repairs, etc.? (Best answer: Yes.)

_____

_____

_____

❏ What fees do you charge? (Normal fees range from 5% to 10% for long-term rentals and 30% plus for short-term rentals.)

_____

_____

_____

❏ Can you (the homeowner) terminate the agreement without cause but with reasonable notice? (Best answer: Yes.)

_____

_____

_____

❏ Can you provide at least three names of clients who will serve as references? (Only acceptable answer: Yes.)

_____

_____

_____

INDEX

A

ABR (Accredited Buyer Representative), 111
ABRM (Accredited Buyer Representative®
  Manager), 111
Abstract, 21
Access to premises, rental, 261
Accommodations tax, 286
Accredited Buyer Representative (ABR), 111
Accredited Buyer Representative® Manager
  (ABRM), 111
Adjustable rate mortgage. *See* ARM
Adjustment periods, for ARM loans, 219
Administration fees, 16
Advance costs, 18–19
Advance payment, on vacation rentals, 268
Advertising for renters, 95, 264, 271, 303
Affordable Monthly Expenditures Worksheet, 39,
  41–45
AFR (Applicable Federal Rate), 193–194
Age of home, repairs and maintenance, 29, 30
AHWD (At Home With Diversity) Realtor®, 111
Alimony payments, budgeting and, 42
Allocating ongoing expenses, co-ownership and,
  242
Alterations to your property, by long-term
  tenants, 264
Amenities, and location, 77, 88
American Home Shield, 31
American Land Title Association, 132–133
American Society of Home Inspectors, 131
Amortized loans, 198, 203, 221–223, 290–291
Annual assessments, 20
Annual Nonessential Expenditures Adjustment
  Worksheet, 175
Antidiscrimination laws, rentals and, 267
Appearance of house, house-hunting and, 85
Applicable Federal Rate (AFR), 193–194
Appraisal
  contingency for, 86

customary fees for, 17
and loan approval, 200, 207–208, 214
working with appraisers, 125–127
Appreciation potential, 87, 100–102
Approval process, mortgage, 214–215
ARM (adjustable rate mortgage)
  cash-out refinance, 178
  compared to fixed-rate, 216–217
  different types of, 222–223
  and flipping properties, 223
  major indices, 219–220
  pros and cons of, 98, 219–221
  rise in interest rates and, 32–33
Assumption fee, 18
At Home With Diversity (AHWD) Realtor®, 111
Attorneys. *See* Real estate attorneys
Auto loans, and budgeting, 42, 49

B

"Balloon" payment, 223
Bankers, 121, 195
Bank loans, combining with private, 193, 207
Bathroom remodel, fixer-upper repair, 143–144
Bed tax, 286
Better Business Bureau, for reviewing contractors,
  153
Board of directors, co-op shareholders, 54, 60
Borrowing. *See* Financing
Borrowing Against Home Equity: Comparison
  Worksheet, 179
Budgeting
  adjusting for a more expensive house, 49–50
  Affordable Monthly Expenditures Worksheet,
    39, 41–45
  current monthly expenses, 40–43, 49
  current monthly income, 38–40
  disposable income, 43
  down payment and, 37–38

and conforming loans, 226
cooperatives (co-op), 8, 54–55, 59–60
and co-ownership, 237
existing homes, 61–63, 71
list of, 53–55
and location, 52
maximum loan amount, 225
multifamily home, 53, 58–59
new build, 61–63, 84
older homes, 29, 30
rentability, 88
single-family homes, 8, 53, 57–58, 225
townhouses, 8, 53–55, 59–60, 278
See also Condominiums; Fixer-uppers
Housing indicators, 69–72, 137
Housing starts, 71
HUD-1 Settlement Statement
line-by-line explanation of, 16–23
predicting closing costs with, 14–16, 26
sample form, 24–25
See also Closing costs
Hybrid ARM, 222

I

Impound account, 20
Improvements, 285, 299–302, 305–306
Income, 214, 225, 298–299
See also Cash flow
Income approach, for current market value, 127
Income tax, 284–285
Indices, ARMs and, 219–220
Individual ownership, of title, 288
Initial costs, 14, 15, 33
See also Closing costs
Initial investment. *See* Down payment
Initial Walk-Through Checklist, 85
Inspections, 17, 22–23, 84, 87, 128
See also Home inspection
Institutional lenders, working directly with, 121
Instructions for the CD-ROM. *See* CD-ROM
instructions

Insurance
borrowing against, 179–180
deducting, 303
dwelling insurance policy, 19, 277, 280
escrow accounts and, 20
flood hazard, 18, 19, 278
hazard, 19, 20, 87, 89, 209, 278
homeowners' insurance, 10, 45–46, 87, 94, 209
home warranties, 29–31
house-hunting and, 89
"loss of rent" coverage, 280
medical liability insurance, 279, 280
mortgage insurance, 17, 20
personal liability, 19
personal property coverage, 278, 280
and private home loans, 200, 207–209
property liability, 19, 95, 279, 280
renting out your house and, 277–280
theft, 19
title insurance, 10, 21, 22, 208–209
See also Liability
Intangible tax, closing cost, 22
Intercom systems, in retiree homes, 91
Interest income/dividends, 40
Interest/interest rates
adjustable rate mortgage, 32, 98, 178, 216, 219–223
advance payment of loan, 19
Applicable Federal Rate, 193–194
cash flow consideration, 98
conforming loans, 224–226
and credit score, 227–229
fixed-rate versus adjustable rate, 216–217, 219–221
overview on, 213, 216
points and, 217–218
private home loans and, 188, 192–194
refinancing, 178
rises in, 32
tax deductions and, 290–291, 293–296
Interest-only loans, 32–33, 198, 222, 223

Borrowing Money From Family or Friends?

Circle Lending℠

The Smart Way to Manage

Loans Between Relatives

and Friends

Use CircleLending when you want to lend to or borrow from someone you know for:

Business loans
To start or grow a business

Real estate loans
To buy, sell, or refinance private property

Personal loans
To pay down debt, buy a vehicle, for education,
for an emergency use, for other personal use.

What our clients are saying:

David, California:
"I had financed my startup business with credit cards, but tapped all those out; and when I found you guys it was a blessing, a way to continue my business. CircleLending allowed me to grab a hassle-free loan with my parents and keep it legit. It made my sister happy because she manages the affairs and all the terms are clear that it wasn't a gift to me."

Kyle, Arizona:
"The funds from friends and family was our first round of financing and let us get the first phase of our business in place. If we hadn't had that money, we couldn't have gotten started."

Money Magazine:
"If you prefer, a company like CircleLending will, for a modest fee, handle the transactions and provide year-end tax statements."

America Online:
"A good source for both borrowers and lenders is CircleLending ... which serves as an intermediary between friends or family members."

VISIT: www.circlelending.com

CALL: 800.805.2472

EMAIL: info@circlelending.com

If you live in – or simply love – the California desert, *Palm Springs Life* is a monthly must read.

SUBSCRIBE TODAY!

Palm Springs Life.

California's Prestige Magazine

www.palmspringslife.com

A Monument to Treasure is about Bobby and his grandfather as they take a journey through the Santa Rosa and San Jacinto Mountains National Monument.

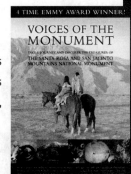

Take your own journey and discover the treasures of the Santa Rosa and San Jacinto Mountains National Monument through this spectacular, high-definition, Emmy Award-winning documentary.

ORDER YOUR COPIES TODAY!

www.monumentaltreasure.com

800.775.PALM

Get the Latest in the Law

① **Nolo's Legal Updater**
We'll send you an email whenever a new edition of your book is published!
Sign up at **www.nolo.com/legalupdater**.

② **Updates at Nolo.com**
Check **www.nolo.com/update** to find recent changes in the law that
affect the current edition of your book.

③ **Nolo Customer Service**
To make sure that this edition of the book is the most recent one, call us at
800-728-3555 and ask one of our friendly customer service representatives
(7:00 am to 6:00 pm PST, weekdays only). Or find out at **www.nolo.com**.

④ **Complete the Registration & Comment Card ...**
... and we'll do the work for you! Just indicate your preferences below:

- -

Registration & Comment Card

NAME _____ DATE _____

ADDRESS _____

CITY _____ STATE _____ ZIP _____

PHONE _____ EMAIL _____

COMMENTS _____

WAS THIS BOOK EASY TO USE?   (VERY EASY) 5 4 3 2 1 (VERY DIFFICULT)

☐ Yes, you can quote me in future Nolo promotional materials. *Please include phone number above.*

☐ Yes, send me **Nolo's Legal Updater** via email when a new edition of this book is available.

Yes, I want to sign up for the following email newsletters:

  ☐ **NoloBriefs** (monthly)
  ☐ **Nolo's Special Offer** (monthly)
  ☐ **Nolo's BizBriefs** (monthly)
  ☐ **Every Landlord's Quarterly** (four times a year)

☐ Yes, you can give my contact info to carefully selected
  partners whose products may be of interest to me.

NOLO

SCND 1.0

Nolo
950 Parker Street
Berkeley, CA 94710-9867
www.nolo.com

YOUR LEGAL COMPANION

MAY   2007